At a time when universities appear focused solely on competing in the higher education market and contributions to national economies, Boni and Walker offer an exciting, imaginative, hopeful and feasible alternative. In this book we are offered concrete examples of how conceptualising the purposes of universities in human development terms can be transformative. A coherent theoretical framework and real-life human development friendly cases exemplify how universities might contribute to social change by emphasising deliberation and participation in university governance; ameliorating social inequalities in access and participation; expanding a broad range of human capabilities; and, fostering human agency towards human development goals.

Monica McLean, *University of Nottingham, UK*

Social and economic change that benefits only elites, while other people's well-being and choices stagnate, is not the kind of 'development' that is worth having. Nor is it only development ethicists like me who think that better is possible. The call for *better* development has become widespread.

Universities and Global Human Development answers with a distinctive call for better education. Other books show how education contributes to development. This one shows how education that contributes to better development is better education. Melanie Walker and Alejandra Boni have given us a well-researched framework with which we can all set new standards for our universities, world-wide.

Jay Drydyk, *Fellow of the Human Development and Capabilities Association, Professor of Philosophy, Carleton University, Canada*

Routledge studies in sustainable development

This series uniquely brings together original and cutting-edge research on sustainable development. The books in this series tackle difficult and important issues in sustainable development including: values and ethics; sustainability in higher education; climate compatible development; resilience; capitalism and de-growth; sustainable urban development; gender and participation; and well-being.

Drawing on a wide range of disciplines, the series promotes interdisciplinary research for an international readership. The series was recommended in the *Guardian*'s suggested reads on development and the environment.

Emerging Economies and Challenges to Sustainability
Theories, strategies, local realities
Edited by Arve Hansen and Ulrikke Wethal

Environmental Politics in Latin America
Elite dynamics, the left tide and sustainable development
Edited by Benedicte Bull and Mariel Aguilar-Støen

Transformative Sustainable Development
Participation, reflection and change
Kei Otsuki

Theories of Sustainable Development
Edited by Judith C. Enders and Moritz Remig

Transdisciplinary Solutions for Sustainable Development
From planetary management to stewardship
Mark Charlesworth

Measuring Welfare beyond Economics
The genuine progress of Hong Kong and Singapore
Claudio O. Delang and Yi Hang Yu

Sustainability and Wellbeing
Human-scale development in practice
Mònica Guillen-Royo

Universities and Global Human Development
Theoretical and empirical insights for social change
Alejandra Boni and Melanie Walker

Universities and Global Human Development

Theoretical and empirical insights for social change

Alejandra Boni and Melanie Walker

LONDON AND NEW YORK

First published 2016
by Routledge
2 Park Square, Milton Park, Abingdon, Oxon OX14 4RN

and by Routledge
711 Third Avenue, New York, NY 10017

Routledge is an imprint of the Taylor & Francis Group, an informa business

British Library Cataloguing-in-Publication Data
A catalogue record for this book is available from the British Library

Library of Congress Cataloging-in-Publication Data
A catalog record for this book has been requested

ISBN: 978-1-138-82245-0 (hbk)
ISBN: 978-1-315-74279-3 (ebk)

Typeset in Sabon
by Wearset Ltd, Boldon, Tyne and Wear

MIX
Paper from
responsible sources
FSC
www.fsc.org   FSC® C013056

Printed and bound in Great Britain by
TJ International Ltd, Padstow, Cornwall

To all the people that make another university possible

Contents

Illustrations

Figures

Tables

Acknowledgements

We are grateful to our colleagues in the Human Development and Capability Association for the fantastic intellectual 'home' and the space the organisation provides us with to deliberate about important development ideas and how to operationalise capabilities expansion in policy and practice. We are also fortunate to enjoy supportive working conditions, Sandra at Ingenio Institute at the Universitat Politècnica de Valéncia and Melanie in the higher education and development research group at the Institute for Advanced Studies and Scholarship at the University of the Free State. We especially want to acknowledge the contributions of our research colleagues in helping us think better, especially: Merridy Wilson-Strydom, Sonja Loots, Sam Fongwa, Felix Lozano, Carola Calabuig, Jordi Peris, Aurora López-Fogues, Sergio Belda, Alvaro Fernández-Baldor, Llanos Gómez-Torres. Our graduate students: Talita Calitz, Oliver Mutanga, Mikateko Hoppener, Tendayi Marovah, Thandi Lewin, Elizabeth Ongera, Patience Mukwambo, Bothwell Mayonga, Faith Makwananzi, Ntimi Mtawa, Vicky Pellicer, Pau Lillo, Maria Ten, Monique Leivas, José Javier Sastre, Estela López, Juan Manuel Rodilla, and Jadicha Sow also present us with new challenges and disagreements through their own human development research projects. Jonathan Jansen as the UFS vice-chancellor has been unwavering in his support of our work on higher education and human development – his confidence in the value of this project is tremendously important to us, as is the support of Lis Lange. We have been fortunate to have received funding from the UFS and the National Research Foundation via Melanie's national research chair in higher education and human development, and from the Mobility and Academic Internationalization VLC-Campus Programme (granted by the Spanish Ministry of Education, Culture and Sport through the International Excellence Campus Programme) in Spain. This combined funding allowed us to meet to discuss the book and to work together on chapters in 2014 and 2015. The book was written in many places: Valencia, Sopeña de Carneros, Bloemfontein and Qwa-Qwa. Sonja, Elizabeth and Phokeng were very patient as we juggled the actions of the gender participatory research work and the writing while in Qwa-Qwa. We also acknowledge funding from the British

Council for the research reported on in Chapter 8 on employability. We are also grateful for the stimulating conversations and collaborations with Monica McLean, Ann-Marie Bathmaker, Andrea Abbas, Elaine Unterhalter, Joan de Jaeghere, Rajani Naidoo, Tristan McCowan, Franziska Trede, Melis Cin, Veronica Crosbie, Paula Ensor, Vivienne Bozalek, Brenda Leibowitz, Enrica Chiappero-Martinetti, Ina Conradie, Jay Drydyk, Alex Frediani, Hans-Uwe Otto, Des Gasper, Andrés Hueso, Gynna Millán, Maria Josep Cascant, Daniel Guijarro, Jethro Pettit, Ilse Osterlaken, Oscar Jara, Joseba Sainz, Fernando Altamira, and many others who have been inspiring for us.

Our thanks to Begoña Arias and Elmarie Viljoen who assisted with preparing the manuscript, while the Routledge editors were always encouraging.

Our much loved dogs – Isis, Lexie and Milo – refused to take writing yet another book seriously, forcing us to break from the writing to take them for brisk walks and play energetic and inventive games. This was good for all of us! For Melanie, Vicki Gilham, Clare Brunner and Chris Brunner, and for Sandra, Eva, Elena(s), Natalia, Marta, are always there, providing love and friendship. Finally, we are as ever aware of the personal debt we owe to Sandra's family and, especially, to our partners, Ian Phimister and Begoña Arias, for helping us to get to 'The End'. We could not have asked for more from them.

Part I

1 Introduction

At the Davos Conference of the World Economic Forum in 2014, Oxfam pointed out that the richest 85 people on the globe – who between them could squeeze onto one double-decker bus – control as much wealth as the poorest half of the global population put together (3.5 billion people). What does this say about us as citizens of our countries and as educators who work in universities? What does higher education as a system have to say about this rather shocking statistic, only one of many in the Oxfam (2014) report? What does higher education have to say in response to Thomas Piketty's (2014: 249) claim that some powerful societies are becoming more and more closed at the top, for example by 2030, the top 1 per cent of the wealthy in the USA will receive 25 per cent of all income, up from 20 per cent in 2010, with similar trends being seen in the UK? This trend is towards a way of organising the world and development that works for the few and that does not work for everyone, yet creates real moral urgencies for developed and developing countries; as the recent and ongoing flow of migrants into Europe also demonstrates, globalisation has eroded the insulation of the North. At issue then, is what does higher education say and do about these global development challenges, which have tremendous impact at the local level and on real people's lives?

Our book on higher education and global human development sets out to acknowledge these problems and inequalities, asking questions about global goals, global values and global ethics, worked out at the level of the university: what kind of society do we want; what is important in a democratic society; and what kind of higher/university education is valuable, relevant and desirable? We do not think that higher education on its own can solve problems of inequality or well-being at the local or global level. We think higher education can, however, make a contribution to better societies with more rather than less human development – that we all should lead good lives – but it is then important to locate debates about higher education in wider development discourses about poverty and inequalities and global concerns, which play out at the national and local level. Here, we make a case for human development and capabilities, which place people at the centre of development and play out in local and national education concerns, but with global development implications and effects. Our primary interest is with universities, but policy generally refers to higher education, which may include university degrees offered in the post-school sector, and tertiary education, which includes universities and also all post-compulsory education. This makes for some difficulty when drawing on global reports, so here we wish to clarify that, at all times, it is the university sector with which we are most concerned, because of its role in producing and disseminating knowledges, its role in national innovation systems and the shaping effect it has for other aspects of higher and secondary education.

In this book we ask, what kind of development do we want to contribute to in making the post-2015 world, and with what global agenda? In light of this, what theoretical approaches, policy analysis and educational processes promote both economic development and individual prosperity in regions and countries, and a broader conception of human flourishing? In particular, what are universities doing when they promote 'development' – and what kind of 'development'? The book aims to answer these and other questions, based on the premise that universities can and should support active, just and sustainable societies. This debate is particularly relevant today, when there are many conversations taking place about inequality, and more specifically post-2015 development agendas, which we think ought to be aligned with inclusive growth, more peaceful societies and quality lifelong education. Recently, in September 2015, the Global Sustainable Development Goals were approved at the United Nations General Assembly. They aim to illuminate development policies for the next 15 years and they have included higher education institutions as development actors. This is certainly a positive addition; but as we will see in Chapter 2, we raise some concerns about the way those goals and their targets have considered universities. Overall, however, we think that equitable and quality higher education is critical for promoting development and sustainable development, potentially advancing knowledge, skills, public-good values and effective participation in public decision-making.

We show here that the role of universities in promoting development has not always been understood in consistent ways, whether offering economic development returns on 'investment', whether mostly for teaching, or research, or having a role in building nations by forming citizens. Policy decisions informed by one or more of these approaches can have far-reaching consequences. For example, before the 1990s, the majority appreciation in powerful global organisations was that higher education generated lower economic and social returns than primary education in developing countries, while in developed countries, universities were regarded as making a social contribution, but access and places were limited in most countries. Today, however, the accumulation, utilisation and commodification of knowledge are perceived as among the principal factors in the process of economic growth and development and are the basis of a country's competitive advantages in the knowledge-based world economy. Higher education has expanded and continues to grow, as does demand for places. However, this may also have weakened public-good and equity commitments in the context of neo-liberal policies, while the gap between rich and poor has also widened considerably, with effects for equality, opportunities and outcomes from higher education.

Yet, beyond the formation of human capital for the economic growth of a country, university education could fulfil other transformative objectives. As highlighted by the group of experts for the Task Force on Higher Education and Society (2000), higher education contributes to the strengthening of civil society and to stimulating democratic governance through the generation of public assets for society, such as new knowledge and secure spaces for the open exchange of ideas about the values that define development. Also, university education can form inspiring public-good leaders in the professions, civil society, business and government; graduates who will act effectively in the political and economic world of the twenty-first century, as well as specialised professionals who can lead, invent, adopt and transfer modern technology to all sectors of society. Here we are reminded of Adam Smith (1759: 259) who wrote in *The Theory of Moral Sentiments* that the human qualities most useful to others are those of 'humanity, justice, generosity, and public spirit'. And, finally, what seems to us most fundamental, higher education increases people's opportunities and options, and therefore contributes directly to human development, human relationships of solidarity, and expanded freedoms of the inhabitants of the world.

Given the potential higher education has for development, it is essential that it gains traction in global development policy. This scenario is complicated by the effects of inequality and austerity policies affecting the global North, leading to a decline in public investment in education, jeopardising access to college for people with fewer resources, and increasing the presence of the private sector in research and education. Global economic developments and, more specifically, a drive to privatisation also affects developing countries, where private universities of variable quality are burgeoning in number to meet the demand for university education. Moreover, corruption and poor governance may constrain quality in higher education. On the other hand, although rather overlooked in global agendas, we also know that the graduates educated in universities are indispensable to development agendas, and it is universities that educate a range of professionals in health, education, science, technology, engineering, and so on.

Thus, we consider it important to explore new juxtapositions between the global North and global South, juxtaposing and integrating the global and the local across these perspectives, and developing a distinctive, in-depth conceptual and empirical understanding of the challenges faced. We do not assume a powerful global North with uniformly well-off populations and high quality universities, or a weak global South with uniformly poor people or low quality universities. Our case study countries of Spain and South Africa problematise this assumption. At the same time, in broad terms, university systems and innovation are much stronger overall in the North than in the South; even weak universities in the North are part of stronger knowledge producing systems. Two statistics from Wade (2003) illustrate this rather starkly: (1) the North is a net producer of patentable knowledge and the South a net consumer by a factor of 1,000s of per cent; (2) tough copyright restrictions double and triple the cost of scientific knowledge contained in research publications and these price escalations widen the gap between North and South in access to scientific knowledge.

Aims and objectives

Overall, our book makes the case for a critical turn in development thinking about universities and their contributions to making a more equal post-2015 world, putting forward a normative approach based on human development, one which can gain a hearing from policy, scholarship, and practitioners dealing with practical issues of research and knowledge, teaching and learning, and community engagement and service – all key university functions operationalised locally but influenced by the global through global university rankings, global policy brokers, a global financial crisis, and so on. In agreement with Manuel Castells, moreover, we are of the view that universities are an important space of freedom in society, which we should preserve for scientific, social and political reasons. As he further explains:

> At the same time we have to earn this autonomy and this freedom every day and use it in the public interest, not in defence of our privileges. [If we cannot do that] the pressures of the society will destroy the university as a space of reflection and innovation.
>
> (cited in Brooks 2011: 10)

We propose a human development approach to take up this challenge and further, because we understand that we cannot talk about sustainable development (which has emerged as the key post-2015 development discourse) if it is not human and vice versa. Sustainability is an intrinsic element of human development. We build and expand substantially on an our earlier edited collection (Boni and Walker 2013) and draw on new research that we have undertaken to now deepen and strengthen the argument that such an approach can elucidate development debates drawing on local, national and international issues and examples to show why higher education matters both in educational and social terms.

Based on this broad aim, the book has three secondary objectives that address the three parts of the book.

The first objective is to deepen the link between universities and development. There is no single answer; various development theories have addressed the university role differently. From the perspective of economic theories of development, the university has the main function of forming human capital. From post-development theories, the university can be seen as a site of social reproduction (and hence, the current unfair global arrangements or unequal societies). The first part of the book concludes with a presentation of the main characteristics of the human development approach in relation to these debates. This normative framework based on values such as diversity, well-being, empowerment, participation and sustainability, among others, and on an idea of human well-being understood as the expansion of human capabilities, overcomes the limitations of other development theories and contributes to essential questions in debates about the university.

The second objective is related to the operationalisation of human development in universities at a more local level, a kind of 'village' level but still connected and able to speak to the global; this is a research-based section that will discuss findings from research projects in South Africa and Spain. This comparative approach will be interesting to readers, as it responds to one of the debates illustrated in the first part of the book: the increasingly blurred distinction between North and South (also noted above), both of which contain people who are oppressed and exploited, and which is a category that has dominated development discourse. It also shows how the ideas set out in the first part of the book can be operationalised in empirical sites, and how these ideas can work in real world, non-ideal settings, to advance (or constrain) human development and justice. South Africa is a middle-income country and as such, could be understood as 'a North' within the African South, where its best universities are highly regarded throughout the continent; however, there are still huge inequalities ('a South') and inequalities in who participates in university education, a significant number of poor (almost half the total population) and serious ecological threats. On the other hand, Spain is an example of a North which, especially in recent years, shows increasing inequality (a South), with a growing percentage of its population living in relative poverty. Its university system is forming graduates who have to migrate to other countries to find work. There are therefore many open questions concerning what should be the role of universities in both countries as examples of South and North, and we believe that juxtaposing South Africa and Spain could help to clarify them.

Therefore, we think it is very helpful to present examples and discuss the role of the university in both contexts, taking into account the premises of human development and to consider the implications for: the purposes of the university, policy, research, and teaching and research that need to be linked with urgent local and global challenges. We also want to highlight the helpfulness of human development for analysing education and university policies. On the one hand, in a context with growing inequalities, we use human development as a framework and philosophy to scrutinise proposed research policy, policy impact at a local level and representations of quality in a university policy. We present and discuss pedagogies that reduce disadvantage, expand capabilities and foster global citizenship, but also look at how universities also reproduce disadvantage. We pay attention to research that allows us do research as and for democratic social change. We present examples of our research and of participation processes developed in partnership with actors inside and outside university.

Our third objective is related to the methodological account we provide, based on our own participatory research, which can serve as a resource for similar research, and also to underline our argument for attention by universities to the question of how knowledge and what knowledge is produced through research, and selected and mediated through teaching and learning, without losing sight of the issue that we need to evaluate which knowledge is more helpful and valuable for human development. What, how and with whom we investigate using human development as our approach are key questions that we respond to in different ways through our research, and in which we have benefited by many other opinions and experiences.

Overall, the book argues for a new arena of engagement with universities and an alternative way of conceptualising the university as a key site of development in order to challenge current development omissions around university education. Moreover, while universities undoubtedly contribute to social reproduction (and hence the current unfair global arrangements or unequal societies), they also open spaces for public-good values formation and public-good contributions through the critical and emancipatory power of knowledge and reason; the usefulness of knowledge for society; and equality, citizenship and democracy. They can foster development grounded in both intrinsic human flourishing as well as human capital formation.

Chapter outlines

The chapters which follow operationalise our aims and objectives. Following this introduction, in Chapter 2, we explore how higher/university education is located and understood in contemporary development debates. We analyse how different actors, especially influential in the development ambit, consider the role for universities in promoting development, and what kind of development they propose. Examples include the World Bank's influential perspective, most especially on Africa and other global South countries. Others include the United Nations Organization for Education, Science and Culture (UNESCO), the Organisation for Economic Co-operation and Development (OECD), the Association of

Commonwealth Universities (ACU), the 2013 High Level Panel Report to the UN, research commissioned on higher education by the UK Department for International Development and the British Council, and what universities ought to do as instruments for the public good.

In Chapter 3, we consider how development theories understand universities. Broadly speaking, debates in development range from positions which equate development with economic growth, through to critical perspectives stressing that uneven development, dependency and inequality are inherent in capitalist development, to ideas of alternative, bottom-up development recognising social and ecological, as well as economic goals, and radical post-developmentalist critiques that often dismiss the entire 'development project' altogether. We also consider gender and development and participatory approaches, and how these have analysed the roles of institutions in promoting (or not) more equitable development in higher education institutions.

In Chapter 4, we make the case for human development for social change oriented universities. Following on the argument developed in the previous chapters and the review of development and higher education, the book turns to a normative account based in human development principles and the capabilities approach. We understand that this approach gives us a comprehensive and multidimensional analysis of development processes and places at the centre issues of equity, diversity, participation and sustainability.

We see this approach as especially pertinent in both developing and developed countries in the face of challenges of growing inequalities, economic challenges, and social cohesion challenges. For us, the focus is on what universities should contribute to building decent societies, which value creating human capabilities for all citizens, so that all may benefit directly and indirectly from universities as a public good. Concepts of well-being and agency, participation and citizenship emerge as critical for advancing universities and development contributions. Amartya Sen's approach of 'comparative assessments of justice' provides us with a way to open out the pessimism inherent in much of the Northern debates to show how universities – even if rather imperfectly in current times – can still be spaces for equity across dimensions of system, institutional, interpersonal and personal, and not only or always drivers for normalisation.

In Part II, we take up empirical examples of university policies and practices. Chapter 5 looks at educational policies using the capability approach. This chapter scrutinises higher education and innovation policies in Europe, Spain, and in South Africa in order to analyse the changes that are occurring from the perspective of human development. This approach allows us to put people at the centre and to show, in a critical way, the consequences – positive and negative – of higher education policies in relation to advancing human development. The policy arena in Spain and South Africa is rather different and in both cases, the informational basis of justice for policy-making also differs. The human development and capability approach offers a robust method of analysis for capturing these differences and could be widely applied by other education policy scholars in the North and the South. We include in our analysis measures taken to address economic development through a research and innovation draft policy; how supranational policies are being shaped at the local level by examining participatory and power dynamics; how 'quality' which we see as crucial for sustainable development is understood; and, the extent to which inequalities and public deliberation are on the agenda of policy-making, or not.

Chapter 6 starts from the position that the twenty-first century University could be committed through knowledge production to solving, rather than merely describing, the challenges of our age, and thus helping to frame a more optimistic global debate. It considers arguments made for a public social science, which informs society about itself and the big issues that shape the future of humanity, and the case for not only good research (knowledge) but 'good for' research, focusing on the production and dissemination of knowledge, what knowledge counts and how it should be produced, and what social innovation looks like from this perspective. This means that universities could foster a democratisation of knowledge, which implies the participation of more and more actors in the social construction of reality and knowledge 'transfer'.

In Chapter 7, we include an analysis and commentary on participatory research methodology from a human development and capability perspective. We also present an innovative approach to analyse participatory research processes – the PARC framework – which pays attention to the expansion of the capabilities and agency of co-researchers, the characteristics of the knowledge produced and the democratic processes that participatory action research processes could enable during and beyond the research process. We then apply this framework to understanding a research process in Spain in 2014, which used participatory digital technologies. We propose that participatory action research, while certainly not the only way to research development, is nonetheless a way of combining teaching and research, which is particularly aligned with human development aspirations.

Moving on to Chapter 8, we address student learning opportunities and outcomes through processes of curriculum and teaching in formal and informal university spaces, with particular attention to disadvantage among students, but also attention to how graduates can develop their values and awareness for contributions to society. We consider how university education can equip students and graduates with the knowledge, skills and public values to exercise work and life choices towards the public good and the strengthening of a democratic public sphere. We draw on empirical research to critique what is problematic but also to show what is possible in forming student agency and ethical concerns. We offer illustrative cases studies of a student-led curriculum and pedagogy, cosmopolitan citizen formation in Spain, and graduate employability in South Africa.

To conclude the book, Chapter 9 draws together the threads of our argument to make a robust but feasible case for universities, which could be for more rather than less human development and social justice in a world of growing inequalities and moral urgencies. We answer our own question regarding how universities understood in this way could look across the dimensions of research, teaching, governance and policy, and what a university which took human development values seriously might do in practice in order to show the transformative possibilities of higher education in forming and sustaining capabilities for a decent society and for human well-being, with global development implications.

Finally this is an aspirational book, in that it looks at higher education and universities in a clear-eyed and critical way but also aspires to higher education, which can advance human well-being, and that for practical purposes, proposes that this aspiration is feasible and possible along many dimensions. That the world is not as we want it to be, or that higher education is currently a rather unequal arena, poses significant challenges, but the greater challenge is not accepting that this is the way things are and will be. Our book offers theoretical and empirical insights, which we hope show the possibility of advancing human well-being through higher education.

References

Boni, A. and M. Walker, eds. 2013. *Universities and Human Development. A New Imaginary for the University of the XXI Century*. Abingdon: Routledge.

Brooks, P. 2011. 'Our universities: how bad? How good?', *New York Review of Books* 24: 10–13.s

Oxfam. 2014. *Even it Up. Time to End Extreme Inequality*. UK: Oxfam. [Accessed 10 December 2015]. www.oxfam.org/sites/www.oxfam.org/files/file_attachments/cr-even-it-up-extreme-inequality-291014-en.pdf.

Piketty, T. 2014. *Capital in the Twenty-First Century*. Cambridge, MA: The Belknap Press.

Smith, A. 1759, 2009. *The Theory of Moral Sentiments*. London: Penguin Books.

Task Force on Higher Education and Society. 2000. *Higher Education in Developing Countries*. New York: World Bank.

Wade, R. 2003. 'What strategies are viable for developing countries today?' *Working Paper Series 1*, Crisis States Programme. Development Research Centre, London School of Economics.

2 Universities from an education and development perspective

In this chapter, we are interested in how universities are understood from an education and development perspective, and whether, or if, this includes the public-good, which we take to include access, equity and quality for, in and through university education, but also without assuming that universities – public or private – will necessarily or consistently work for public-good interests (see Walker and McLean 2013). Indeed, under current challenges of inequality, contributions may be patchy, but this is no reason not to set out high aspirations for global development and social changes arising from universities with commitments to the public good. A higher education for one person has impact well beyond one life but affects families and siblings, educating more people out of poverty and into employment. Such aspirations encourage both personal and social goals so that higher education could be both a place to form and achieve aspirations, and be aspirational itself towards public-good forms of development locally and globally. Just because aspirational higher education goals appear demanding is no reason to give up. There is no reason not to aim high just because we know that failure or patchiness along some dimensions – access, equity, quality – is possible, even likely. At the same time, it is necessary to think as clearly as we can about the challenges, as well as in later chapters (see especially, Chapters 6, 7 and 8), to consider realisable aspirational possibilities in particular contextual conditions, or we may be either disheartened or naively optimistic.

Moreover, that higher education matters for development is indicated by the increasing demand for higher education (McMahon 2014; Schofer and Meyer 2005; UNESCO 2012; Unterhalter and Carpentier 2010). According to the European Commission (cited in McMahon 2014), the number of students enrolled in higher education worldwide is forecast to rise from almost 100 million in 2000 to over 400 million in 2030. While the UNESCO (2012) statistics available are for tertiary education, which includes all post-compulsory education, the figures are striking nonetheless. In 2012, the number of students in tertiary education was: Africa – 11,650,258; Asia – 104,741,971; Europe – 32,524,016; North America – 27,814,783; South America – 17,690,901; and, Oceania – 1,655,158.

The number of female students enrolled in tertiary education in 2012 globally was 99,089,651. In 2012, there were four million students studying abroad, representing 1.8 per cent of tertiary enrolment. Central Asia is home to the most mobile student population growing from 67,300 in 2003 to 156,600 in 2012. Sub-Saharan Africa is the second, growing from 204,900 in 2003 to 288,200 in 2012. The highest destination countries were in the global North, for example, USA (18 per cent), UK (11 per cent), Australia (6 per cent) and Germany (5 per cent), suggesting both peril (brain drain) and promise (brain circulation). This leads us therefore to ask the development question: what are all these millions of students learning to be, to know, to do, and to value, with what effect for public services, well-being and development at local, national and global levels?

Thus, in this chapter, we want to analyse the contribution that universities can make to a more equal and fairer society, taking into account that access to higher education is improving, although not necessarily always in a desirable or fairer way. First we discuss the global development agenda with regard to higher education specifically. We follow by reviewing selected studies that highlight the contributions universities can bring to the development of people. We then position ourselves in an understanding of universities for a public good that expands real opportunities available to different social groups in any society, connecting universities to development agendas and addressing the tremendous problems the world faces today. Finally, we take account of the significant challenge of inequality as a substantial element in constraining public-good aspirations of universities.

Higher education and global development debates

Leading global development agencies, such as UNESCO, Oxfam, United Nations Development Programme (UNDP), the World Bank, and many others, tell us that education is tremendously important for development and equality, for individuals and for societies. Turning to these global agencies and their agendas, in the recently published UNESCO Report (2014: 1) on their proposed post-2015 goals for sustainable development, Ban Ki-Moon emphasised that: 'Education is a fundamental right and the basis for progress in every country.... With partnership, leadership and wise investments in education, we can transform individual lives, national economies and our world'. Notably, such efforts are to be directed not at any development but to the challenges of poverty, climate change and sustainable development. Education can then be a development 'multiplier'. Similarly, UNESCO Director-General Irina Bokova, in the same commentary declared that 'the evidence is unequivocal: education saves and transforms lives' (UNESCO 2014: 1). UNESCO's post-2015 cross-sector global development goals of ending poverty, inclusive sustainable development and decent work, healthy lives, renewable and modern energy, gender equality, reduction of inequalities in and between countries, environmental resilience, and peaceful, just societies all require educational contributions and efforts. We think they require that higher education is also recognised as a key development actor.

Global higher education and development policy, driven by the World Bank as the biggest funder, has not been static, but this policy has not necessarily fostered human development. At times, the developmental role of universities has been recognised, only to disappear and reappear. In a detailed review of shifting policy (and see Obamba 2013), Lebeau and Sall (2011) highlight the part played by international agencies, focusing primarily on the World Bank and UNESCO as the two major global policy players. They rehearse policy and policy changes since 1946; our intention here is not to detail this but to draw on their work to highlight the most significant shifts and reversals. Lebeau and Sall (2011: 129) note that higher education has been at the margins of UNESCO's agenda, but further claim that the two organisations: 'have so far produced, for good or bad, the most influential reflection of the articulation of higher education and economic development'. From earlier support for universities and development, by the 1970s public universities, they say, went into decline as major donor agencies decided that they had not delivered on 'development'. The World Bank's influence in higher/education at the same time, 'increased spectacularly' (Lebeau and Sall 2011: 134) with the result that non-compulsory tertiary education became 'a long-term absentee', given that the World Bank had decided that the focus should be on primary education because their human capital calculations showed the highest returns from this investment.

In a significant reversal, which Lebeau and Sall (2011: 135) date from 1994, they argue that the World Bank now places higher education 'at the heart of its anti-poverty and development strategy', and by its 2002 report, terms such as 'globalisation' and 'knowledge economy' had become key higher education policy terms in its reports. In *Constructing Knowledge Societies* the World Bank (2002) emphasised that the advancement and application of knowledge is key to development, together with the role to be played by tertiary education in this and in building technical and professional capacity. In the World Bank's 2003 report, it emphasised this focus by addressing lifelong learning in the global knowledge economy, and specifically the challenges for developing countries. Major international agencies and bilateral donors now converged on the role of higher education in knowledge production. By now, the World Bank was emphasising human capital growth, productivity, skills and quality, 'pushing' an agenda of 'diversification, privatization and regionalization' (Lebeau and Sall 2011: 139).

More recently, the World Bank has shifted the emphasis in their Education 2020 strategy to learning for all and learning outcomes, but this is perhaps a less radical shift than Obamba (2013) claims. The discourse is still economic: 'Invest early. Invest smartly. Invest for all' (World Bank, quoted in Obamba 2013: 103). It is still an economic knowledge-based development paradigm: poverty reduction is through economic growth and science–technology innovation. Moreover, Obamba (2013: 105) concedes that asymmetries in the global knowledge-based economy (and higher education systems) between the global North and South could endure if 'not radically reconfigured to become more truly equitable and inclusive'. It may be that only certain universities will do well, and will be well funded; it may be that the development emphasis both widens slightly but also narrows to a focus on science and technology or research areas, such as food security, in which some countries in the North have a vested interest; or that research capacity is selectively fostered. This could apply globally; as Naidoo (2015: 17) points out:

> there are connections between high status universities in low income countries which are detached from their surroundings and linked to higher education power centres of the North and the black holes of under-resourced institutions located in the richest countries of the North but dislocated from power.

Such a scenario is more likely to perpetuate uneven and combined development, she argues.

UNESCO does offer a more aspirational higher education development agenda, grounded in the values of the United Nations Universal Declaration on Human Rights on higher education which emphasises that 'higher education shall be equally accessible to all on the basis of merit' (article 26, paragraph 1). In the light of the World Bank's neo-liberal and 'far from empowering' agenda, Lebeau and Sall (2011: 139) noted the 1998 UNESCO World Declaration on higher education, which was based on a more inclusive and expansive approach and defence of higher education than the World Bank. This was followed by the setting up in 2004 of a UNESCO Forum on Higher Education Research and Knowledge, based on the need to strengthen systems of higher education and research in 2004; it lasted until 2009. By this time, say Lebeau and Sall (2011: 142), there was 'increasing recognition of the importance of higher education for the achievement of the global goals of the international societies'. However, UNESCO (in Lebeau and Sall 2011: 143) promoted the more inclusive idea of a 'knowledge society', which 'encompasses much broader social, ethical and political dimensions' against a 'narrow, fatalistic technological determinism'. The situation is further complicated by the mushrooming of private higher education, which today enrols more than 60 per cent of students in a number of countries, including Brazil, India and South Korea. Lebeau and Sall (2011: 144) thus suggest that the 2009 UNESCO conference was something of a 'last desperate attempt to rescue and restore the notion of the public good in higher education'. Echoing this, is the commentary by De Sousa Santos (2010: 274, 281) of the perverse declining interest in public universities as a 'public good produced by the state' so that, he suggests, the university 'is a collective good without strong allies'. Finally, Lebeau and Sall (2011: 144) conclude that global institutions have shaped the higher education landscape in developing countries 'in a very significant way'. The World Bank, they note, still adheres to a largely human capital approach, with UNESCO keeping space open for a more critical approach to development. Thus, in global policy terms, what 'development' in and through higher education means is by no means decided.

Turning to more developed countries, Van der Wende (2011) outlines the role of the OECD as another global player in higher education policy, especially in the face of globalisation and internationalisation trends, which affect all higher education institutions in some way, even though national policy-making still matters. Most national policy-makers, he suggests, want institutions 'to be more competent for the global era'; global knowledge economy-oriented higher education is crucial for 'the competitiveness of the nation', attracting, for example highly skilled workers and international students (Van der Wende 2011: 99). The OECD operates as a kind of think-tank for its member states, focusing on producing research, comparative statistics, policy analysis and in-depth country reports, which Van der Wende (2011: 102) describes as 'mechanisms of persuasion'. Increasingly the OECD has 'assumed the role of policy actor' (Van der Wende 2011: 103), shaping and reshaping policy and translating this into 'messages' for governments.

Van der Wende suggests that the OECD sits somewhere in the middle ideologically between the World Bank and UNESCO, but lacks the financial clout of the World Bank. Moreover, the World Bank focuses on developing countries and the OECD on richer countries. There is cooperation, however, with the World Bank in a shared human capital approach to higher education as an engine of economic growth. Van der Wende (2011) suggests that the OECD position has also shaped the work of the European Commission, citing the Lisbon Council support for the economic returns to higher education as being instrumental to economic recovery. As the Council report (in Van der Wende 2011: 109) stated: 'If, for instance, all the OECD countries in Europe could raise their educational performance to Finland's level, the result could be an aggregate GDP increase of US$200 trillion'. Van der Wende concludes that the OECD is an advocate for a predominantly neo-liberal reading of globalisation, with education positioned as producing human capital for economic development. But she also points out that the OECD is not static and that the destabilising effects of economic globalisation have increased concerns for social cohesion and 'balancing globalization'.

Notwithstanding these various reports, Unterhalter *et al.* (2013) suggest that universities have in the past not attracted strong global/human development policy advocates, such as we found for primary education in the

Millennium Development Goals (MDGs).[1] They outline possible reasons for the relatively light attention to higher education, including: the unfinished business of universal primary education for all (more urgent than 'elite' university education); the unresolved problem of quality of learning in schools; the urgency of escalating youth unemployment; and, the contestations around the significance of higher education, whether it 'delivers' development and how this can be 'proved'. Higher education may be implicit but this is instrumental towards explicit development goals, which are seen to be the priorities. For example, we could say that higher education is important, and yet not foregrounded, for all the High Level Panel (HLP) goals reported to the United Nations (2013) as a contribution to the post-2015 goals process: (1) leave no-one behind; (2) put sustainable development at the core; (3) transform economies for jobs and inclusive growth; (4) build peace and effective, open and accountable institutions for all; and, (5) forge a new [symmetrical] global partnership.

For its part, UNESCO (2013) identified six educational imperatives for post-2015, which do not exclude higher education but which do not foreground the sector either: equity at all levels of education, quality education and learning at all levels, gender equality, lifelong learning and opportunities to acquire knowledge and skills for sustainable development, global citizenship and the world of work. UNESCO notes with concern the growing barriers in developing countries for access to higher education by the urban poor, but also notes the potential of investments in higher education to pay economic development dividends. Nonetheless, while UNESCO offers a 'deep rooted understanding of universities as having a profound role in bringing about social and economic change, it does not appear to be driving a global debate around this' (Unterhalter *et al.* 2013: 27), confirmed also by Lebeau and Sall (2011) in their account of UNESCO's involvement in higher education. The World Bank, as noted earlier, has now placed secondary and higher education at the heart of its anti-poverty activities, and the development of higher knowledge is now seen as crucial for economic growth to reduce poverty, through learning, knowledge, science, technology and innovation, but the World Bank may not necessarily align well with the post-2015 normative approach. Nonetheless, overall in Unterhalter *et al.*'s (2013) assessment of post-2015 proposals, they suggest that neither UNESCO nor the World Bank have specific policies on higher education as a stand-alone goal.

More promising is the 'Zero Draft' of the Sustainable Development Goals (United Nations 2015) approved in a General Assembly of the United Nations in September 2015.[2] Higher education appears in a clearer way in several targets related to Goal 4, which is specifically devoted to education. The following is the proposed broad statement for Goal 4: *Ensure inclusive and equitable quality education and promote lifelong learning opportunities for all*, while the following are the targets relate to higher education:

- By 2030, ensure equal access for all women and men to affordable and quality technical, vocational and tertiary education, including university.
- By 2030, increase by [x] per cent the number of youth and adults who have relevant skills, including technical and vocational skills, for employment, decent jobs and entrepreneurship.
- By 2030, eliminate gender disparities in education and ensure equal access to all levels of education and vocational training for the vulnerable, including persons with disabilities, indigenous peoples and children in vulnerable situations.
- By 2030, expand by [x] per cent globally the number of scholarships available to developing countries, in particular least developed countries, small island developing States and African countries, for enrolment in higher education, including vocational training and information and communications technology, technical, engineering and scientific programmes, in developed countries and other developing countries.
- By 2030, ensure that all learners acquire the knowledge and skills needed to promote sustainable development, including, among others, through education for sustainable development and sustainable lifestyles, human rights, gender equality, promotion of a culture of peace and non-violence, global citizenship and appreciation of cultural diversity and of culture's contribution to sustainable development.

This proposal suggests that higher education has indeed gained a more prominent role in the global debate, acknowledging thus that the continuum between all levels of education is positive for development.

However, to make the global goals debate more complex, this acknowledgement could also be detrimental for higher education. As Fukuda-Parr *et al.* (2014: 20) explain, global goals can shape the way development is (mis)understood, 'with reductionist consequences for how development and poverty were construed', compared with earlier debates in the 1990s. To take a higher education example of how reductionist target setting might work, countries may overlook the arts and humanities, unless they can prove their economic worth or their centrality to science and innovation; or, the distinctiveness of higher knowledge as both an intrinsic and instrumental good could be diminished in the search for immediate development solutions. 'Universities and development' could come to mean something other than the expansive goals of equality, solidarity and freedom in a focus on simplicity, measurability and achievability of goals and targets (Fukuda-Parr *et al.* 2014). We comment further on the challenge of indicators in Chapter 5.

This is not a simple debate, and for higher education to be visible in the post-2015 agenda undoubtedly has pros and cons. What we want to argue here is that, even if universities do not feature as a stand-alone goal in making the post-2015 global policy agenda, they do contribute substantially to development through the graduates they educate, their engagement in development research, and in promoting critical thinking and democratic values. The challenge lies in 'so what' and 'what now', with regard to universities and development. This section has attempted to address both of these questions in arguing for the significance of universities to development agendas, for the importance of ideas, innovation and imagination in finding solutions to problems of poverty and disadvantage, for the role of universities in educating professionals with knowledge skills and also public-good values, but also for the recognition and protection of the distinctiveness of the university higher knowledge project. Here the appeal to global development agenda may be weak in its drive for more immediate targets and results; university knowledge and training is for medium- and long-term development agendas and for a public space of critical reasoning (De Sousa Santos 2010). It does not offer quick and easy solutions.

Benefits for development from higher and university education

Having considered how universities feature in education and development debates and appear in global development agendas, we acknowledge that higher education cannot do everything, and that it cannot compensate for severe inequality in society, but this does not mean it cannot do anything, as we will examine in this section. Graduates educated in universities are indispensable to development agendas, educating a range of professionals in health, education, science, technology, engineering, and so on (Walker and McLean 2013). Skilled cadres of professionals are needed to staff, lead and deliver accountable and effective public services, while science and technology innovations emerging from universities are crucial for addressing problems of water, sanitation, preventable diseases, food security, etc. As Unterhalter *et al.* (2013: 13) state: 'Basic education cannot adequately be delivered, particularly to the poorest and taking account of inequalities, without a simultaneous expansion of secondary and tertiary education'. Similarly, the UNESCO assistant Director-General for education, Dr Qian Tang (in McMahon 2014: 1), has stressed the urgent need for more higher education in developing countries, saying, 'everyone in Africa tells me they need higher education to help primary schools and therefore the socio-economic development of their country'. This is reiterated globally by UNESCO (2009: 10): 'At no time in human history was the welfare of nations so closely linked to the quality and outreach of their higher education systems and institutions'.

However, for global policy agendas, the social returns to higher education are more elusive and harder to measure than those from schooling, which makes higher education less attractive as a measurable global policy goal, unlike primary education in the MDGs. Nonetheless, we can find evidence pointing to measurable, if complex benefits. McMahon and Oketch (2013) examine the effects of human capital skills, created through higher education, on life chances over the life cycle, both in increased earnings and skills through gaining higher educational qualifications. They also look at private benefits such as health (individual and family), longevity and happiness, and social benefits, including democratisation, civil rights, political stability, reduced crime, health and welfare costs, and new ideas. They augment standard social rates of return data to obtain new estimates of total returns relative to costs, including non-market outcomes, in which case they find that 'narrower' social rates of return of 13.6 per cent for Bachelor's programmes are expanded to twice that. In his earlier study of the USA, McMahon (2009) similarly showed that a college degree brings better job opportunities and higher earnings but it also leads to non-market benefits, both social and private. Higher education, he claims, improves democracy and sustainable growth, and generates social benefits, such as reduced crime. He argues that measuring and valuing both market and non-market benefits of higher education relative to the costs 'cannot be overstated' in the face of underinvestment, and warns that if this is not done 'higher education's service to the public good is seriously at risk' (McMahon 2009: 329).

Oketch *et al.* (2014) have also reviewed the impact of tertiary education (which is not limited to universities but includes all post-compulsory education) on development; they assess the evidence linking tertiary education to a wide range of economic and human development outcomes in low- and lower-middle-income countries (LLMICs). They point to evidence of a range of positive outcomes and likely impacts across a range of LLMICs, suggesting that tertiary education appears to have a stronger impact on economic growth than was previously assumed, with some studies suggesting that it has a stronger impact than do lower levels of education. In addition to having a strong impact on the earnings of graduates, there is some evidence, they suggest, that tertiary education has a positive impact on productivity in the workplace, although significant barriers to impact remain. Moreover, even though research output in universities in LLMICs is generally low, and there is limited transfer of technology to local industries, the proportion of workers with higher education within a given context appears to increase the likelihood of technological uptake and adaptation. They further point out that tertiary education provides a range of broad, measurable benefits to graduates relating to health, gender equality and democracy, among other areas. In addition, it contributes to the strengthening of institutions, and the formation of professionals in key development areas, such as health and education.

Research also suggests the social value added by higher education in Africa, including job creation, good economic and political governance, increased entrepreneurship and better intergenerational mobility (Sawahel 2014: 1). In Africa, many universities, except for South Africa, were badly affected by World Bank policies, which promoted the neglect of higher education, so that research has called for the 'revitalisation' of universities (see, e.g. Sall *et al.* 2003; Singh 2011) in the light of possibilities for knowledge-driven development, which is now regarded as crucial to development trajectories in Africa (Singh 2011). Employability, employment and individual economic opportunities are critical: professionals without jobs cannot use their knowledge and skills to contribute to society; unemployed graduates will not be socially mobile and are likely to be dissatisfied with their lives: a graduate without job prospects is a wasted national resource in any developed or developing country.

But there are also wider benefits. Sall *et al.* (2003) discuss African universities in civil society, explaining that, while they may have reproductive effects, they also have the potential as part of the public sphere to hold the state and business accountable and provide critical discussion and direction on changes in society. Importantly, they note that universities produce most of the people employed at the higher echelons of the public and private sector. The social significance of university expansion lies in graduate social mobility and integration into the labour market, both critical for the transformation roles and functions of universities (Sall *et al.* 2003). However, they note that the choices and experiences of young people in higher education in Africa will be critical to whether it fulfils a reproductive role for privilege and private advantages, or also encompasses a transformative role for well-being across society.

In a developed countries context, Brennan *et al.* (2013) reviewed the literature for the Department for Business Innovation and Skills in the UK on the wider benefits of higher education unrelated to the economic sphere, but which nevertheless may have significant impacts at the individual and societal levels. They found that much of the literature focuses on the significance of gaining a higher education qualification for progression in the labour market and for the resultant effects on lifestyle and aspirations, but there is also a significant literature illustrating differences between higher education graduates and other members of society on a range of other dimensions. The most frequently cited ones are: citizenship (expressed in attitudes towards voting); civic engagement (propensity to volunteer, participation in public debates, mutual trust and tolerance towards 'the other'); crime (educational attainment leads to lower crime rate); health (positive correlation between education and health); and general well-being. The benefits from higher education, they say, are not limited to people who are or have been students but extend to wider society, for example, influencing changes in consumption patterns and attitudes to diversity and multiculturalism.

A UNESCO (2014) briefing paper provides further examples where higher education seems to make a difference. According to UNESCO, higher education contributes to ending poverty and powerlessness in the workplace, equipping individuals with competencies and skills that are needed in the labour market, but also with job security. For instance, in El Salvador, whereas only 5 per cent of workers with less than primary education have an employment contract, 50 per cent of those with secondary and tertiary education work under secure signed contracts. More education, and also higher education is one way of enhancing gender equality and empowerment. Women with higher education are less likely to get married or have children at an early age, and have a significantly lower fertility rate in sub-Saharan Africa. In Pakistan, while only 30 per cent of women with no education believe they can have a say over the number of their children, the share increases with levels of education, rising to over 70 per cent among women with higher education. Nussbaum (2004: 337) underlines the case for the significance of university education for gender equality in that university-educated women 'are far more likely to be able to influence debates at a national level as well as have access to the more influential and higher paying jobs'. More education also contributes to sustainable environmental practices. For example, in the Netherlands, people with a higher level of education tend to use less energy, even taking account of their income. A study of households in ten countries that are members of the OECD found that those with higher education tended to save water and energy. Finally, higher education is good for justice: as a catalyst to promote human rights, justice and the rule of law; and a mechanism that can promote political pluralism, and tolerance.

There is then evidence that higher and university education can make a difference to individuals and to more inclusive societies. Moreover, university education uniquely conserves, disseminates and advances scholarly knowledge through teaching and research, and this too matters for global development agendas and universities' contributions. 'Higher knowledge' is prized in modern societies, in that it constitutes a 'potent source of innovation and development' (Morrow 2009: 117) and hence, new ideas and new thinking; it encourages doubt, not certainty, imagination and critical thinking. Such innovation is foregrounded in knowledge economy policies, which need the expertise and the experts produced in higher education, Morrow (2009: 31) argues, as a 'springboard from which to leap into the future'. He further points out that the value of professional training is precisely in its relationship to higher knowledge:

> It is the flexibility and openness to new ideas that universities at their best engender that which should characterize professional knowledge – a far cry from the mechanical application of learning skills that will then be mechanically applied. Professional knowledge is thus closely linked to higher knowledge.
>
> (Morrow 2009: 136)

Thus, what global development agendas might be most interested in, in relation to higher education – professional education and training of graduates and scientists who can take forward development – requires a foundation in scholarly knowledge and expertise, and universities are key sites for producing this knowledge through evidence, argument, peer review and publication.

University graduates, as McMahon (2009) explains, do seem to lead better lives with more opportunities and agency, and countries with more university education seem to do better than those with less. There is sufficient evidence that universities are key sites of and for development, distributing higher knowledge and understanding, and shaping life chances and hence advantages. Who gets it and what they do with, and which countries have more (or less) of it is then significant in global debates and partnerships. While universities undoubtedly contribute to social reproduction (and hence to the current unfair global arrangements or unequal societies), they also open spaces for public-good development contributions through the critical and emancipatory power of knowledge and reason; the usefulness of knowledge for society; and equality, citizenship and democracy. They can foster intrinsic human flourishing as well as human capital formation, so that development is inclusive, human and well-being led. As the ACU confirmed at its 2010 conference (McGregor 2010) and the then President of Association of African Universities (AAU) further emphasised, universities play a pivotal role, so that there can be no question of the contribution of higher education to development goals (Mohamedbhai 2007).

Higher education attainment is also linked to more positive perceptions of good health, levels of interpersonal trust, participation in volunteering activities, and the belief that an individual can have an impact on the political process. From here we can say that countries with less higher education risk diminishing social cohesion and well-being. But it also matters how education and skills are distributed across the population. Countries with proportionally fewer low-skilled adults and more high-skilled adults do better in terms of economic output and social equality than countries with a similar average level of skills but with larger differences in skills proficiency across the population. Education and skills have thus become increasingly important dimensions of social inequality; but they are also an indispensable part of the solution to this problem. Education can lift people out of poverty and social exclusion, but in order to do so, educational attainment has to translate into social mobility. Inclusive societies thus need education systems that promote learning and the acquisition of knowledge and skills in an equitable manner. 'Education and skills', Gurria (2014) argues optimistically, 'hold the key to future wellbeing and will be critical to restoring long-term growth, tackling unemployment, promoting competitiveness, and nurturing more inclusive and cohesive societies'.

Higher education and public-good goals

On the other hand, it may not matter if higher education does not feature that prominently in global development agendas, if we agree with Marginson (2016) that 'what happens with incomes, wealth, labour markets, taxation, government spending, social programmes, and urban development are overwhelmingly more important' than what happens in universities. But we are not ready to give up on higher education or to extrapolate an Anglo-American societies argument to all societies. We think that there is still a powerful argument available about what ought to be the aims of universities and for public reasoning about the real opportunities available to different social groups in any society, connecting universities to development agendas and the tremendous problems the world faces today – environmental challenges, social injustices, armed conflicts, intolerance, abuses of and lack of respect for human rights – and that higher education should have an active role, engaged in local and global spaces, to foster and support a just and sustainable society. Holmwood (2011: 4) argues that to diminish this public value of higher education, is to diminish 'our life in common'. Similarly, Nixon (2011) makes the argument for universities as central to the well-being of civil society and its citizens and to public reasoning, all of which require a fair and equitable system of higher education. While he offers a critique of the current commodified state of higher education, he also suggests that higher education can educate people 'who are not only efficient and effective in their use of acquired knowledge, but who can use that knowledge to make complex choices regarding the right uses and application of that knowledge' (Nixon 2011: 26). He claims that we would know 'when the public had returned' because we would see real people with different backgrounds and aspirations, sharing commitments to each other and the world, bringing resources for their own flourishing and that of others to a 'republic of learning', which would respond to these new and diverse ways of knowing towards 'a collective purposes, a common idiom and possible futures' (Nixon 2011: 132). The public-good function of universities is also realised through the education of professionals as citizens who will interchange value with society through the exercise of their professional responsibilities, acting with ethical awareness and civic commitment – 'public-good' professionals (Walker and McLean 2013). Understanding professional education as educating people to be able to contribute to the common welfare connects the singular public good of higher education to the notion of plural public-goods. 'Public-good' captures, as Leibowitz (2012) suggests, the idea that a university as a whole leans consistently towards the values, practices and policies of social justice and inclusion both within the institution and in its external dealings.

More specifically, Nussbaum (1997) argues for liberal higher education, which could exemplify this public-good orientation through the 'cultivation of humanity' by developing in students three core capacities: critical self-examination, the ideal of the world citizen, and the development of the narrative imagination. The first is a capacity for critical examination of oneself and one's traditions – the 'examined life' – which requires a critical perspective on our beliefs, traditions and habits, reasoning logically and testing ideas for consistency, correctness and accuracy of judgement as a democratic citizen. Discussions around bioethics, religion, history and physics could all adopt such a method. Second, Nussbaum (1997: 10) argues, we need to develop the ability to see ourselves as 'world citizens', not only belonging to a local community, but also as bound to all other human beings 'by ties of recognition and concern in a global world'. Again, this could be applied in a philosophy or anthropology class but also in a biology class discussing genetically modified foods and their impact on food security. Third, is the cultivation of a 'narrative imagination', by which Nussbaum means the ability to think what it might be like to be in the place of a person different from oneself across dimensions of country, social class, gender, ethnicity, and so on, to read such people's stories intelligently, and to understand the emotions and desires that someone so placed might have.

Bok (2006) also proposes a set of goals for undergraduate education: learning to communicate; learning to think; building 'character'; preparation for citizenship; living with diversity; preparing for a global society; acquiring 'broader interests'; and preparing for a career (listed as the last of his goals). He is clear about the importance of preparing students for career choices, but as only one of a number of multidimensional learning outcomes, even though graduates' careers 'will have a great deal to do with defining who they are, how satisfied they feel about their lives, and how comfortably they will live' (Bok 2006: 281). Taken together, these goals and their realisation would constitute a coherent education, which included but went beyond occupational preparation to prepare students to live full lives as widely informed, reflective human beings. As Bok (2013) notes, economic stagnation and a lack of opportunity are problems, but so are low voting rates, civic apathy, disregard for ethical standards, and indifference to art, music, literature and ideas. It is, he says, the responsibility of educators in universities to help students live (and choose) satisfying, responsible lives.

Thus, some things emerge as significant for higher education as a public good: that fostering meaningful lives are important; that what we might call the knowledge and critical thinking project is crucial to what makes higher education; that multidimensional goals, including but not reduced to work, are important for a full life; that affiliations with others near and far should be fostered; that engagement with wider communities and the role of universities in society, if well done, is potentially powerful; and that higher education educates graduate-professionals who will go out into the world, who can have an impact on individuals, communities and society, so that the cultivation of graduates' public values orientation matters.

Inequality challenges to universities and public-good commitments

However, Gurria (2014) points to a problem: data shows that the benefits of the expansion in education have been shared inter-generationally only by the middle-class, with the children of low-educated families increasingly excluded from the potential benefits. In Piketty's (2014) closed societies in which wealth is concentrated in fewer and fewer hands, this looks rather difficult. It may be that the benefits of higher education are rather unevenly spread, favouring the already advantaged; both Marginson (2016) and McCowan (2015) seem to confirm this. Thus, we are especially concerned with the specific global challenge of uneven (broadly between North and South) and combined development (countries which are both advanced and less developed) and the increase of inequalities both in the global South and North for public-good aspirational goals. As we pointed out at the beginning of the chapter, one of our major concerns here is the relationship between universities, development and advancing or constraining equality to, in and through education. Turning to inequality challenges, which may undermine public-good orientations or, conversely, foreground them as needing attention by higher education, we consider two South African examples to illustrate the point. First, according to Oxfam (2014), the two richest South Africans, Johan Rupert and Nicky Oppenheimer, together have the same wealth at around ZAR155 billion, as the bottom 50 per cent of the population. Such harsh inequalities if allowed to persist will definitely limit the opportunities of most young South Africans to approach anywhere near higher education. Such conditions also affect health, political participation, and constrain aspirational pathways. Moreover, as Oxfam (2014: 16) notes in its report, extreme inequality 'corrupts politics, hinders economic growth and stifles social mobility.... It squanders talent, thwarts potential and undermines the foundations of society'. These conditions are not good for universities and their public-good contributions. On the other hand, in a recent debate among some South African universities Prins Nevathulu (in UCT 2014), current Vice-Chancellor of the Cape Peninsula University of Technology, argued that universities should guard against merely producing students who exacerbate present social inequalities. He pointed out that South Africa has one of the world's worst Gini coefficients (a measure of inequality) (see Atkinson 2015: 22), and asked: 'Do universities produce students who are going to exacerbate these divisions between the very rich and the very poor?' In different ways, the examples raise the question of development for whom, and the obstacles inequality puts in the way of higher education.

Recently, there have been a number of books and reports published detailing growing inequalities in the distribution of wealth, particularly over the last 30 years or so (e.g. Atkinson 2015; OECD 2012; Piketty 2014). Piketty (2014: 571) in his study of developed economies, argues robustly that 'the consequences for the long-term dynamics of the wealth distribution are potentially terrifying', especially – as his book demonstrates – in societies where wages are unequal, and where the top 10 per cent have pulled away from the rest, leading to concentrations of capital (wealth) with severe intergenerational effects. Atkinson (2015) also argues that equality of opportunity is intergenerational – not only a matter of the here and now but of the future and of the impact of the past in shaping opportunities, thereby calling into question advancing fair opportunities in higher education access and participation. These are not books specifically on higher education, even though they may touch on, as Piketty does, the role education and training played in increasing incomes in developed countries following the Second World War. Indeed, he concedes that over time, 'the main force in favor of greater equality has been the diffusion of knowledge and skills' (Piketty 2014: 22).

But in his view, higher education may no longer play this role. Piketty is thus less sanguine that higher education always advances mobility (and we add, public-good development) in the face of high or growing inequality, notably the unequal and unfair distribution of wealth and income, which constrains equality of opportunity. For example, he argues that in the USA, parental income 'has become an almost perfect predictor of university access' (Piketty 2014: 485), with the most degrees being awarded to the children of parents in the top quartile of income, and the highest returns coming from elite higher education. Piketty (2014: 85) further points out that the challenge of unequal access to higher education 'is one of the most important problems that social states must face everywhere in the twenty-first century'. This is very significant, given that higher education is assumed to constitute a significant driver for social mobility and a better life globally; but this may now not be the case everywhere. Sen's (1999) confidence that a 'good' education can make a dramatic difference to human abilities and achievement, that it can transform individual lives and contribute to social change, including in the direction of equity and social justice – may not hold for all lives if we follow Piketty and the educational application of his arguments to unequal university access in Anglo-American societies provided by Marginson (2016). At stake is that in unequal societies, education will be unequal, more reproductive and less transformative, as Bourdieu and Passeron (1977) argued some four decades ago, and as sociological studies of higher education have continued to demonstrate.

This inequality challenge should be considered for its impact on public-good contributions, taking into account globalisation and how it is affecting higher education, not only from an economic point of view but also socially, culturally and politically. Marginson (2011), one of the leading commentators on higher education and globalisation, points to a real strain between an economically instrumental policy agenda for universities and more expansive development. The former is far better embedded and advanced so that Marginson (2011: 31) claims: 'Notions of capability and public goods are readily transferred to the global dimensions. But these ideas are not dominant. Mainstream thought about higher education is led by neo-liberalism, which emphasises the market economy'. Nonetheless, other commentators, among them Sen (2002), argue that 'globalism' has not been only an unalloyed burden and the question to ask is: how fair are the benefits? Globalism, argues Sen, has brought benefits and gains including, we think, in the arena of university education: expanded student access, more diverse students, more gender equity, more interaction and mobility internationally fuelling graduate capacity building and research collaborations, and economic opportunities and employment. On the other hand, there are also inequalities globally in access to and the quality of higher education, in some (but not all) regions, significant graduate unemployment, and certainly a drive by economic policy-makers to cast universities as contributing primarily to economic growth and national innovation systems, obscuring other purposes of higher education in relation to development. Yet, such shifts are neither hegemonic nor uniform and whatever policy intentions are, they do not wholly determine actual practices.

We are especially interested in this question of inequality and higher education from the point of view of aspirational goals regarding what universities ought to aim for and do, as well as Sen's (2009) pragmatic idea of comparative assessments in actual practices and lives, so that we identify the spaces for more transformation rather than less, for more equity rather than less, and for more agency expansion rather than less to allow for grounds for action and optimism. We are interested therefore in approaches which take us beyond the necessary but insufficient critiques of globalisation and neo-liberalism effects in higher education. Such critique highlights injustices well but does not indicate direction or spaces of more justice, which we think is needed if higher education is to be oriented towards models of social justice in policy and action. On the other hand, we do not claim that higher education can solve the problems of society, inequality or well-being but we also need to understand growing inequality gaps and take them into account so that we align higher education analysis to wider development issues, challenges and strategies.

Concluding thoughts

We still want to argue for higher education as a public-good and an arena that ought to be taken seriously in development and global policy. Unterhalter *et al.* (2013) helpfully advocate for a 'continuum' of education stretching from primary, through secondary, to post-secondary education and where the supportive links between different phases of learning are fully recognised and understood. In other words, there is a feedback loop from higher education into primary and secondary education in the way higher education educates teachers and other professionals who contribute to overall well-being in children's health and other development sectors. They also outline ten case study countries where there is both rising economic growth and expanding higher education to suggest at least a correlation between the two, even if direct causality cannot be claimed. The literature reviewed illustrates, they say, that as complex as they are, the links between economic growth and poverty eradication and addressing inequalities can be made by focusing on secondary and post-secondary education.

Meanwhile in higher education, we need still to advance an agenda of reform and change, which has at least the potential to influence wider social change, as Unterhalter (2006) argues in relation to gender equity in higher education having a social impact. We take some inspiration from Atkinson who shows, as an economist, what could be done now to reduce inequality. As he states, 'The world faces great problems, but collectively we are not helpless in the face of forces outside our control. The future is very much in our hands' (Atkinson 2015: 1). We can ask the same question of higher education reform or policy that Atkinson asks of economic change or policy: who gains and who loses? If inequality is being perpetuated over the course of generations, why does this inequality persist (and by implication why we as agents allow this). What can higher education do? What we need is to think as well as we can about these questions and about what matters for a decent society, conceptualising an approach to higher education, which is globally ambitious and locally relevant and transformative.

Having considered the higher education perspective on development, in the next chapter we consider how development theories have understood higher education and universities, before turning in Chapter 4, to proposing a foundation of human development and capabilities for universities.

Notes

1 The MDGs which ran until 2015 were: eradicate poverty and hunger; achieve universal primary education; promote gender equality and empower women; reduce child mortality; improve maternal health; combat HIV/AIDS, malaria and other diseases; ensure environmental sustainability; develop a global partnership for development.
2 The 2030 Development Agenda, *Transforming our World*, includes 17 development goals, which in different ways will require the contributions of graduate professionals'. For example, in addition to Goal 4, other goals include: 'Ensure availability and sustainable management of water and sanitation for all'; 'Ensure access to affordable, reliable, sustainable and modern energy for all'; and 'Take urgent action to combat climate change and its impacts'.

References

Atkinson, T. 2015. *Inequality. What Can Be Done?* Cambridge, MA: Harvard University Press.

Brennan, J., N. Durazzi and T. Tanguy. 2013. *Things We Know and Don't Know about the Wider Benefits of Higher Education: a Review of the Recent Literature.* [Accessed 2 July 2015]. www.heer.qaa.ac.uk/.

Bok, D. 2006. *Our Underachieving Colleges: A Candid Look at How Much Students Learn and Why They Should Be Learning More.* Princeton: Princeton University Press.

Bok, D. 2013. *Higher Education Misconceived.* [Accessed 14 July 2014]. www.project-syndicate.org/commentary/derek-bok-on-policymakers--misconceptions-of-the-role-of-higher-learning.

Bourdieu, P. and J-C. Passeron. 1977. *Reproduction in Education, Society and Culture.* London: Sage.

De Sousa Santos, B. 2010. 'The university in the twenty-first century: towards a democratic and emancipatory university reform'. In *The Routledge International Handbook of the Sociology of Education*, edited by M. Apple, S. Ball and L.A. Gandin, 274–82. Abingdon: Routledge.

Fukuda-Parr, S., A. Yamin and J. Greenstein. 2014. 'The power of numbers: a critical review of Millennium Development Goal targets for Human Development and Human Rights', *Journal of Human Development and Capabilities* 15(2–3): 105–17.

Holmwood, J. (ed.) 2011. *A Manifesto for the Public University.* London: Bloomsbury Academic.

Gurria, A. 2014. *Secretary-General's Report to Ministers.* Paris: OECD. [Accessed 15 October 2014]. www.oecd.org/about/secretary-general/SG-Annual-Report-to-Ministers-2014.pdf.

Lebeau, Y. and E. Sall. 2011. 'Global institutions, higher education and development'. In *Handbook on Globalization and Higher Education*, edited by R. King, S. Marginson and R. Naidoo, 129–47. Cheltenham: Edward Elgar.

Leibowitz, B. (ed.) 2012. *Higher Education and the Public Good.* Stellenbosch: SUNMedia.

Marginson, S. 2011. 'Imagining the global', In *Handbook on Globalization and Higher Education*, edited by R. King, S. Marginson and R. Naidoo, 10–39. Cheltenham: Edward Elgar.

Marginson, S. 2016. 'Higher education and inequality in Anglo-American societies'. In *Student Equity in Australian Higher Education: Twenty Five years of a 'Fair Chance for All'*, edited by M. Brett, A. Harvey and C. Burnheim. Dordrecht: Springer.

McCowan, T. 2015. 'Three dimensions of equity of access to higher education', *Compare.* DOI: 10.1080/03057925.2015.1043237.

McGregor, K. 2010. 'Higher education a driver of the MDGs'. *University World News*, 2 May 2010. [Accessed 5 January 2014]. www.universityworldnews.com/article.php?story=20100501081126465.

McMahon, M. 2014. 'He should get the lion's share in post-2015 education goals'. *University World News Global Edition*, 306. [Accessed 15 February 2015]. www.universityworldnews.com/article.php?story=20140206618041568O&mode/.

McMahon, W. 2009. *Higher Learning, Greater Good: The Private and Social Benefits of Higher Education*. Baltimore: Johns Hopkins University Press.

McMahon, W. and M. Oketch. 2013. 'Education's effects on individual's life chances and development: an overview', *British Journal of Educational Studies* 61(1): 79–107.

Mohamedbhai, G. 2007. 'Higher education contribution to the UN Millennium Development Goals', *Global University Network for Innovation*, 18 October 2007. [Accessed 17 December 2013]. www.guninetwork.org/resources/he-articles/higher-education-contribution-to-the-millenium-development-goals.

Morrow, W. 2009. *Bounds of Democracy*. Pretoria: HSRC Press.

Nixon, J. 2011. *Higher Education and the Public Good*. London: Continuum.

Naidoo, R. 2015. 'Transnational perspectives on higher education and global well-being'. *Valuing Research into Higher Education: Advancing knowledge, informing policy, enhancing practice*. SRHE 50th Anniversary Colloquium, 26 June 2015, pp. 14–16. [Accessed 18 September 2015]. www.srhe.ac.uk/downloads/SRHE_50Programme_web.pdf

Nussbaum, M. 1997. *Cultivating Humanity. A Classical Defence of Reform in Liberal Education*. Cambridge, MA: Harvard University Press.

Nussbaum, M. 2004. 'Women's education: a global challenge', *Signs: Journal of Women and Culture in Society* 29(2): 325–55.

Obamba, M. 2013. 'Uncommon knowledge: World Bank policy and the unmaking of the knowledge economy in Africa', *Higher Education Policy* 26: 83–108.

OECD. 2012. *Divided We Stand*. Paris: OECD.

Oketch M., T. McCowan and R. Schendel. 2014. *The Impact of Tertiary Education on Development: A Rigorous Literature Review*. London: Department for International Development.

Oxfam. 2014. 'Even it Up. Time to End Extreme Inequality'. United Kingdom: Oxfam. [Accessed 10 December 2015]. www.oxfam.org/sites/www.oxfam.org/files/file_attachments/cr-even-it-up-extreme-inequality-291014-en.pdf.

Piketty, T. 2014. *Capital in the Twenty-First Century*. Cambridge, MA: The Belknap Press.

Sall, E., Y. Lebeau and R. Kassimir. 2003. 'The public dimensions of the University in Africa'. *Journal of Higher Education Africa* 1(1): 126–48.

Sawahel, W. 2014. 'USAID's transformative strategy for higher education'. *University World News* 129, 11 April 2014.

Schofer, E. and J. W. Meyer. 2005. 'The worldwide expansion of higher education in the twentieth century'. *American Sociological Review* 70: 898–920.

Sen, A. 1999. *Development as Freedom*. Oxford: Oxford University Press.

Sen, A. 2002. 'Globalism'. *The American Prospect*, 1 January 2002. [Accessed 5 January 2013]. www.sas.upenn.edu/~dludden/SenGlobalism.htm.

Sen, A. 2009. *The Idea of Justice*. London: Allen Lane.

Singh, M. 2011. 'The place of social justice in higher education and social change discourses', *Compare* 41(4): 481–94.

UNESCO. 2009. *Trends in Global Higher Education: Tracking an Academic Revolution*. Paris: UNESCO.

UNESCO. 2013. *Position Paper on Education Post-2015*. Paris: UNESCO.

UNESCO. 2014. *Sustainable Development Begins with Education: How Education Can Contribute to the Proposed Post-2015 Goals*. [Accessed 26 July 2015]. www.globaleducationfirst.org/4443.htm/.

UNESCO Institute for Statistics. 2012. *Higher Education Statistics.* [Accessed 22 July 2015]. www.uis.unesco.org/Home/Education/.

University of Cape Town (UCT). 2014. *Monday Paper* 33(2): 1.

United Nations. 2013. 'A new global partnership: eradicate poverty and transform economies through sustainable development'. *The Report of the High Level Panel of Eminent Persons on the Post-2015 Development Agenda.* New York: United Nations. [Accessed 12 December 2013]. www.post2015hlp.org.

United Nations. 2015. *Zero Draft of the Outcome Document for the UN Summit to Adopt the Post-2015 Development Agenda.* [Accessed 24 July 2015]. https://sustainabledevelopment.un.org/?page=view&nr=1064&type=13&menu=1634.

Unterhalter, E. and V. Carpentier, eds. 2010. *Whose Interests Are We Serving? Global Inequalities and Higher Education.* New York: Palgrave Macmillan.

Unterhalter, E., R. Peppin Vaughan and A. Smail. 2013. *Secondary, Post-Secondary and Higher Education in the Post-2015 Discussions.* London: British Council.

Unterhalter, E. 2006. 'New times and new vocabularies: theorising and evaluating gender equality in Common Wealth higher education', *Women's Studies International Forum* 29: 620–8.

Van der Wende, M. C. 2011. 'Global institutions: The Organisation for Economic Co-operation and Development'. In *Handbook on Globalization and Higher Education*, edited by R. King, S. Marginson and R. Naidoo, 95–114. Cheltenham: Edward Elgar.

Walker, M. and M. McLean. 2013. *Professional Education, Capabilities and the Public Good: The Role of Universities in Promoting Human Development.* London: Routledge.

World Bank. 2002. *Constructing Knowledge Societies. New Challenges for Tertiary Education.* Washington DC: World Bank.

World Bank. 2003. *Lifelong Learning in the Global Knowledge Economy: Challenges for Developing Countries.* Washington DC: World Bank.

3 How development theories understand universities

In this chapter, we consider development, which is too seldom linked to higher education (and of course vice-versa). Thus, we find development ideas in development studies, innovation studies, welfare economics, development ethics, and so on. This is to miss an opportunity for expanding the reach and responsiveness of our education conceptual repertoires. Thus, we describe how different development theories have considered the university, its goals, social function and practices, both in the area of teaching and of research and community engagement, selecting development theories and approaches that are most widely acknowledged in the field of development studies (Willis 2011). In these different theories, development is conceptualised differently and will generate different policy frameworks and priorities, for example development as economic growth, development as participation, development as gender equity, sustainable development, market-friendly development, and so on (McCowan 2015).

Our purpose, following on from Chapter 2, is to locate universities as a key site in debates about development in society, both in the local and global realms, and to work to bring together higher education language in the previous chapter and development language in this chapter. To dislocate higher education and universities from wider development discourse, as Naidoo (2011: 55) suggests, 'constrains the development of research and policy on the potential of higher education to contribute to development'. We need to draw from development to locate and make the case for the role of higher education in development. We also need fresh approaches to explore and understand educational inequality, and wider attention to development can help us with this (as did Piketty's work in the previous chapter). Moreover, development intersecting with education requires that we take a normative stand regarding both what we take to be a decent society (development to what end?) and, following on this, a normative stand on universities (universities to what development ends?), and from here, what should be our priorities. We are aware of the general and limited nature of our analysis, given the wide range of our subject of study; nevertheless, we deemed it appropriate to write this chapter as the university is not well covered in development theories.

The first group of theories includes theories of economic development, elaborated from the 1940s onwards and concurring with the birth of an international cooperation (development) system. Theories which are economically oriented include modernisation theory, dependency theories, new-growth theories and neo-liberalism, the latter related to the globalisation phenomenon. The second group includes various alternative approaches to development (Willis 2011), ranging from sustainable development, gender in development, participation and citizenship. All of them have considered the university in a different way from economic theories and, even although it has not been a central institution in their analyses, they have indeed made interesting proposals reflecting on the mission of the university. We conclude this chapter with post-development and post-colonial approaches which, beyond making a direct criticism of the very concept of development, have put forward relevant analyses about the political economy of knowledge and the re-valuation of local knowledge.

Economic development theories: modernisation and dependency

The purpose of an economic theory of development is to unravel the causes, mechanisms and consequences of economic growth, particularly in countries with low per-capita income (Bustelo 1998). The approach foregrounds economic growth as the policy driver for poverty eradication, beginning in the 1940s, with the disasters caused by the 1930s Great Depression and Second World War in mind. The period witnessed a cycle of economic expansion led by the USA, whose economy represented almost half of world trade production and whose Federal Reserve held 80 per cent of the world's gold reserves (Unceta and Yoldi 2000). The idea was, Streeten (2004: 68) explains, that economic growth is a benign force, and market forces (the demand for labour, rising productivity, rising wages, lower-priced consumer goods) would spread the benefits of economic growth 'widely and speedily'. As Griffin (2001) suggests, the modern development economy has dealt with material enrichment and with how to expand the volume of the goods and services produced. It was assumed that any increase in the per-capita gross national product would reduce poverty and would raise the general level of well-being and living standards of the population.

However, instead of being a means to reach development, economic growth began to be considered the end-goal. While there was debate, it focused on how to accelerate growth and, more marginally, on a more equal distribution of the goods or benefits of growth. The Kuznet's curve suggested that the early stages of economic growth are anyway accompanied by inequality, but eventually a turning point is reached and growing incomes generate greater equality (Streeten 2004). However, as Streeten (2004: 69) points out, 'there was no automatic tendency for increasing incomes to be spread widely'.

At about the same time, decolonisation and the Cold War aligned the new decolonised countries with the interests of either the capitalist or the socialist block (Griffin 2001), thereby initiating different development programmes driven by cooperation agencies in the most industrialised countries and various multilateral institutions (such as the World Bank). The first development economists (such as Nurkse 1961; or Rostow 1960) supported modernisation theory; the implicit goal of their theories was to reproduce the experience of developed countries; that is to replicate the industrialisation process and labour utilisation. Development was viewed as an ahistorical process, without conflicts, where modernity was always positive and tradition always negative (Bustelo 1998). In their analyses, the state and the market are the key development actors (Willis 2011), and no significant role is attributed to other institutions, including the university. However, these modernisation approaches were strongly criticised by dependency theories (Amin 1974; Prebisch 1959) as ahistorical, technicist and only focused on an internal diagnosis of the problems of developing countries, ignoring how they become inserted into and are shaped by international economic dynamics. According to dependency theorists, developing countries are societies that are structured in a different way and which, after being colonised, are forced to take on the capitalist production mode to play a role that suits industrialised countries as suppliers of raw materials and importers of manufactured products. The proposed solutions included changing the peripheral countries' insertion into world markets as a basic condition to break through the obstacles of the modernisation and development process.

However, as Unceta (2001) highlights, we cannot say that dependency approaches contributed new proposals to what had been the main dimensions in existing conceptions: those which linked it to economic growth, productive investment and industrialisation. Nonetheless, the development debate in some places, for example, the Institute of Development Studies at Sussex University, did turn to the question of income redistribution and how redistribution might combine with strategies for growth (Streeten 2004). In none of these approaches did the university play a significant role in development. Indeed, as we showed in the previous chapter, university education was not supported by the World Bank at this time. However, in some developed countries, the university was often a significant space for researchers tackling questions of growth and sometimes of inequality. It was not seen to be a driver of economic development itself, but could be the location for economic policy development, as was the case of the Chicago School of economics with its emphasis on reduced government intervention in the economy, which came to be taken up in Thatcherite economic policies (Alkire and Ritchie 2007).

Also falling under this group of theories are the 'new growth theories' of the 1980s (Streeten 2004), in which the emphasis shifted from growth arising from productive factors and technological progress to the behaviour of people, with an emphasis on human capital and higher levels of education. Better-educated people were seen to be more productive, innovative and efficient. This approach had been anticipated by rising investments and expansion in higher education in the USA and the UK from the 1960s, driven partly by equity concerns, and by the conceptualisation of 'human capital theory' in the 1960s by Becker (1964) as the basis for increased incomes. More education, it was argued, meant higher wages. At this point, universities enter the economic development arena rather firmly, anticipating neo-liberal moves to come. Marginson (2015: 7) argues that the effect was to create 'impossible' expectations of higher education, which now 'became responsible not just for personal development and social justice, but universal career success, private enrichment and collective economic growth'. Thus, in some developed countries at least, higher education was being firmly linked to economic growth for good or ill, although university education continued to be marginalised for low-income countries.

Neo-liberalism and globalisation

The 1990s witnessed the emergence of a new neo-liberal orthodoxy, where development was understood to turn on markets driving economic liberalisation, accompanied by privatisation, deregulation and reduced government spending on public services, and the state's having to support or sustain markets but not replace them (Bustelo 1998). For developing countries, the 'Washington Consensus' emerged in the late 1980s to refer to a set of economic policy prescriptions that constituted a standard reform package promoted for developing countries. It was led by institutions, such as the International Monetary Fund (IMF) and the World Bank, and encompassed policies, such as macro-economic stabilisation, opening up of trade and investment, and the expansion and prevalence of market forces. The term 'Washington Consensus' has thus come to be used fairly widely to refer to a more general orientation towards a strongly market-based approach enshrining the principles of neo-liberal economic policy (Sanahuja 2001; Williamson 1990).

This neo-liberal orthodoxy goes hand in hand with globalisation, a concept (as also noted in Chapter 2) contested in terms of its meaning, form and implications (Kothari *et al.* 2002). Giddens (2001: 245) uses the term 'stretched' to describe the new relationship between 'local involvements' and 'interaction across distance' in which geographical boundaries are blurred, and flows of movements of people, information, capital and goods have become faster. Examples include transnational forms of production, around-the-clock financial markets, and supranational organisations, such as the European Union. While globalisation has the effect of minimising the state's role in driving national economies, the state nonetheless plays a crucial role in providing the conditions, laws and institutions to maximise economic participation and competition in global markets. At a political level, Scheuerman (2010) argues that it is no longer self-evident that democracy and justice can only be pursued in the domestic arena; domestic and foreign affairs are now irrevocably intertwined. For development policies and practices, globalisation has had important implications; first, as highlighted in several reports (Oxfam 2014; UNDP 1999; UNDP 2014) its benefits have been tremendously uneven having reinforced social exclusion among individuals and groups in the South as well as the North. On the other hand, some see global benefits. Norberg (2001), for example, argues that the diffusion of capitalism has lowered poverty rates and created opportunities for growth and employment all over the world, raising living standards and increasing life expectancy.

From an economic point of view, globalisation has brought important changes in the relation between: (1) state and capital – the state is expected to deliver neo-liberal policy; privatisation (e.g. expanding higher education through private provision) is an example of how an international agenda is forced on states by multilateral donors; (2) labour and capital involving de-industrialisation and job reductions in developed economies and the relocation of jobs from the 'core' to the 'periphery'. Meanwhile, the advent of the information society is responsible for producing the phenomenon of insecure employment; (3) changes in core-periphery relations have been produced by restructured production chains that create forms of global networking, and a new social-core periphery hierarchy resulting in the creation of advantaged elites and insecure middle groups, while entirely excluding some of the 60 per cent of the developing countries from the benefits of capitalist expansion (Hoogvelt 1997, cited in Kothari *et al.* 2002: 32).

Sen (2002) is not sympathetic to claims that the poor are better off because of globalisation, as noted in the previous chapter, he asks of globalisation: who benefits? For Sen, dispensing with a market economy is not the solution to reducing poverty and inequalities, rather it is that a market economy can be seriously defective in its operations, and the globalisation of markets on its own is a 'very inadequate approach to world poverty'. Moreover, he notes that the outcomes of dealing in markets (however fair or not they are) are 'massively influenced' by public policies, so that public action can 'radically alter the outcome of local and global relations'. For Sen, then, it is precisely the reach of globalisation and the abundant opportunities that flow that 'makes the question of fairness in sharing the benefits of globalisation so critically important'.

For universities, the globalisation process has been extremely relevant. We touched on this in Chapter 2, but here we want to highlight some implications from a development perspective. As UNESCO (2009: 7) notes, higher education cannot opt out of the new global environment, describing globalisation as 'the reality shaped by an increasingly integrated world economy, new information and technology, the emergence of international knowledge networks, the role of the English language, and other forces beyond the control of academic institutions', all of which have 'profoundly affected higher education' in contradictory ways. As we examined in Chapter 2, the World Bank (2002) has positioned higher education at the core of economic growth, radically changing its initial recommendations, which emphasised primary and secondary education (World Bank 1991). In its report on The East Asian Miracle, the World Bank (1993) acknowledges its own previous prescriptions were too simplistic and, among other causes, the 'miracle' was seen to be possible due to the investment in human capital, especially in primary and secondary education, but also in university technical training. In 2002, the World Bank emphasised the unique importance of higher education institutions for development through economic growth and poverty eradication by training a qualified labour force, generating new knowledge and providing the capacity to access existing stores of global knowledge for local use. It (2002: 5) claimed now that 'sustainable transformation and growth throughout the economy are not possible without the capacity-building contributions of an innovative tertiary education system'. This change of perspective is partly explained by globalisation and the enhancement of the knowledge economy. As Etkowitz and Klofsten (2005: 244) argue: 'Whereas industry and government were the primary institutions of industrial society; university, industry and government [the triple helix] constitute the key institutional frameworks of post-industrial, knowledge-based societies'.

In this context, a major investment in science, technology and innovation has been proposed by many development institutions. Among them, the OECD (2000), has stressed the importance of links between science and industry because innovation requires more external and more multidisciplinary knowledge as technologies have become extremely complex. Also, universities seek engagement with industries to ensure good prospects for their students, to keep curricula up-to-date and to obtain research support. The main benefit for firms is improved access to well-trained human resources, new scientific knowledge, networks and problem-solving capabilities. OECD's vision is similar to that of authors who argue that university–industry–government interaction can also be identified as a key factor in regional or territorial development (Alburquerque 2008; Etkowitz 2005).

The key point to be made in the era of neo-liberal policies and globalisation (whether their effects are more or less negative for development and for education) is that the university has moved centre stage as a key policy instrument in a way which did not happen in the earlier period when modernisation and dependency theories held sway.

Sustainable development

Sitting somewhat at odds with neo-liberalism, in 1987 with the publication of the *Brundtland Report* (WCED 1987), the idea of sustainable development to refer to development and the environment began to take hold at the global level (Calabuig 2014). The United Nations World Commission on Environment and Development (WCED), set up for the purpose of producing the Brundtland report, concluded that ecological and social failures showed common cause and required common responses (Kemp *et al.* 2005). Several events over the past decades have paved the way for further discussions; global summits and documents, such as the United Nations Millennium Declaration, make it possible to better understand the cross-cutting nature of the multilateral sustainability agenda (Barton 2006). In the 1992 UN Conference on Environment and Development (the Rio Summit), special attention was paid to development and the environment and subsequent summits have focused on issues such as population, poverty and social deprivation, gender inequality and urbanisation, among other things. Currently, due to the growing global consensus on the origins of climate change, conferences or 'climate summits' are becoming more frequent and more relevant. Recently, the 2012 Conference on Sustainable Development, Rio + 20, established once again the links between development and sustainability and in the post-2015 development agenda, a proposal for new Sustainable Development Goals is under discussion. Early efforts to make the concept of sustainable development operational have focused on economic and environmental dimensions, but evidence in recent years suggests a greater interest in taking social, ethical and values dimensions into account (Froger *et al.* 2004). This is driven by an increasing awareness that sustainability problems cannot be solved solely by scientific knowledge (Selman and Parker 1997).

Sustainability as applied to or relevant for higher education can be interpreted in a number of ways. Whether the focus is on implementing sustainability, such as reducing a university's ecological footprint and improving its sustainability performance, or reflecting on the mission of higher education for sustainable development, such as the role higher education can play in global transformation towards sustainable futures, sustainable development challenges higher education to contemplate its vision, mission, purpose and relevance (Beringer and Adomßent 2008). Calls have been made for a more transformative whole-systems response, which places ethical sustainability at the heart of higher education's *raison d'être* (Sterling 2013: 18): an epistemic and paradigmatic reorientation of universities towards sustainability, which fundamentally changes the make-up and ideology of the higher education system itself. However, 'greening the campus approaches' tend to be dominated by project-based operations initiatives, while a systematic linking of academia – research and teaching – with sustainable facilities management and operations remains the exception (Beringer and Adomßent 2008). Additionally, new public management coming out of neo-liberal ideology has often been viewed as antithetical to the purpose and responsibilities of higher education associated with a more transformative agenda.

Turning to university education as a site where sustainability might be relevant, unlike earlier nature or conservation studies that dominated approaches to environmental education, complex forms of 'environment' have been outlined in recent debates (Kopnina 2012), privileging a mainstream discourse on sustainability absent from earlier practices (Anderson 2012). Fien (2002) makes the case for a different kind of knowledge both rational and non-rational, which is markedly different from Western knowledge, which separates fact from value. Quoting Robottom and Hart, Fien (2002: 252) highlights an appropriate form for environmental education research:

> [It] is one which includes consideration of both human consciousness and political action and thus can answer moral and social questions about educational programs which the dominant form [research paradigms] cannot. It is one which is more consistent with the ecophilosophical view – which encourages individuals to be autonomous, independent critical and creative thinkers, taking responsibility for their own actions and participating in the social and political reconstruction required to deal intelligently with social/environmental issues within mutually interdependent and evolving social situations.
>
> (Robottom and Hart 1993: 51–2)

A further important contribution from the sustainability community is its stress on inter- and trans-disciplinarity for effective sustainability-oriented research and teaching (Posch and Steiner 2006). With the traditional single disciplinary approach it is not possible to capture the complex nature of the problems and their solutions. Hence, a paradigm shift towards an holistic problem-solving approach involving systems thinking is needed. Working in real-world cases requires also a strong interaction between academics and practitioners in order to promote a mutual learning process (and see Chapters 6 and 8). It can be seen as a move from science on/about society towards science for/with society (Scholz and Marks 2013: 236). Academic expertise needs to be viewed as being on the same level as the more practical experience and values of non-scientists, and decisions on strategies for sustainable development need to be taken together with stakeholders (Posch and Steiner 2006: 281). The latter can help to identify the relevant problems, to define sustainable development scenarios, and to contribute by expressing their expectations and ideal views (Tobias 2003).

We will return to these elements in Chapter 4, in reviewing commonalities between sustainable and human development in an attempt to integrate the contributions of both approaches to examine the role and functions of higher education institutions. What is clear at this point, is that universities potentially have a key role to play in advancing sustainable development through their teaching, research and community activities, but equally it is not clear how many universities embrace this agenda holistically as opposed to contenting themselves with greening initiatives. The latter are a good start but should not be the end of sustainable development as taken up by universities.

Gender and development

Women-oriented policies in international development have moved on from the initial invisibility of gender needs and interests, to the present consideration of gender subordination as an obstacle to development (Moser 1991; Murguialday 2014; World Bank 2012). During the early years of international cooperation projects, the institutions responsible for promoting development simply did not 'see' women; two conceptual and empirical assumptions made women invisible to planners. First, there was a lack of information on what women's roles and needs were in society. Second, there was an assumption that men were the breadwinners and women and children the dependents with no productive economic (development) role (Kothari 2002). The first explicit appearance of women as recipients of development projects was still associated with the recognition of their reproductive roles and responsibilities and, in particular, the consideration of low-income mothers as a 'vulnerable sector'. When planners 'saw' women, the first need they recognised was related to the care of children. The second way to 'look' at women, the women in development approach, recognised their productive roles socially and economically, and became common in developmental planning in the early 1970s (Murguialday 2005).

Since the early 1990s, and as a result of feminist efforts in the South and North to include the discussion of gender inequality in development agendas, a new way of understanding the participation of women in development processes has emerged, the gender and development (GAD) approach. The term 'gender' is used by feminists to emphasise that differences and inequalities between men and women are socially constructed, rather than biologically determined. The main focus of GAD is not women per se but the socially constructed relations between men and women which hold women back (Kothari 2002) and the persistence of 'sticky' gender norms (World Bank 2012). The GAD approach demands a re-examination of development processes shifting the emphasis of the analysis and proposals from being centred on women to being focused on gender, and particularly on the unequal power relations between genders (Murguialday 2014). A key assumption of the GAD strategy is that nothing is neutral in terms of gender, and all projects, including the technical, have a gender dimension, so that regardless of whether it is a project with women or with men, women's projects affect the position of men, and vice versa. Therefore, the GAD strategy aims to analyse social processes and institutions that lead to inequalities between men and women, the asymmetric development of capacity of both genders, and the different access to resources and power that are thus generated, including how this may shift over time. In addition, GAD is also a political proposal in that it requires a commitment to building equitable gender relations, including questioning the concept and practice of development as a process of economic growth that can lead 'underdeveloped' societies towards the current model of society in the developed North. An operationalisation of the GAD approach is 'gender mainstreaming' (also called 'gender integration or incorporation'), which is based on the principle that the gender order of a society can be changed through deliberate and focused interventions at every level. This proposal was first made at the Third World Conference on Women in Nairobi (1985). In the Beijing Conference (1995), gender mainstreaming was explicitly endorsed by the Platform for Action, which states that 'governments and other actors should promote an active and visible policy of mainstreaming a gender perspective in all policies and programs, so that, before decisions are taken, an analysis is made of the effects on women and men, respectively'. The World Bank (2012) now explicitly recognises gender equality as a core development objective in its own right, but adds that it is also 'smart economics'.

With regard to the university, work on gender and development has included attention to gender structures and proposals for changing gender in universities. Higher education is not separate from gender structures in society, but will be influenced by gender equality in the wider society. Education systems help produce culture, society and personal identity, and where a society contains gender inequalities, these will be reproduced inside and through education, but these structures of exclusion can also be changed, although with difficulty. Historical research has found that universities are masculinist in their history and origins (Noble 1992), and despite significant gains by women in the twentieth and twenty-first centuries, including massively expanded access to university in most countries (World Bank 2009), the pattern of male power continues. Statistics reflect how men dominate senior university positions globally, and particular hegemonic masculinities are the norm in management and academic work (Blackmore 2002). Studies have focused on horizontal and vertical segregation, which characterises university institutions. Vertical segregation refers to women being concentrated in lower-level positions; horizontal segregation explains how women tend to be concentrated in activities and/or areas of knowledge that are traditionally considered 'typical' of women (Díaz-Martínez and Dema-Moreno 2013). Different internal and external factors have been indicated as a cause of these segregations: unequal social structures, culture and organisational dynamics (Díaz-Martínez and Dema-Moreno 2013; Sánchez-Apellániz 1997; Wasburn 2007). Eveline (2000, quoted in Blackmore 2002) focuses the feminist gaze on the 'glass escalator' that facilitates male academics (and managers) moving up higher and faster (better perhaps than metaphors of the glass ceiling, sticky steps or slippery floors holding women down). Perhaps the strategy is to focus on relations of advantage – to recognise that one party may have significant advantage over the other, thus turning the gaze away from discourses about women's disadvantages, often constructed as only women's problems. However, while acknowledging women as a group, we also need to recognise how women are also marked internally by differentiation along class, racial and ethnic, age, ability and sexual preferences (Bacchi 2000).

Mama (2004: 122) evokes the subversive and transformative spirit of feminist studies, pointing out two important contributions of southern feminists: first, an insistence on being constantly alert to the politics of location and diversities of class, race, culture, sexuality and so on; second, to build an understanding of the connections between the local and global, between the micro-politics of subjectivity and everyday life, and the macro-politics of global political economy. This reflects a commitment to a certain holism, to challenging and subverting the disciplinary and locational fragmentations, which have tended to demarcate and circumscribe the theorising of gender and gender relations. In such ways, the university might contribute to gender and development efforts.

Participation in development

Since the beginning of the idea of development, participatory approaches have been present in developing thinking and practice. Nonetheless, concepts, motivations and applications of participation have evolved and changed radically in development discourse. During the 1950s and 1960s, modernisation theory largely ignored participation. The only exception to this was the idea of 'community development' that sets up spaces of participation for people to improve their living standards with the provision of technical services to stimulate their initiative, self-help and mutual help. In the 1960s and 1970s, a radical shift occurred in the understanding of participation, thanks to the prevalence of popular political movements of the time. It was at this time that the entire concept of development was being questioned by dependency theorists, the 'Third World' and non-aligned countries (Cornwall 2006).

It was in this context that participation was related to popular education and political activism thanks to the work of pedagogues such as Paulo Freire, Orlando Fals-Borda and Augusto Boal, who were disseminating the notion of emancipatory pedagogy. Building on the work on liberatory theology, they argued for participation and mobilisation to address passivity, generating critical awareness and combating structural causes of inequalities (Frediani *et al.* 2015). Given that these structures of oppression are rooted in oppressed people's own beliefs, it is through participation that people become active subjects of knowledge and action, and begin to build their own human history by engaging in processes of authentic development (Goulet 1989). This transformative process that leads to empowerment and emancipation is articulated through various methods, among which is participatory action research as developed by Fals-Borda (see Chapter 8). This is aimed at developing self-consciousness in the poor and oppressed for the progressive transformation of their environment. It enables the emergence of a counter power that allows them to move towards shared goals of social change in a participatory political system (Peris 2014).

In the 1980s, with the rise of neo-liberal theories, we witness a different approach to participation, based on the reduced role of the state, the increasing role of development NGOs as service providers, and the concept of empowerment understood as the access of the poor to markets are key to this vision of participation in development. In the 1980s, organisations such as the World Bank, supported community participation as an instrument for reducing costs of programmes and shifting the burden of delivery from the state to communities. Self-help housing programmes were, for example, initiatives using the rhetoric of participation with the intent to implement a more successful cost-recovery strategy. Participation moved away from addressing structural causes of inequalities, to an operational fix, and the concept moved away from a political realm, to a technical one. Communities were encouraged to join the implementation of projects, and were contracted to implement projects, thus becoming deliverers of services, rather than actors in social transformation. Communities' areas of work were confined to their own backyard, and participation did not mean a genuine stake in spaces where key decisions that affected a wider and larger context were made (Frediani *et al.* 2015). In this framework of participation in development, the critical counterpoint was provided by an approach developed around the writing of Robert Chambers (1994). Chambers exposes the arrogance behind the erroneous assumption within international development projects that the external experts know more. In contrast, he proposes considering people as active subjects rather than beneficiaries, with valuable knowledge and experience in the planning and solving of their own problems. For this, it is necessary to limit the role of experts and to invite development professionals to 'unlearn' their attitudes in order to put 'the last ones first', valuing and recognising the role of indigenous knowledge and experiences (Chambers 1997).

More recently, discourses on participation have shown the intent to safeguard the radical roots of participation by associating it with normative notions of development, such as empowerment and citizenship. Hickey and Mohan (2004) and Gaventa (2006) call for the re-politicisation of the idea of participation and for it to recover its transformative potential by linking it to citizenship and contributing to the deepening of democracy through participatory governance systems. In this sense, participation is no longer understood as a tool to make development interventions more efficient but as a process for resolving social conflicts democratically (Peris 2014). Democratic citizenship is achieved through the exercise of not only civil and political rights but also of social rights, which must be attained through participation processes (Gaventa 2006). In this regard and with the intention of placing power relationships at the centre of the discussion, the accountability of governance systems becomes a key issue, 'not only regarding the few actors who design and control them, but also the many who make up societies' (McGee 2010: 16). Taking this line of argument further, Hickey and Mohan (2004: 12) argue that 'participation must be ideologically explicit and tied to a coherent theory of development'; they propose radical citizenship as the theoretical framework that can safeguard participation from its populist capture. Their recommendation also stresses the need to focus on agency and structure, thus revealing relations of power locally and underlying processes reproducing social injustices. The focus on citizenship takes a political perspective on participation to high-light the importance of political rights in the process of development. On the one hand, this is the strength of this approach, contributing towards political change in the thinking and practice of development. On the other hand, it falls short of an operational approach to development that can generate practices and policies beyond the political arena (Frediani *et al.* 2015).

Participatory approaches have been influential inside universities, although, as with other approaches to development presented here, such approaches are not mainstreamed, and universities may be an obstacle to participation (Taylor and Boser 2006). Nonetheless, Taylor and Fransman (2004) advocate for the potential of universities in becoming key actors for individual and social change by providing an enabling environment in which teaching and research become integral and valued through partici-patory processes; participation itself is a desirable outcome in order to challenge established power relations. They recognise three key areas where universities could promote greater participation in learning and teaching: (1) bridging theory and practice; (2) linking universities and com-munities; and (3) participatory methods for more effective learning. Taking the last of these, a basic concept of participatory learning is that indi-viduals participate in generating their own personal theories, which are rel-evant to their contexts. These emerge through the experience of practice, and then go on to inform further practice. The relationship between theory and practice seems to work best when a variety of stakeholders are able to participate at different levels of the process, especially through the use of experiential learning methods and activities (Kolb 1984). Many adult edu-cators consequently assert that experiential, hands-on learning activities offer a powerful medium for promoting transformative learning (Taylor 1998) and for bridging theory and practice.

Such an approach may require an exploration of alternative approaches to the traditional classroom, such as drama-based activities, or even moving the learning experience into the community. Community-based learning and action research methods can enable the participation of indi-vidual actors in generating their own personal and contextually relevant theories, which are grounded in (as well as informing) practice (Taylor and Fransman 2004). Participatory and collaborative learning shifts the traditional dichotomies of the learner–teacher relationship in education. Mezirow (1991) emphasises the role of the educator as a facilitator of subjective transformation, helping learners focus on and examine the assumptions that underlie their beliefs, feelings and actions, assessing the consequences of these assumptions, identifying and exploring alternative sets of assumptions and testing the validity of assumptions through effective participation in reflective dialogue. Mezirow also stresses the critical reflections of the educator in their learning process. Teachers can (and should) learn through their teaching, but also from the students they teach as well. Transformation itself may only occur much later; the educative process may in effect sow the seeds which contribute to such longer-term processes (Taylor and Fransman 2004).

Ansley and Gaventa (1997) and McEwan (2001) make an interesting contribution to the role that participatory and more democratic research (participatory action research, collaborative research, participatory inquiry, practitioner research, etc.) can play in universities. They argue that it is a global model, both in the South and North, that shares three characteristics: (1) the development of a new role for researchers, who do not simply mine facts 'objectively' but facilitate joint and reciprocal work; (2) a recognition of the part that grassroots reflection and inquiry have played in the development of knowledge; and (3) an insistence that research be linked not only to the process of knowledge building, but also to education and action, especially for the less powerful. For universities that wish to shift their research priorities in this direction, Ansley and Gaventa (1997) caution as follows. First, universities must appreciate that they are not reaching out to a research void – community groups have developed their own research and knowledge capacities in different ways. Second, participatory activities are primarily about new forms of research and should be rewarded and acknowledged in a similar way to more traditional research – working with communities in a democratic and collaborative way takes time and makes demands at least as great as those that traditional researchers face. Third, participation with others involves moving over, making space, and in some instances, sharing or giving up certain kinds of power. There are many examples of such university–community collaborations, such as grassroots representation on advisory groups for research centres, citizen participation in research teams, co-ownership of data by community research partners, etc. These forms of participation in turn can affect other institutional procedures, such as the protection of academic freedom, intellectual property rights, confidentiality, and protocols relating to human subjects. Rather than being ignored or routinised through deadening procedures, these challenges should be injected into debates about research in administrative halls, faculty offices and classrooms. And, the final point, leaders who want to promote research for democracy and democratic research must be prepared for conflict. Passionate disagreement about hard questions is a sign of a robust democracy. In a robust democracy, people argue over the allocation of power and resources. Research partnerships with the less powerful in communities may well lead to conflict, sometimes with the very corporations or government agencies upon which universities are increasingly dependent for funds and good will.

Post-colonial and post-development approaches

Post-colonialism and post-development constitute powerful critiques of 'development' and an increasingly important challenge to dominant ways of apprehending North–South relations (McEwan 2001). Post-colonial approaches problematise the ways in which the world is known, challenging the unacknowledged and unexamined assumptions at the heart of Western disciplines that are profoundly insensitive to the meanings, values and practices of other cultures. They challenge the meaning of development as rooted in colonial discourse, which depicts the North as advanced and progressive and the South as backward, degenerate and primitive (Said 1978). One of the main failures of this development discourse is its limited historical analysis and its unreflective nature, partly engendered through the imperative to achieve development goals and targets (Kothari 2002). This ahistoricism is continually legitimated by the pervasive representation of development as Western philanthropy, as a humanitarian mission that bears no resemblance to the perceived inequalities and exploitations of empire. Thus, development can only be 'good' when set against a colonialism that was 'bad'. This dichotomy absolves those of us teaching, researching and advising in the fields of development studies and education of the responsibility of examining the ways in which we may be perpetuating and entrenching notions of Western superiority, difference and inequality (Kothari 2005). Post-colonial studies go hand-in-hand with radical feminism – the focus is on challenging masculinist and Eurocentric knowledge, power and practice that is present in development discourses and preventing the radical outlook of alternative practices from being co-opted by dominant agendas that reinforce, rather than challenge, the orthodoxy (Cornwall 2006; Kothari 2002; McGee 2002). Post-colonialism feminisms, therefore, have the potential to contribute to the critical exploration of relationships between cultural power and global economic power. Moreover, they point towards a radical reclaiming of the political that is occurring in the field of development and in the broader arena of societal transformation (McEwan 2001).

Post-developmental approaches share with post-colonialism, a critique of dominant development discourse. USA President Truman's speech in 1945 is considered by post-developmental theorists as the beginning of the era of development. By using for the first time the word 'underdeveloped', Truman changed the meaning of development and created 'a euphemism, used ever since to allude either discreetly or inadvertently to the era of American hegemony' (Esteva 2010: 2). From the start, development's hidden agenda was regarded as a project for Westernisation of the world. The result has been a loss of diversity. Market, state and science have been the great universalising powers, and administrators, experts and educators have expanded their reign. Moreover, the spreading monoculture has eroded viable alternatives to industrial, growth-oriented societies and hindered humankind's capacity to meet an increasingly different future with creative responses (Sachs 2010).

According to Escobar (2005), development discourse of this kind has operated through two mechanisms: (1) the professionalisation (including in universities) of developmental problems, which has included the emergence of expertise and fields to deal with all aspects of 'underdevelopment' (including Development Studies); and (2) the institutionalisation of development through the vast network of organisations dedicated to development planning, which provide systematic knowledge through projects and interventions.

> Institutional practices such as project planning and implementation give the impression that policy is the result of discrete, rational acts and not the process of coming to terms with conflicting interests, a process in which choices are made, exclusions effected and world views imposed. There is an apparent neutrality in identifying people as 'problems', until one realizes, first, that this definition of 'the problem' has already been put together in Washington or some capital city of the Third World, and, second, that problems are presented in such a way that some kind of development programme has to be accepted as the legitimate solution.
>
> (Escobar 2010: 154)

Escobar (2005: 19) stresses the importance of challenging this 'vision' in three ways. The first is through the ability to create different discourses and representations that are not mediated by the constructions of development (ideologies, metaphors, language, premises, etc.). The second is the need to change practices of knowing and doing and the 'political economy' of truth that defines the development regime. The third is the need to multiply production centres and agents of knowledge production to make visible forms of knowledge produced by those who are supposedly the 'objects' of development so that they can become subjects and agents. Thus both post-colonial and post-development approaches question deeply the kind of knowledge that has been created by universities, specifically in the field of development studies. As Crush (1995) suggests:

> development texts are 'avowedly strategic and tactical', promoting and justifying certain interventions and delegitimizing and excluding

others. Power relations are clearly implied in this process; certain forms of knowledge are dominant and others are excluded. The texts of development contain silences.

(quoted in McEwan 2001: 103)

Concluding thoughts

In the previous pages, we have described how different development theories understand the role of the university; from economic theories that see universities as essential institutions for the production of human capital and economic growth, competitiveness and technological progress, to more critical approaches of policy, university system and relations and practices inside universities. These approaches bring into the discussion the importance of values connected with environmental and social sustainability, diversity and its relevance to address the lack of participation opportunities as a driver to foster a different way of understanding teaching and learning and knowledge production.

Furthermore, these approaches are questioning the hegemonic view of governing, teaching, researching and engaging with external actors prevailing in higher education institutions today (see Chapter 2).

In the next chapter, devoted to the characterisation of human development, we will resume all these contributions to advance the conceptualisation of a transforming vision of the university. While it may not be easy to dislodge the economic growth/neoliberal/globalisation university, without an alternative vision and imaginary we cannot begin to re-think how development understands universities.

References

Alburquerque, F. 2008. 'Innovation, knowledge transfer and territorial economical development: a pending politics', *Arbor-Ciencia Pensamiento Y Cultura* 184(732): 687–700.

Alkire, S. and A Ritchie. 2007. 'Winning ideas: lessons from free market economics', *OPHI Working Paper* 6. Rochester, NY: Social Science Research Network. [Accessed 3 October 2015]. http://papers.ssrn.com/abstract=1815256.

Amin, S. 1974. *Accumulation on a World Scale; a Critique of the Theory of Underdevelopment*. New York: Monthly Review Press.

Anderson, E. N. 2012. 'Tales best told out of school: traditional life-skills education meets modern science education'. In *Anthropology of Environmental Education*, edited by H. Kopina. New York: Nova Science Publishers.

Ansley, F. and J. Gaventa. 1997. 'Researching for democ & democratizing research', *Change: The Magazine of Higher Learning* 29(1): 46–53.

Bacchi, C. 2000. 'The seesaw effect: down goes affirmative action, up comes workplace diversity', *Journal of Interdisciplinary Gender Studies* 5(2): 64–83.

Barton, J. R. 2006. 'Sustentabilidad Urbana Como Planificación Estratégica', *EURE* 32(96): 27–45.

Becker, G. S. 1964. *Human Capital: A Theoretical and Empirical Analysis*. Chicago: University of Chicago Press.

Beringer, A. and M. Adomßent. 2008. 'Sustainable university research and development: inspecting sustainability in higher education research', *Environmental Education Research* 14(6): 607–23.

Blackmore, J. 2002. 'Globalisation and the restructuring of higher education for new knowledge economies: new dangers or old habits troubling gender equity work in universities'? *Higher Education Quarterly* 56(4): 419–41.

Bustelo, P. 1998. *Teorías contemporáneas del desarrollo económico* [Contemporary theories of economic development]. Madrid: Editorial Síntesis.

Calabuig, C. 2014. *Sustainable Development*. GDEE Project, European Commission. [Accessed 30 September 2015]. http://gdee.eu/index.php/resources/courses-2.

Chambers, R. 1994. 'The origins and practice of participatory rural appraisal'. *World Development* 22(7): 953–69.

Chambers, R. 1997. *Whose Reality Counts?: Putting the First Last*. London: Intermediate Technology.

Cornwall, A. 2006. 'Historical perspectives on participation in development', *Commonwealth & Comparative Politics* 44(1): 62–83.

Crush, J. 1995. 'Introduction'. In *Power of Development*, edited by J. Crush. London: Routledge.

Díaz-Martínez, C. and S. Dema-Moreno. 2013. 'Las mujeres y la ciencia. La escasez de mujeres en la academia. Un caso de histéresis social'. [Women and science. Shortage of women in the academy. A case of social hysteresis], *Vida Científica* 6: 149–56.

Escobar, A. 2005. 'El "postdesarrollo" como concepto y práctica social'. [Post-development as concept and social practice). In *Políticas de Economía, Ambiente y Sociedad en Tiempos de Globalización* [Policies of Economic, Environment and Society in Globalization Times], edited by D. Mato, 17–31. Caracas: Facultad de Ciencias Económicas y Sociales, Universidad Central de Venezuela.

Escobar, A. 2010. 'Planning'. In *The Development Dictionary a Guide to Knowledge as Power*, edited by W. Sachs, 145–60. 2nd edition. London: Zed Books. [Accessed 30 September 2015]. www.credoreference.com/book/zeddev.

Esteva, G. 2010. 'Development'. In *The Development Dictionary a Guide to Knowledge as Power*, edited by W. Sachs, 1–23. 2nd edition. London: Zed Books. [Accessed 30 September 2015] www.credoreference.com/book/zeddev.

Etkowitz, H. 2005. *Tripplehelix*. Stockholm: SNS Press.

Etkowitz, H. and M. Klofsten. 2005. 'The innovation region: towards a theory of knowledge-based regional development'. *R&D Management* 35(3): 243–55.

Fien, J. 2002. 'Advancing sustainability in higher education: issues and opportunities for research', *Higher Education Policy* 15(2): 143–52.

Frediani, Alex A., J. Peris and Alejandra Boni. 2015. 'Notions of empowerment and participation: the contribution of the capability approach'. In *The Capability Approach, Empowerment and Participation*, edited by D. Clark, M. Biggeri and Alex A. Frediani, forthcoming. Basingstoke: Palgrave.

Froger, G., P. Meral and V. Herimandimby. 2004. 'The expansion of participatory governance in the environmental policies of developing countries: the example of Madagascar', *International Journal of Sustainable Development* 7(2): 164–84.

Gaventa, J. 2006. 'Triumph, deficit or contestation?: deepening the "deepening democracy" debate', *IDS Working Paper* 264. [Accessed 30 September 2015]. http://opendocs.ids.ac.uk/opendocs/handle/123456789/4064.

Goulet, D. 1989. 'Participation in development: new avenues', *World Development* 17(2): 165–78.

Griffin, K. 2001. 'Desarrollo humano: orígenes, evolución e impacto'. [Human development: origins, evolution and impact]. In *Ensayos Sobre el Desarrollo Humano* [Essays on Human Development], edited by P. I. Güell and K. Unceta, 25–40. Barcelona: Icaria Editorial.

Giddens, A. 2001. 'Dimensions of globalisation'. In *The New Social Theory Reader: Contemporary Debates*, edited by S. Seidman and J. C. Alexander, 244–52. London: Routledge.

Hickey, S. and G. Mohan. 2004. *Participation, from Tyranny to Transformation? Exploring New Approaches to Participation in Development*. London: ZED Books. [Accessed 30 September 2015]. http://site.ebrary.com/id/10231429.

Kemp, R., S. Parto and R. B. Gibson. 2005. 'Governance for sustainable development: moving from theory to practice', *International Journal for Sustainable Development* 8(1/2): 12–30.

Kolb, D. A. 1984. *Experiential Learning: Experience as the Source of Learning and Development*. Englewood Cliffs, NJ: Prentice-Hall.

Kopnina, H. 2012. *Anthropology of Environmental Education*. Hauppauge, NY: Nova Science Publishers.

Kothari, U. 2002. 'Feminist and postcolonial challenges to development'. In *Development Theory and Practice: Critical Perspectives*, edited by M. Minogue and U. Kothari, 35–51. Basingstoke: Palgrave.

Kothari, U., ed. 2005. *A Radical History of Development Studies. Individuals, Institutions and Ideologies*. London: Zed Books.

Kothari, U., M. Minogue and J. DeJong. 2002. 'The political economy of globalization'. In *Development Theory and Practice: Critical Perspectives*, edited by M. Minogue and U. Kothari, 16–34. Basingstoke: Palgrave.

Mama, A. 2004. 'Demythologising gender in development: feminist studies in African contexts', *IDS Bulletin* 35(4): 121–4.

Marginson, S. 2015. 'Higher education and inequality in Anglo-American societies'. In *Student Equity in Australian Higher Education: Twenty Five Years of a "Fair Chance for All"*, edited by M. Brett, A. Harvey and C. Burnheim, forthcoming. Singapore: Springer.

McCowan, T. 2015. 'Theories of development'. In *Education and International Development: An Introduction*, edited by T. McCowan and Elaine Unterhalter, 31–48. London: Bloomsbury Academic.

McEwan, C. 2001. 'Postcolonialism, feminism and development: intersections and dilemmas', *Progress in Development Studies* 1(2): 93–111.

McGee, R. 2002. 'Participating in development'. In *Development Theory and Practice: Critical Perspective*, edited by M. Minogue and U. Kothari, 96–112. Basingstoke: Palgrave.

McGee, R. 2010. 'Procesos de desarrollo, participación, gobernanza, derechos y poder' [Development processes, participation, governance and power]. *Cuadernos de Investigación en Desarrollo*. Valencia: GEDCE. [Accessed 30 September 2015]. www.mastercooperacion.upv.es/images/mcad/cuad_inv1.pdf.

Mezirow, J. 1991. *Transformative Dimensions of Adult Learning*. San Francisco: Jossey-Bass.

Moser, C. 1991. 'La planificación de género en el Tercer Mundo: enfrentando las necesidades prácticas y estratégicas de género' [Gender Planning in the Third

World: Addressing Practical Needs and Gender Strategies]. In *Una Nueva Lectura: Género en el Desarrollo* [Anew Reading: Gender in Development], edited by V. Guzmán, P. Portocarrero and V. Vargas. Lima, Perú: Ediciones Entre Mujeres: Flora Tristán.

Murguialday, C. 2005. *Las mujeres en la cooperación para el desarrollo* [Women in development aid]. Vitoria: Servicio Central de Publicaciones del Gobierno Vasco.

Murguialday, C. 2014. 'Gender perspectives and interculturality'. *GDEE Project*, European Commission. [Accessed 30 September 2015]. http://gdee.eu/index.php/resources/courses-2.

Naidoo, R. 2011. 'Rethinking development: higher education and the new imperialism'. In *Handbook on Globalization and Higher Education*, edited by R. King, S. Marginson and R. Naidoo, 40–58. Cheltenham: Edward Elgar.

Noble, D. 1992. *A World without Women*. New York: Alfred A. Knopf.

Norberg, J. 2001. *In Defense of Global Capitalism*. Sweden: Timbro. [Accessed 30 September 2015]. http://site.ebrary.com/id/10379723.

Nurkse, R. 1961. *Problems of Capital Formation in Underdeveloped Countries*. New York: Oxford University Press.

OECD. 2000. 'Science, *Technology and Innovation in the New* Economy', *Policy Brief, OECD Observer*, 12. [Accessed 28 September 2015]. www.oecd.org/publications/Pol_brief/.

Oxfam. 2014. *Even It up: Time to End Extreme Inequality*. Oxford: Oxfam GB. [Accessed 30 September 2015]. www.oxfam.org/sites/www.oxfam.org/files/file_attachments/cr-even-it-up-extreme-inequality-291014-en.pdfOxfam.

Peris, J. 2014. 'Participation, governance and citizenship'. *GDEE Project*, European Commission. [Accessed 30 September 2015]. http://gdee.eu/index.php/resources/courses-2.

Posch, A. and G. Steiner. 2006. 'Integrating research and teaching on innovation for sustainable development', *International Journal of Sustainability in Higher Education* 7(3): 276–92.

Prebisch, R. 1959. 'International trade and payments in an era of coexistence, commercial policy in the underdeveloped countries', *American Economic Review* 49(2): 251–73.

Robottom, I. and P. Hart. 1993. *Research in Enviromental Education: Engaging the Debate*. Geelong: Deakin University.

Rostow, W. W. 1960. *The Stages of Economic Growth, a Non-Communist Manifesto*. Cambridge: University Press.

Sachs, W. 2010. *The Development Dictionary a Guide to Knowledge as Power*. 2nd edition. London: Zed Books. [Accessed 30 September 2015]. www.credoreference.com/book/zeddev.

Said, E. W. 1978. *Orientalism*. London: Routledge and Kegan Paul.

Sanahuja, J. 2001. 'Del interés nacional a la ciudadanía global: la ayuda al desarrollo y las transformaciones de la ciudadanía global' [From national interest to global citizenship: development aid and global citizenship transformations]. In *La Cooperación al Desarrollo en un Mundo en Cambio: Perspectivas Sobre Nuevos Ámbitos de Intervención* [Development Aid in a Changing World], edited by J. Sanahuja and M. Gómez, 53–127. Madrid: CIDEAL.

Sánchez-Apellániz, M. 1997. *Mujeres, Dirección y Cultura Organizacional* [Women, Management and Organizational Learning]. Madrid: Centro de Investigaciones Sociológicas; FEDEPE.

Scheuerman, W. 2010. 'Globalization'. In *Stanford Encyclopedia of Philosophy.* Stanford, CA: Stanford University. [Accessed 30 September 2015]. http://plato. stanford.edu/entires/globalization/.

Scholz, R. and D. Marks. 2013. 'Learning about transdisciplinarity: Where are we? Where have we been? Where should we go?' In *Transdisciplinarity: Joint Problem Solving Among Science, Technology, and Society An Effective Way for Managing Complexity,* edited by K. J. Thompson, W. Grossenbacher-Mansuy, R. Häberli, A. Bill, R. W. Scholz and M. Welti, 236–52. Basel: Birkhauser.

Selman, P. and J. Parker. 1997. 'Citizenship, civicness and social capital in local agenda 21', *Local Environment* 2(2): 171–84.

Sen, A. 2002. 'Globalism'. *The American Prospect* 1 January 2002. [Accessed 30 September 2015]. www.sas.upenn.edu/~dludden/SenGlobalism.htm.

Sterling, S. R. 2013. 'The sustainable university: challenge and response'. In *The Sustainable University: Progress and Prospects,* edited by S. Sterling, L. Maxey and H. Luna, 17–50. Abingdon: Routledge.

Streeten, P. 2004. 'Shifting fashions in development dialogue'. In *Readings in Human Development: Concepts, Measures and Policies for a Development Paradigm,* edited by S. Fukuda-Parr and A. K. Shiva Kumar. New Delhi: Oxford University Press.

Taylor, E. W. 1998. 'The theory and practice of transformative learning a critical review', *Information Series 374.* Columbus, OH: ERIC Clearinghouse on Adult, Career, and Vocational Education, Center on Education and Training for Employment, College of Education, the Ohio State University.

Taylor, P. and S. Boser. 2006. 'Power and transformation in higher education institutions: challenges for change', *IDS Bulletin* 37(6): 111–21.

Taylor, P. and J. Fransman. 2004. 'Learning and teaching participation: exploring the role of higher learning institutions as agents of development and social change'. *Working Paper 219.* Brighton: Institute of Development Studies.

Tobias, S. 2003. 'Do we make better land use decisions by inter- and transdisciplinary work?' In *Interdisciplinary and Transdisciplinary Landscape Studies: Potential and Limitations,* edited by B. Tress, G. Tress, A. van der Valk and G. Fry, 59–63. Wageningen: Delta Series 2. [Accessed 30 September 2015]. http://edepot.wur.nl/15144.

Unceta, K. 2001. 'Perspectivas para el desarrollo humano en la era de la globalización'. [Human development perspectives in a globalization era]. In *Ensayos Sobre el Desarrollo Humano* [Essays on Human Development], edited by K. Unceta and P. I. Güell, 401–26. Barcelona: Icaria Editorial.

Unceta, K. and P. Yoldi. 2000. *La Cooperación al Desarrollo: Surgimiento y Evolución Histórica* [Development Cooperation: Origins and Historical Evolution]. Vitoria-Gasteiz: Gobierno Vasco.

UNDP. 1999. *Human Development Report 1999.* New York: UNDP.

UNDP. 2014. *Human Development Report 2014.* New York: UNDP.

UNESCO (ed.) 2009. *Trends in Global Higher Education: Tracking an Academic Revolution.* Paris: UNESCO.

Wasburn, M. M. 2007. *Mentoring Women in Faculty: An Instrumental Case Study of Strategic Collaboration.* Oxford: Taylor and Francis.

WCED. 1987. *Report of the World Commission on Environment and Development: 'Our Common Future'.* New York: World Commission on Environment and Development. [Accessed 28 September 2015]. www.un-documents.net/our-common-future.pdf.

Williamson, J. 1990. *Latin America Adjustment. How Much Has Happened?* Washington: Institute for International Economics.

Willis, K. 2011. *Theories and Practices of Development.* New York: Routledge. [Accessed 26 September 2015]. www.123library.org/book_details/?id=75730.

World Bank. 1991. *World Development Report.* Washington DC: World Bank.

World Bank. 1993. *The East Asian Miracle: Economic Growth and Public Policy.* New York: Oxford University Press.

World Bank. 2002. *Constructing Knowledge Societies: New Challenges for Tertiary Education.* Washington DC: World Bank.

World Bank. 2009. *The World Bank Annual Report 2009 Year in Review.* Washington DC: The World Bank. [Accessed 27 September 2015]. www.worldbank. icebox.ingenta.com/content/wb/bk17946.

World Bank. 2012. 'Gender equality and development'. *World Development Report.* Washington DC: World Bank. [Accessed 30 September 2015]. http://site. ebrary.com/id/10506397.

4 A foundation of human development and capabilities for higher education

The World Social Forum at Port Alegre in Brazil in 2001 reminded us that another world is possible (Fisher and Ponniah 2003). Thus far, we have considered how the university is understood and located in contemporary higher education and development debates; now we consider another possible imaginary. We have considered how the dominant view of higher education as a driver of competitive economic growth and development, supported by a highly skilled educated workforce, pulls away from the more expansive view of universities as a space for the public good as described in Chapter 2. In practice, the debate is complex and not as simple as this on the ground, but this captures the broad tension. We also explored development theories in Chapter 3 and how universities and higher education are positioned in these, noting that in modernisation theories, higher education was not seen as significant for economic development, but from the 1990s became increasingly prominent for human capital formation. At the same time, a range of alternative perspectives on development were sketched, more aligned with public, social and common good values.

We now outline in this chapter, key ideas from human development (Haq 2003), its theorisation as capabilities and functionings formation (Sen 1999; Nussbaum 2000) and its global reach and responsiveness (Sen 2009; Nussbaum 2006). This constitutes, we think, currently the most convincing development theory and, while capturing the imperatives of economic development and human capital formation, subsumes them within a wider and ethically inclusive frame in which people's well-being individually, in nations and globally, is the end purpose of development, rather than profit or GDP. It is these ideas that we elaborate in the chapter, foregrounding individual well-being and agency in and through universities, so that universities might be understood as generative capability multipliers when individual students flourish. We suggest further that when this individual flourishing is oriented to others and the public good, this in itself will reduce both personal and social inequalities and contribute to sustainable human relationships, and if aggregated over countries, also to global development and well-being.

The chapter demonstrates thus, how a foundation of human development and capabilities offers a tremendous resource to support universities committed to the public good in their own countries and also to global development. We propose in this chapter that human development and, inside this, the capability approach can comprehensively contribute to defining and characterising what a good university should be, the kind of social change universities should work towards, and how this can be responsive to the world and pressing development challenges. In the next section, we give an introduction to the human development approach and the underpinning values, followed by a description of what we consider are the core elements of its theorisation as capabilities: capabilities and functionings, conversion factors, agency and public deliberation. Finally, we present some indications of how this approach could be helpful in analysing educational interventions and also contributing to global development.

A human development framework

Although the appearance of the Human Development Report (HDR) of the United Nations Development Programme (UNDP) in 1990 marks a fundamental milestone for the dissemination of the concept of human development, the origins of this theory go back to the 1970s, with the conceptualisation of the basic needs approach applied to development processes (Streeten 2003). This approach represented a shift in economic development thinking, in that it introduced concerns about the social aspects of development, participation, the depletion of natural resources, etc. Development policies produced under this current of thought influenced the need for redistribution of the benefits of development (Chenery *et al.* 1974). However, as Griffin (2001: 28) reminds us:

> both redistribution from growth and basic needs continued to be addressed from a development perspective focused on consumer goods: only intended to ensure that a greater share of the benefits derived from increased production came to groups with lower incomes.

In the next decade, observing the impact of structural adjustment programmes, it was UNICEF that drew attention to the need to redesign structural adjustment programmes to protect the poor from the serious deterioration of revenues and cuts in basic social services. This approach was described as 'adjustment with a human face'. It represented a major challenge in facing dominant mainstream thought and did more than any other publication to put people first in development planning (Griffin 2001: 28).

A further relevant milestone for the introduction of human development coming from outside universities was the entrance of Mahbub Ul Haq of Pakistan as a special advisor to the general manager of the UNDP in 1989.

Haq (2003: 17) explained that social arrangements must be judged by the extent to which they advance the human good, citing Aristotle who argued that, 'wealth is evidently not the good we are seeking for it is merely useful and for the sake of something else'. As Haq (2003: 17) elucidated, 'the basic purposes of development is to enlarge people's choices'; such choices are dynamic and encompass the economic, social, cultural and political. Haq has been key to the creation of the Human Development Reports (HDR) of the UNDP, popularising the concept of human development along the focal themes chosen each year for the last 25 years (e.g. Migration, Rethinking Work for Human Development), as well as individual country reports. The first Report proposed indicators for the measurement of development different from those that had been employed up to that point and which used a measure only of economic growth (captured as GDP or average income). Thus, the first page of the first Human Development report published in 1990 famously reads:

> People are the real wealth of a nation. The basic objective of development is to create an enabling environment for people to live long, healthy and creative lives. This may appear to be a simple truth. But it is often forgotten in the immediate concern with the accumulation of commodities and financial wealth.
>
> (UNDP 1990: 1)

While economic growth is necessary, it is not on its own sufficient for multidimensional flourishing, or as the single measure of good lives. As the first Human Development Report explained, human development is a process of enlarging people's choices of which the most critical are to be able to lead a long and healthy life, to be educated and to enjoy a decent standard of living. Additional choices include political freedom, guaranteed human rights and self-respect, such as being able to mix with others without being ashamed to appear ill-dressed in public. Alkire (2010) explains that human development sets priorities among goals, integrating several principles at the same time. Commonly used principles include poverty reduction, equity, efficiency, voice and participation, sustainability, respect for human rights and fostering the common good. Human development is thus multidimensional and its components are crucially interconnected. Alkire outlines the most recent and expanded definition of human development as follows:

> Human development aims to enlarge people's freedoms to do and be what they value and have reason to value. In practice, human development also empowers people to engage actively in development on our shared planet. It is people-centred. At all levels of development, human development focuses on essential freedoms: enabling people to lead long and healthy lives, to acquire knowledge, to be able to enjoy a

decent standard of living and to shape their own lives. Many people value these freedoms in and of themselves; they are also powerful means to other opportunities.

(Alkire 2010: 43)

Turning back to Haq (2003), he had been convinced that a single but composite measure of human development was needed in order to convince policy-makers that they should evaluate development by improvements in human well-being, not economic growth alone or as the main end of development. To this end, he worked closely with Amartya Sen and other development economists to produce the Human Development Index (HDI). The HDI is a summary measure of average achievement in key dimensions of human development: (1) health: life expectancy at birth; (2) education: combined measure of mean of years of schooling for adults aged 25 years and expected years (maximum of 18 years) of schooling for children of school entering age; and (3) standard of living: measured by gross national income per capita. The HDI is the geometric mean of normalised indices for each of the three dimensions. The UNDP explains that the HDI can be used to question national policy choices, asking how two countries with the same level of per capita income can end up with different human development outcomes. These contrasts, it suggests, can stimulate debate about government policy priorities. Using just the HDI, Table 4.1 provides some indicative examples from the 2014 HDR (UNDP 2014):

As the UNDP makes clear the HDI does not reflect on inequalities, poverty, human security, empowerment, and so on, and certainly intuitively and experientially from what we know of our own countries, Spain and South Africa, there are many lives that do not go well at all, even though Spain has a high HDI and South Africa a medium HDI.[1]

Plurality of dimensions

What is clear from Haq and Alkire's definitions is that human development conceives of multidimensional good lives and a plurality of important dimensions, beyond the economic and even the HDI. These plural dimensions and underpinning values constitute a crucial anchor and guard against easy domestication when applying the ideas to universities. All the values matter, and support and reinforce each other. The UNDP's standard definition of dimensions of human development covers: (1) empowerment,

Table 4.1 Illustrative examples of the Human Development Index (HDI)

Very high HD	Norway, USA, UK, **Spain**
High HD	Mexico, China
Medium HD	Botswana, **South Africa**, India
Low HD	Angola, Mozambique

meaning the expansion of capabilities (ability to attain valued ends), expansion of valued functionings (attained valued ends) and participation (sharing in specifying priorities); (2) equity in distribution of basic capabilities; (3) security; and (4) sustainability of people's valued attainments and opportunities. Penz *et al.*'s (2011) work on human development ethics slightly extends this list by highlighting human rights and cultural freedom. Arguably, these are already largely subsumed within the UNDP formulation within the range of valued ends to be promoted, equitably distributed, sustained and secured, but are now further highlighted by them. In a more detailed definition of the central values of human development, Alkire and Deneulin (2009: 36–7) identify four interlocking principles of equity, efficiency, participation and empowerment, and sustainability and elaborate each as follows:

1 *Equity* draws on the concept of justice, impartiality and fairness and incorporates a consideration for distributive justice between groups. In human development, we seek equity in the space of people's freedom to live valuable lives. It is related to, but different from, the concept of equality, which implies equality of all people in some space. In human development, equity draws attention to those who have unequal opportunities due to various disadvantages and may require preferential treatment or affirmative action.

2 *Efficiency* refers to the optimal use of existing resources. It is necessary to demonstrate that the chosen intervention offers the highest impact in terms of people's opportunities. When applying this principle, one must conceive of efficiency in a dynamic context since what is efficient at one point in time may not necessarily be efficient in the long run.

3 *Participation and empowerment* is about processes in which people act as agents – individually and as groups. It is about the freedom to make decisions in matters that affect their lives; the freedom to hold others accountable for their promises, the freedom to influence development in their communities. Whether at the level of policy-making or implementation, this principle implies that people need to be involved at every stage, not merely as beneficiaries or spectators, but as agents who are able to pursue and realise goals that they value and have reason to value.

4 *Sustainability* is often used to introduce the durability of development in the face of environmental limitations but is not confined to this dimension alone. It refers to advancing human development such that progress in all spheres – social, political and financial – endures over time. Environmental sustainability implies achieving developmental results without jeopardising the natural resource base and biodiversity of the region and without affecting the resource base for future generations. Financial sustainability refers to the way in which development is financed without penalising future generations or economic stability.

Social sustainability refers to the way in which social groups and other institutions are involved and support development initiatives over time, and avoid disruptive and destructive elements. Cultural liberty and respect for diversity are also important values that can contribute to socially-sustainable development. In education sustainability requires quality in processes and to secure educational achievements.

As Alkire and Deneulin point out, these four principles are not exhaustive; other values, such as responsibility or justice, could be also considered. However, we agree with Ibrahim (2014) that an intervention inspired by the human development approach should incorporate all the four dimensions; even if its main focus is on one dimension of value, the others must also be considered in relation to the main value chosen. For example, efficiency should not be considered on its own.

This is one of the key differences with previous approaches to development that we analysed in Chapter 3. Compared with those, we consider that human development offers a broader perspective: it is multidimensional, more integral and integrative, and in its conception is able to reflect and to integrate, in a balanced way, the values that underline the other approaches. Efficiency is one of the core values of economic theories of development, but human development considers it limited if taken on its own, and always shaped by the other principles. Sustainability is intrinsic to human development, which is consistent with the most recent versions of sustainable development (Froger *et al.* 2004): a desirable development process should be both human and sustainable. With participatory approaches to development, human development shares the key pillar of empowerment and process, adding to the other dimensions. Gender is included into the equity umbrella, although there are other aspects of gender approaches that are not specifically considered in general human development analysis, such as the relations between micro- and macro-politics. Finally, with post-development and post-colonial approaches we observe more differences: human development refers to development, while post-development argues against this concept, its metaphors, discourses and practices. Human development, in its general interpretations, does not pay explicit attention to historical processes, while post-colonial approaches target them. (Although we do also need to say that both Sen and Nussbaum draw extensively on history and historical examples to make their arguments.) However, instead of considering those differences as irreconcilables, our proposal is try to bring elements of these approaches to a better understanding of universities, especially when we address the knowledge and teaching activities of higher education institutions in Chapters 6, 7 and 8.

Core elements of the capability approach

Human development is theorised through the capability approach and the two concepts are closely interwoven; human development seeks to expand people's capabilities and expanding capabilities in turn advances human development nationally and globally. Robeyns (2005: 94) succinctly summarises the capability approach as a 'broad normative framework for the evaluation and assessment of individual well-being and social arrangements, the design of policies, and proposals about social change in society', in which the means are instrumental to the ends of enabling people's well-being. Here, we explore why a capabilities approach grounded in human development is our preferred analytical framework to investigate higher education and development in the direction of more equality and more justice.

Sen's (1992) capability approach is clear: freedom is both the primary end and the principal means of development, and freedom is grounded in both well-being (the opportunity or capability aspect) and agency (the process aspect). Sen explains:

> Freedom can be valued for the substantive opportunity it gives to the pursuit of our objectives and goals. In assessing opportunities, attention has to be paid to the actual ability of a person to achieve those things that she has reason to value ... on what the real opportunities for achievement are for the persons involved. This "opportunity aspect" of freedom can be contrasted with another perspective that focuses in particular on the freedom involved in the process itself.... This is the process aspect of freedom.
>
> (Sen 2002: 10)

As Deneulin (2014: 34) sums up: 'A person is free when she or he has the opportunity to function (as a human being) and to pursue goals he or she values'.

Capabilities and functionings

Sen's approach was developed in answer to the question 'Equality of what?' When we assess or measure equality, what is it that we are looking at (the problem of what we place in the evaluative space – income, happiness, freedoms), and how do we justify our focus? Sen's response is to insert freedoms or what he calls 'capabilities' into the evaluative space, that is to understand and measure development as a process of expanding the real freedoms (the capabilities or well-being freedoms, the opportunity aspect of freedom) that people enjoy to be and do what they have reason to value (their functionings or well-being achievements). Once opportunities are in place, a person chooses the options – the functionings – they most value. Well-being is then understood in terms of how a person can function – or what a person can actually succeed in being and doing.

Conversely, ill-being would point to development failures and constraints. However, two people may demonstrate the same functioning, for example attaining a university degree, but have differing capabilities; it is the capabilities that reveal inequalities. One graduate may have been funded by her parents, been able to live on the campus, attended a good school which had prepared her well for university, and found achieving the degree relatively easy. The other student may have struggled financially before winning a scholarship, and been to a poor quality school which left her under-prepared for university so that achieving her degree meant tremendous struggle. If we look only at functionings, we may miss the capability differences which point to actual opportunities and inequalities between the two students. Furthermore, although Sen proposes an approach to individual freedom, Stewart (2005) has pointed out the importance also of considering groups, in which case we could aggregate across social groups to establish broad social inequalities which public policy ought to address.

Resources and contexts

Resources of different kinds – what Robeyn's (2005: 98) calls 'goods' matter as the means to achieve functionings, for example: the good of a quality school; the good of a supportive family for higher education; the good of public transport to travel safely; the good of income to pay for university; social norms about gender, and so on. As she explains further, these material and non-material goods, 'shape people's opportunity sets, and the circumstances that influence the choices that people can make from the capability set' and 'should receive a central place in capability evaluations' (Robeyns 2005: 99). Moreover, while income is not regarded as an end in itself – it can only be a proxy for capabilities – Sen is nonetheless concerned that our freedoms should include freedom from material want, and basic capabilities for freedom from want and deprivation. Unlike Nussbaum (2000), he does not specify what the threshold of these should be but leaves this open to debate and context. The main point is that the capability approach acknowledges the integration of resources (including economic growth) and opportunities, but always arguing that instruments to enhance human freedom must be 'appraised precisely ... in their actual effectiveness in enriching the lives and liberties of people' (Dreze and Sen 2002: 3). The further crucial point is that this requires us in evaluating people's capabilities 'to scrutinize the context in which economic production and social interactions take place, and whether the circumstances in which people choose from their opportunity sets are enabling and just' (Robeyns 2005: 99). Thus, both Nussbaum and Sen would advocate a focus on what Nussbaum (2000: 83–85) calls 'combined capabilities', that is 'internal capabilities' (such as being able to think critically), together with the external conditions that effectively enable that person to exercise this capability.

Agency

If capability is freedom of opportunity, agency is freedom of process. Agency refers to the ability of the individual to pursue and achieve the objectives they value. An agent is 'someone who acts and makes change happen' (Sen 1999). As Deneulin (2014: 27) explains, 'wellbeing depends not only on what a person does or is, but on *how* [author's emphasis] she achieved that functioning, whether she was actively involved in the process of achieving that functioning or not'. The process is thus significant. For example, take two students who choose to study teacher education, we should ask how did they decide and who decided? Did each student arrive independently at this choice; did a teacher or parent tell one or both of them to make this choice; did the government make the decision by offering a generous bursary? Who, in short, chose the functioning of enrolling into teacher education and what was each student's underlying capability to choose? Sen (1992: 150) explains: 'The crucial question here, in the context of wellbeing, is whether freedom to choose is valued only instrumentally, or is also important in itself'. In other words, being able to make one's own choices matters intrinsically. Because people as agents will choose the life they have reason to value, this makes capabilities 'an agency-based and opportunity-oriented theory' (Biggeri and Ferrannini 2014: 2).

Crocker and Robeyns (2009: 6) helpfully point out that not only should individuals exercise their agency by shaping or determining their own lives, but it is by exercising joint agency that communities can and should select, weigh and trade-off capabilities, functionings and other normative considerations. What is important is that people individually and collectively conduct their lives, sometimes realising or helping realise each other's goals, sometimes by forming joint interventions and exercising collective agency. According to Crocker and Robeyns (2010), exercising agency requires a number of elements: (1) *Self-determination*: the person decides for herself rather than someone or something else making the decision (to enrol in teacher education, for example). (2) *Reason orientation and deliberation*: the person bases her decisions on reasons, such as the pursuit of her aspirations and goals. (3) *Action*: the person performs or has a role in performing some action. (4) *Impact in the world*: the person brings about (or contributes to bringing about change in the world). Deneulin and Alkire (2009: 37) add two more components to this ideal of agency: a person who exercises agency can pursue well-being or other objectives that somehow should be reasonable (this component is also emphasised by Drydyk 2013), plus they emphasise the responsibility of the agent in wanting to achieve her goals, so that agency is linked to responsible choices and actions, as well as to reasoning.

Agency freedom is then a central concept, together with the focus on each person as of moral worth and hence, a concern with what each person is able to be and do in reasonably choosing a good life. While, the capability approach appears to support an individual maximising calculus (what I have reason to value being and doing for my own good life), nonetheless agency obligations to others directs this maximising calculus to take into account the improvement of the well-being of others as a means to my own well-being. Thus, Sen (2008: 336) argues that being advantaged 'inescapably' generates obligations to be responsible for promoting democratic values, social justice and fundamental human rights because 'capability is a kind of power, and it would be a mistake to see capability only as a concept of human advantage, not also as a concept in human obligation'. From Sen's perspective, if someone has the power to make a change that he or she can see will reduce injustice in the world, there is a strong case for doing so.

Indeed, Deneulin (2014: 45) makes this explicit in arguing that 'living well and acting justly go together'. What I have reason to value as significant to my own good life then includes advancing the well-being of others. Agency includes 'other-regarding' goals, meaning goals which concern the good lives of others, so that agency carries an obligation to use one's power to enhance human development.

This is consistent with higher education as a public good – doing something for others, based on an individual foundation of well-being and agency, as well as doing something for oneself, supported by the human

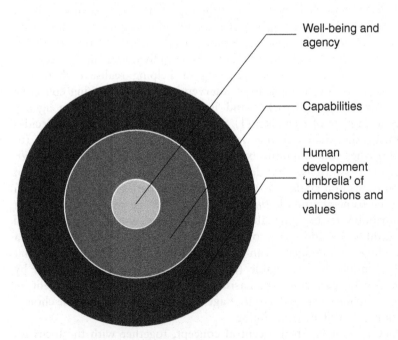

Well-being and agency

Capabilities

Human development 'umbrella' of dimensions and values

Figure 4.1 Core elements of human development and capabilities.

development dimensions and values sketched earlier. As Deneulin (2014) notes, other-regarding agency introduces a language of justice insofar as acting justly is to work to transform social, economic and political conditions and structures so that people are able to live dignified lives in a shared world. In this way, acting justly also takes us towards global development. To ask what kind of life a person is leading and is able to lead, and to work to change the conditions that do not enable good lives is logically to tackle global development and the inequality challenge highlighted in Chapter 2.

Human dignity

Nussbaum's (2000: 78–80; 2011) approach is slightly different from Sen's in that she defines a list of ten universal human capabilities as fundamental entitlements in a just society, and locates human dignity as foundational to her approach. She thus aims to develop a partial theory of justice, with her list of capabilities constituting the political principles that should underlie a state's constitution. Her argument is that if we are for social justice we need to say more about the content of justice (although one could argue that Sen's instrumental freedoms and his emphasis on public reasoning do in fact do this). Both Sen and Nussbaum are helpful and we are not especially concerned here with the differences, although we do think Sen's strong emphasis on public reasoning is important; on the other hand Nussbaum's list and her emphasis on human dignity also enables an entry into the debate from which point one can agree or disagree with her approach. We think incorporating human dignity as a core element of the approach adds value insofar as inequality and unequal development reduces and removes dignity from many people; even in what appears to be the more elite space of higher education, dignity can be reduced in the face of unfair educational arrangements. More important than the differences, we think, is Nussbaum's reminder that:

> All over the world, people are struggling for a life that is fully human, a life worthy of human dignity. Countries and states are often focused on economic growth alone, but their people, meanwhile, are striving for something different: they want meaningful human lives. They need theoretical approaches that can be the ally of their struggles, not approaches that keep these struggles from view.
>
> (Nussbaum 2012: 1)

Human development and capabilities is such a theory, and one which illuminates the policy struggles for access, equity and quality in universities, casts a fresh lens on research practices (Chapter 6), and above all opens up the aspirations and efforts of students towards meaningful and good lives.

Conversion factors and equality

In the capability approach, we focus on the ends of development, that is people's well-being and resources and commodities as the means to those ends. The approach aims for greater precision and attention to micro-data at the level of the individual and each person's valued and achieved functionings, as well as the underlying capabilities to develop and choose these functionings. This requires, according to Sen (1999), an enriched 'informational basis of judgement in justice', capturing what people are actually able to be and to do, but also through the concept of capability, what freedoms different people have for genuine choices among alternative possibilities. Diversity among people is always understood as constitutive of the richness and normalness of human being-ness – people are diverse in their humanity and such diversity ought not to be the grounds for discrimination or inequalities.

This is recognised in the emphasis on having a plurality of functionings; which functionings are valued will vary from person to person. (Setting aside at this point a common core of opportunities and functionings, which are distinctive to higher education as education, and should be opportunities for all, see Walker 2006a.) But we also need a mechanism to understand how each person 'converts' her bundle of resources into freedoms to achieve, across dimensions of the personal, social and environmental (Sen 1999). The concept of conversion connects individual lives to social and policy arrangements and the historical context in order to illuminate social norms (of race, gender, class and so on), and how they shape our everyday lives and our capacity to take advantage of opportunities. We need information about each person's bundle of resources and commodities (their means to achieve), the personal and social conversion factors which shape their capabilities (their freedoms to achieve), and their choices which convert capabilities into actual achievements and realised agency (Bonvin and Favarque 2006). As Bonvin and Favarque (2006) explain, the possession of a certain amount of commodities acts as the means to achieve, but cannot guarantee real possibilities to choose because of the intervention of personal and social conversion factors (see Chapter 8 for an empirical application).

By connecting individual lives to social and policy arrangements conversion captures what gender theories in development (and others) place in the front line of their analysis: the connection between micro- and macro-politics. If the opportunity to develop capabilities and valued functionings is uneven, we look to wider arrangements to understand what is unjust and needs to be changed to enable well-being in each life. For Sen, the idea is to create appropriate social arrangements to develop the freedoms to choose a life one has reason to value. It is then important to note that, although sometimes overlooked in account of the capability approach, Sen (1999: 38) also outlines five 'instrumental freedoms' (also see Chapters 5 and 8) that are crucial to 'the overall freedom people have to live the way they would like to live' and to live more freely (for a higher education application, see Flores-Crespo 2007): (1) *political freedoms*, e.g. democracy, the freedom to scrutinise and criticise authorities, to enjoy a free press and multi-party elections; (2) *economic facilities*, e.g. people's opportunity to have and use economic resources or entitlements; (3) *social opportunities*, e.g. people's ability to have health care, to be educated, and to live in a society where others also enjoy these goods; (4) *transparency guarantees*, e.g. the ability to trust others and to know that the information one receives is clear and honestly disclosed; and (5) *protective security*, e.g. social protections for vulnerable people that prevent abject deprivation. Instrumental freedoms provide the conditions for capabilities to develop. The view taken of development is vivid and multidimensional taking account of, 'links between the material, mental, and social well-being, or to the economic, political and cultural dimensions of human life' (Crocker and Robeyns 2009: 65). The further implication is that the full development of people's capabilities and functionings will be difficult if these conditions are not in place, so that we need to work simultaneously to expand and secure instrumental freedoms in the democratic dispensation implied by Sen, and expand and secure people's capabilities which in turn will secure instrumental freedoms in a virtuous circle. This is potentially radical and certainly must require a critical analysis and action around current global conditions if some global institutions and global power relations reduce the development space (or we might say, instrumental freedoms and citizen well-being and agency) of low income countries (Wade 2003).

Public deliberation

In Sen's (2009) thinking, deliberation, critical scrutiny, public debate and therefore a thick democracy are central elements. Among many statements to this effect, he writes that, 'When we try to determine how justice can be advanced, there is a basic need for public reasoning, involving arguments coming from different quarters and divergent perspectives' (2009: 392) and, 'bad reasoning can be confronted by better reasoning' (2009: xviii). Enabling subjugated voices to be heard would be especially important in development debates. This rich emphasis on public reasoning would change how we engage in the theory and practice of development, as well as how we think about equality and justice. It should then be a priority in development policies to consolidate democratic structures, while basic economic and social needs are met.

According to Sen (1999), there are three arguments to support the primacy of political freedom and democracy for development; Crocker (2008: 299–308) gives us a detailed description of these arguments for democracy and public deliberation. First, democracy has an intrinsic value;

it is intrinsically good because it enables people to participate politically and this freedom is something people have reason to value intrinsically. From this perspective, freedom of political participation is emphasised, not the activity itself. Second, democracy has an instrumental value because, 'democracies have an important instrumental role in enhancing the hearing that people get in response to their claims to political attention, including the claims of economic needs' (Dreze and Sen 2002: 24). Finally, democracy has a constructive value insofar as it provides institutions and processes in which people can learn from each other and construct and decide on the values and priorities of the society. Crocker (2008: 303–6), based on Sen's writings, gives us examples of these kinds of collective choices; we outline six relevant for higher education:

1   *The choice of agents and participants*: who should be a member of the group and who or what is to make (further) choices? Should the group make its own choices and make them deliberatively or should it choose to have some other agent or authority make them? Sen assumes that people who are most affected by a decision should make the decision.
2   *The choice of the process and decision-making*. Groups have a choice from among several collective decision-making procedures, including some form of democratic decision-making.
3   *The choice of agency versus well-being*. When the community exercises its agency and make its *own* decision, this choice is the social version of an individual's choice between the opportunity aspect of freedom (capabilities) and the process aspect of freedom (agency).
4   *The choice between functioning or capability*. Within the space of well-being, a community sometimes must choose between a functioning, such as its members being healthy now (through curative medicine) and a capability, such as being made free from ill-health (through preventive medicine).
5   *The choice between functionings (or capabilities) now and functioning (or capabilities) in the future*. Crocker's examples, we think, are examples of tragic choices – ill-health now or ill-health in the future – and we prefer the example of university students who may have to choose between the freedom now to have a wonderful social life (which could be very agreeable) or the opportunity to study for good grades (which may seem less agreeable but is crucial for future capabilities and functionings). There is no reason why students cannot be involved in public reasoning to understand the better choice, or any trade-off.
6   *The choice of distributive and other values*. A community can and should choose criteria of distribution, and has the freedom to value and sometimes prioritise some values upon others.

The important point that Crocker notes is that for each kind of choice – effectively practical valuational debates – Sen endorses public dialogue and scrutiny and democratic processes which extend beyond representative democracy.

All this has important implications for higher education: we need to pay attention not only to the capabilities and functionings which we would like to expand among a university community and external groups linked with this community, but also who decides and how which are to be the capabilities and functionings, and how external structural factors influence the process of decision-making. There are also significant implications for processes of university governance, for higher education public policy, even for systems of deciding on university league tables and donor decisions that seriously affect universities.

Drawing on complementary ideas

In our view, the capability approach and public reasoning could also be strengthened further by being aligned with other approaches rooted in participatory approaches to development (see Chapter 3). To give some examples, following Frediani *et al.* (2015), participatory processes could be helpful because they can facilitate the sustained ability to identify and analyse problems, formulate and plan solutions, mobilise resources and implement actions (Leal and Opp 1998: 7–8), with the objective of improving people's effective freedoms. Moreover, the notion of participation as empowerment provides the capability approach with a deeper understanding of power within society at a structural and institutional level and thus makes interesting contributions to the notion of democracy as a central aspect of human development. Such an approach could contribute to the application of capability-oriented initiatives by providing critical lenses on collective mechanisms of decision-making for social benefits and service distribution. Gaventa (2006) contributes examples of how to engage with the concept and practice of participation reflexively, providing resources on how spaces of participation can reveal, navigate and reshape relations of power. This has much in common with the concerns of the capability approach for 'deepening' democratic processes, and shows how participatory approaches allow a better understanding of the 'disruptive effects of power imbalances in participatory and democratic mechanisms' (Deneulin 2009: 190). However transparent it might seem, any public debate involves hidden or invisible power relationships.

Assuming that Gaventa's (2006) invisible power is rooted in our imagination, beliefs and assumptions, the experience of participatory approaches demonstrates how creating conditions of freedom and equality for a democratic deliberation process is not only a question of developing cognitive and communicative abilities or overcoming social or economic difficulties, but also of incorporating critical and reflective practices that enable people to question beliefs and previous assumptions to get rid of tacitly imposed restrictions. Feminist movements have offered us the clearest demonstration of how overcoming inequalities among men and women is a transformational process, whereby deeply rooted social values and beliefs have to be challenged (see Chapter 3). Participatory approaches demonstrate that in order to tackle this issue, we must engage in reflective practices to generate a deep self-questioning process of the principles that guide human relationships and which may question the very basis of the current social order. Gender studies in particular have demonstrated the social construction of relationships, power and gender identities and the implications for inequalities between the sexes (Frediani *et al.* 2015).

These contributions from participatory and power theories, gender approaches and also post-development and post-colonial perspectives, remind us that the capability approach is a framework rather than a theory. This makes it both flexible but also vulnerable to domestication. Because it is not a theory of justice it does not directly address what Rainer Forst (2014: 24) calls 'the first question of justice', that is 'the question of power' (see Chapter 8). The approach is therefore more robust when firmly located within human development values, which include participation and empowerment, and in education could be moored by identifying worthwhile capabilities (Walker 2006a). Second, the capability approach does not deal well with the socialness of well-being, which makes it open to capture by individualised and decontextualised accounts of well-being and by individualised solutions, whether by one university, or a unit, or a group. For example, at the University of the Free State in South Africa, the campus is fully gated to ensure the safety of students while on campus. Entry to the campus is via an access card. The students are safe on campus but as soon as they leave they are vulnerable to muggings and the general lack of human security in a violent society; women are especially affected. The on-campus security is an important response but longer-term public policy around public safety would be needed to move beyond a privatised solution that normalises an abnormal way of living and ultimately does not secure people's capabilities.

Education is also deeply relational and requires a concept of relational well-being, we learn with, from and through others. Education is also always historical and contextual and this needs to be taken into account; we cannot say that, because something goes well in one university that it will go well in another university. Finally, it might be thought that the capability approach underplays the contribution of economic factors. This we think is incorrect – what the approach says is that income distribution and commodities or resources are important conversion variables and need to be taken into account when considering people's well-being, but also that attention only to the economic does not settle the challenges of well-being and agency. The focus on multidimensional well-being, as we see it, requires that we attend to the economic, the social and cultural and the policy/political by working iteratively from lives to structures, histories and contexts, with due attention to power, and always adopting a multidimensional approach and method. Moreover, Sen (1999) discusses economic arrangements in many places, for example his discussion of two approaches, which have been successful in rapidly reducing human mortality: 'growth-mediated', which works through fast economic progress accompanied by using economic prosperity to expand relevant health services, and 'support-led', which focuses on a programme of social support (health care, education, etc.). Nonetheless, choosing between these alternative pathways for Sen demands public discussion and a foundation of relevant capabilities and functionings, including economic literacy.

Human development, the capability approach and education

Although in the following chapters we will expand our analysis of the contribution of the human development and capability approach to higher education, here we would like to highlight some characteristics of the approach (complemented with other perspectives as we noted above) that make it especially interesting for analysing educational scenarios. First, we emphasise that Sen considers that education forms human capital but, 'The benefits of education exceed its role as human capital' (Sen 1999: 294). McCowan and Unterhalter (2013: 143) suggest two main ways in which capabilities have a bearing on education: (1) relating to the distributional aspect of education; and (2) its substantive values and content. With regard to equality, they argue that the general position on equality taken by the capability approach can be applied to educational settings: 'Just as the approach rejects an emphasis on equality of initial resources or of preference satisfaction, so it rejects in education an approach of equal treatment or equal attainment regardless of individual or group differences' (McCowan and Unterhalter 2013: 143). This has to do with the concept of conversion factors, those personal, social and environmental characteristics (Sen 1999) that intersect different dimensions, which we noted earlier. Students for example, could differ: (1) along a personal axis (e.g. gender, age, class, etc.); (2) along an intersecting external of environmental axis (wealth, climate, etc.); and (3) along an inter-individual or social axis. Additionally, students with the same outcome (e.g. passing an exam) may have had very different opportunities, so cannot be judged in the same manner (Unterhalter *et al.* 2007). Consequently, as Unterhalter points out, thinking in terms of capabilities raises a wider range of issues than simply looking at the amount of resources or commodities people have. Because of interpersonal diversity, 'people need a different amount of resources in order to transform these into the functioning of being educated' (Unterhalter 2009: 166).

The second contribution to education by the human development and capability approach refers, first, to the capability multiplier role of education. Education is valuable for its democratic contributions; it can teach us to reason and deliberate with others in an informed and critical way.

Education has interpersonal effects in opening up opportunities for others, for example, younger brothers or sisters or people in the communities of which we are a part. From a social perspective, education can have empowerment and distributive effects, for example, disadvantaged groups can increase their ability to resist inequalities and get a fairer deal in and through education. Crucially, having a good education affects the development and expansion of other capabilities so that an education capability expands other important human freedoms. Education thus includes both market and non-market goods and both need to be captured for a full account (Boni and Arias 2013; Walker 2006a).

Third, capabilities can have implications for curriculum and pedagogies. In this aspect, the capability approach in education has strong links with other progressive educational ideas of Rousseau, Dewey and Freire (Flores-Crespo 2007). These approaches and the capability approach have in common concerns with the voices of those who have to struggle to be heard and included. Further, it is concerned with human flourishing and how equality and social arrangements have to change. Therefore, when we teach about the capability approach, we need to keep in mind that our pedagogy ought to be consistent with the core principles of the approach itself. It ought to be both a critical and a humanising pedagogy (Walker 2009: 264).

The last contribution of the capability approach to education has to do with values. It is not just that education should promote particular political and moral values, but that it is inescapably charged with those values (McCowan and Unterhalter 2013) and also forms values (Vaughan and Walker 2012; see also Chapter 8). In the previous pages, we have proposed four fundamental values that should be at the core of any development process: efficiency, equity, participation and empowerment, and environmental sustainability. In the following chapters, we see how those values could be relevant to evaluate policies and practices, as well to inspire human development and capability-friendly actions.

Another relevant contribution of the human development and capability approach to education has to do with idea of citizenship, which relates primarily to three aspects: deliberation, the acknowledgement of heterogeneity and the emphasis on agency (McCowan and Unterhalter 2013). We have explored all of these ideas previously, including how key elements of the human development and capability approach need to be complemented with other approaches (participatory, gender and historical approaches mainly). Any idea of citizenship rooted in the human development and capability approach should consider a deep democratic way of taking decisions, with adequate mechanisms that allow the real participation of people, paying special attention to the most marginalised groups who, due to personal and social conversion factors, have fewer opportunities to participate in the decision-making process.

We also think that universities could make contributions to global justice. If universities commit to advancing the 'intuitive idea of life that is worth the dignity of the human being' (Nussbaum 2006: 70) and through education, help secure the necessary capabilities, they could contribute indirectly and directly to the principles Nussbaum (2006: 319–22) outlines for a just global structure, specifically: (1) cultivating a forceful global public sphere (which following Sen would rest on having robust public reasoning and public participation at all levels up to and including the global); (2) institutions and individuals should focus on the problems of the disadvantaged in each nation and region (as Chapter 2 showed through fostering public good values, and Chapters 5, 6, 7 and 8 show through policy, research and student learning); and (3) supporting education as key to the empowerment of those who are currently disadvantaged (as we argued in Chapter 2, higher education is a significant global and local development actor across the continuum of education provision). Sen's (2009) concern for global justice proposes that we need to be able to scrutinise our own societies from a distance as Adam Smith's 'impartial spectators' in a global public dialogue, which Sen argues (2009) is central for world justice and requires a foundation of well-reasoned public participation in civil society. In turn, this requires education, and particularly higher education in its contribution to graduate formation and citizenship (Walker and McLean 2013; see also Chapter 8).

Actual lives

We close the chapter by considering the very micro-level of student learning and individual flourishing. This may seem rather fine-grained but we think it underlines the crucial foundation of capabilities – what does each person succeed in being and doing – and we should not lose sight of this, even if global development seems far off (mistakenly we think) from individual lives. Consider then the lives of Ntabiseng and Janet who have both attained the grades to come to university. On the surface, they appear to have opportunities, which have enabled them to access higher education. But they both face inequalities beyond having the grades for attending university. Do we give them more money? Do we ask how satisfied they are? Do we ask what each can be and do? What would development theories outlined in Chapters 2 and 3 and in this chapter have to say first, to Ntabiseng, a black working-class student at the University of the Witwatersrand (Wits) in South Africa in response to her comments on her learning experiences:

> In Drama, they say all these names of people who have written theories about drama and films and you find that you don't know them. But other people, who have had the privilege [of good schools], know them. It just scares you. Sometimes the lecturer acts as if we know these things.... In class when we were asked a particular question, I could not answer because ... but I could not show that I don't

know.... [Also] when we were in class drawing and the lecturer would walk around to comment.... I could see he would go to some people and make detailed comments but when he came to me he said very little and I felt that perhaps my level of competition was lower than others. I couldn't stand the pressure.... So I only stuck to what I knew, and if I got 50 per cent then I was happy and would not struggle to get 80 or something like that.

(quoted in CHE 2009: 273)

Or to Janet, a first generation student in her final year of a degree in sociology and social policy at an elite UK university:

I won't do as well as everyone else [this year], even though I have done in the past. I don't know why, I just seem to lack that confidence.... I emailed my lecturer for advice about the marker's comments on an essay I wrote, but her response was unhelpful; she just sent it back saying, 'Well, I haven't seen the work, I didn't mark the essay, I can't really comment', and said that perhaps it's more my problem and that I'm finding it difficult to adjust to university work. [So] when we had to choose between a dissertation and an extended essay in our final year I chose the essay because I didn't think I could cope with doing a long piece of research, but after I'd chosen the essay, I found out that everyone else on my course was doing the dissertation, and I felt kind of inferior.

(quoted in Walker 2006b: 12)

We think economic growth theories prioritised by global agencies for higher education in Chapter 2 may have little to say to both students, but that the alternative theories, which we sketched in Chapter 3 – gender, participation and even post-development approaches – could be significant for Ntabiseng and Janet being able to participate meaningfully in their own development, but they do not tell us about the kind of life each person is able to lead.

Financial resources do have to be in place. But once they are in place, and even if each person is given an equal amount, this would still not tell us about their freedoms to convert their bundle of resources into actual achievements. For poorer students, they would need more resources, as they cannot rely on families to assist them now or in the future, indeed they are likely to be called on themselves to finance the education of younger siblings. But they also need more than financial aid. Resources – on their own – would not tell us that Ntabiseng and Janet need more supportive conditions to learn well and confidently than students from advantaged backgrounds. Sen's argument holds that income and economics are not a proxy for *all* aspects of human development in higher education, or the plural good things (not just a single measure, such as income) that make up a flourishing life. There are many, indeed millions of students in higher education (see Chapter 2); we think human development and capabilities is a rich theoretical approach that can be the 'ally' (Nussbaum 2012: 1) of Ntabiseng and Janet and their struggles, and can keep the struggles of disadvantaged students in view right up to the global level.

Concluding thoughts

We have seen that for human development and capabilities, GDP or average income, the resources that a university has, or even the average allocation per student would not tell us enough about distribution to each student, or about forms of inequality beyond the economic, such as students' opportunities for meaningful participation in their own education. Nor does the contemporary neo-liberal logic of a human capital focus on higher education for economic growth (Chapter 2) tell us much about student aspirations, of their struggles for higher-level skills and knowledge, how these and other things are important in their lives and identities, or what the circumstances are that have affected their access to and participation in higher education and future employment (as we elaborate on empirically, in Chapter 8). Moreover, to focus only on the economic is to strengthen neoliberal discourse and its world of unequal power relations. Thus, the question we ask is: once sufficient resources are in place, have we done enough to implement higher education which is equitable and transformative? Are the richest universities in the world also the most enabling of all students' well-being and agency and the public-good?

We recognise the strain between a global dominant human capital policy agenda for universities and human development. Nonetheless, higher education still has a potentially transformative role, of renewing our common world, of inserting something new and unforeseen into our flawed world (Arendt 1954). As Arendt (1954: 11) writes of the possibility of education: 'Without newcomers [students] who are introduced into the world and taught to love it as their own, the world will die out'. Higher education ought to and can make a real difference to the lives of young people from all kinds of backgrounds; it especially opens out opportunities for women and working class youth; it makes possible something new emerging in the pedagogical space between teaching and learning. A capabilities-friendly approach to higher education practices, achievements and policy constitutes the theoretical approach that enables us to think well about what socially just universities ought to look like for the individual development of Ntabiseng, Janet and many others, and for social development. Higher education ought to be a generative capability multiplier, with flourishing effects for individuals, communities and societies. It ought to be what our universities aim for, human development values should guide change actions, and it should be supported by public policy arrangements.

Note

1 There have been subsequent developments and additions to the HDI (see UNDP 2010) in the form of: (1) an inequality adjusted HDI (IHDI), which takes into account not only the average achievements of a country on health, education and income, but also how those achievements are distributed among its population by 'discounting' each dimension's average value according to its level of inequality. (2) A gender inequality index (GII) measures gender inequalities in three aspects of human development – reproductive health, empowerment and economic status. (3) A gender development index (GDI) measures gender gaps in human development achievements in three dimensions of human development: health, education and command over economic resources. (4) The multidimensional poverty index (MPI), first published in the 2010 HDR, complements monetary measures of poverty by considering overlapping deprivations suffered by people at the same time to show the number of people who are multidimensionally poor and the number of deprivations with which poor households typically contend.

References

Alkire, S. 2010. 'Human development: definitions, critiques and related concepts', *Human Development Research Paper* 2010/01. New York: UNDP.

Alkire, S. and S. Deneulin. 2009. 'The human development and capability approach'. In *An Introduction to the Human Development and Capability Approach*, edited by S. Deneulin and L. Shahani, 22–49. London: Earthscan.

Arendt, H. 1954. *The Crisis in Education*. [Accessed 8 November 2014]. http://learningspaces.org/files/ArendtCrisisInEdTable.pdf.

Biggeri, M. and A. Ferrannini. 2014. *Sustainable Human Development*. Houndmills: Palgrave Macmillan.

Boni, Alejandra and M. B. Arias. 2013. 'People first. Rethinking educational policies in times of crisis using the capability approach'. *Scuola Democratica* 3: 797–816.

Bonvin, J.-M. and N. Favarque. 2006. 'Promoting capability for work: the role of local actors'. In *Transforming Unjust Structures: The Capability Approach*, edited by S. Deneulin, N. Sagovsky and M. Nebel, 121–34. Dordrecht: Springer.

CHE (Council on Higher Education). 2009. 'Access and throughput in South African higher education: three case studies', *Higher Education Monitor No. 9*. Pretoria: CHE.

Chenery, H. B., M. S. Ahluwalia, C. L. G. Bell, J. H. Duloy and R. Jolly. 1974. *Redistribution with Growth*. Oxford: Oxford University Press.

Crocker, D. A. 2008. *Ethics of Global Development: Agency, Capability, and Deliberative Democracy*. Cambridge: Cambridge University Press.

Crocker, D. and I. Robeyns. 2009. 'Capability and agency'. In *Amartya Sen, Contemporary Philosophy in Focus*, edited by C J. Morris, 60–90. Oxford: Oxford University Press.

Deneulin, S. 2009. 'Democracy and political participation'. In *An Introduction to the Human Development and Capability Approach: Freedom and Agency*, edited by S. Deneulin and L. Shahani, 185–206. London: Earthscan.

Deneulin, S. 2014. *Wellbeing, Justice and Development Ethics*. London: Routledge.

Deneulin, S. and S. Alkire. 2009. 'A normative framework for development'. In *An Introduction to the Human Development and Capability Approach: Freedom and Agency*, edited by S. Deneulin and L. Shahani, 19–31. London: Earthscan.

Dreze, J. and Amartya K. Sen. 2002. *India: Development and Participation.* Oxford: Oxford University Press.

Drydyk, J. 2013. 'Empowerment, agency and power'. *Journal of Global Ethics* 9(3): 249–62.

Fisher, W. and T. Ponniah, eds. 2003. *Another World is Possible. Popular Alternatives to Globalization at the World Social Forum.* London: Zed Books.

Flores-Crespo, P. 2007. 'Situating education in the human capabilities approach'. In *Amartya Sen's Capability Approach and Social Justice in Education*, edited by Melanie Walker and E. Unterhalter, 45–66. Houndmills: Palgrave Macmillan.

Forst, R. 2014. *Justice, Democracy and the Right to Justification.* London: Bloomsbury.

Frediani, Alex A., J. Peris and Alejandra Boni. 2015. 'Notions of empowerment and participation: the contribution of the capability approach'. In *The Capability Approach, Empowerment and Participation*, edited by D. Clark, M. Biggeri and Alex A. Frediani, forthcoming. Houndmills: Palgrave.

Froger, G., P. Méral and V. Herimandimby. 2004. 'The expansion of participatory governance in the environmental policies of developing countries; the example of Madagascar', *International Journal for Sustainable Development* 7(2): 164–84.

Gaventa, J. 2006. 'Finding spaces for change. A power analysis', *IDS Bulletin* 37(6): 23–33.

Griffin, K. 2001. 'Desarrollo humano: orígenes, evolución en impacto'. In *Ensayos Sobre el Desarrollo Humano*, edited by K. Unceta and P. I. Güell, 25–40. Barcelona: Icaria.

Haq, ul M. 2003. 'The human development paradigm'. In *Readings in Human Development*, edited by S. Fukuda-Parr and A. V. Kumar, 17–34. Oxford: Oxford University Press.

Ibrahim, S. 2014. 'Introduction. The capability approach: from theory to practice: rationale, review and reflections'. In *The Capability Approach: From Theory to Practice*, edited by S. Ibrahim and M. Tiwari, 1–29. Houndmills: Palgrave Macmillan.

Leal, P. and R. Opp. 1998. *Participation and Development in the Age of Globalization.* Ottawa: Canadian International Development Agency.

McCowan, T. and Elaine Unterhalter. 2013. 'Education, citizenship and deliberative democracy: Sen's Capability Perspective'. In *Education for Civic and Political Participation. A Critical Approach*, edited by R. Hedtke and T. Zimenkova, 135–44. New York: Routledge.

Nussbaum, M. 2000. *Women and Human Development.* Cambridge: Cambridge University Press.

Nussbaum, M. 2006. *Frontiers of Justice.* Cambridge, MA: The Belknap Press.

Nussbaum, M. 2011. *Creating Capabilities. The Human Development Approach.* Cambridge, MA: The Belknap Press.

Nussbaum, M. 2012. 'Creating Capabilities: The Human Development Approach'. Mimeo of lecture delivered at the University of the Free State, Bloemfontein, December 2012.

Penz, P., J. Drydyk and P. S. Bose. 2011. *Displacement by Development. Ethics, Rights and Responsibilities.* Cambridge: Cambridge University Press.

Robeyns, I. 2005. 'The Capability Approach: a theoretical survey', *Journal of Human Development*, 6 (1): 93–114.

Sen, A. 1992. *Inequality Re-examined*. Oxford: Oxford University Press.

Sen, A. 1999. *Development as Freedom*. Oxford: Oxford University Press.

Sen, A. 2002. *Rationality and Freedom*. Cambridge, MA: Harvard University Press.

Sen, A. 2008. 'The idea of justice', *Journal of Human Development*, 9(3): 331–42.

Sen, A. 2009. *The Idea of Justice*. London: Allen Lane.

Stewart, F. 2005, Groups and capabilities. *Journal of Human Development*, 6 (2): 185–204.

Streeten, P. 2003. 'Shifting fashions on development dialogue'. In *Readings in Human Development*, edited by S. Fukuda-Parr and A. V. Kumar, 68–81. Oxford: Oxford University Press.

UNDP. 1990. *Human Development Report 1990: Concept and Measurement of human Development*. New York: Oxford University Press.

UNDP. 2010. *Human Development Report 2010: 20th Anniversary Edition. The Real Wealth of Nations: Pathways to Human Development*. New York: Oxford University Press.

UNDP. 2014. *Human Development Report 2014: Sustaining Human Progress: Reducing Vulnerabilities and Building Resilience*. New York: UNDP Publications.

Unterhalter, E. 2009. 'Education'. In *An Introduction to the Human Development and Capability Approach*, edited by S. Deneulin and L. Shahani, 207–27. London: Earthscan.

Unterhalter, E., R. P. Vaughan and M. Walker. 2007. 'The capability approach and education'. *Prospero* 13(3): 13–21.

Vaughan, R. P. and M. Walker. 2012. 'Capabilities, values and education policy', *Journal of Human Development and Capabilities* 13(3): 495–512.

Wade, R. 2003. 'What strategies are viable for developing countries today?', *Working Paper Series 1*, Crisis States Programme, Development Research Centre, London School of Economics.

Walker, M. 2006a. *Higher Education Pedagogies*. Maidenhead, UK: Open University Press and the Society for Research into Higher Education.

Walker, M. 2006b. 'Identity, Learning and Agency'. Unpublished paper, University of Sheffield, UK.

Walker, M. 2009. 'Appendix 1: Teaching the human development and capability approach: some pedagogical implications'. In *An Introduction to the Human Development and Capability Approach*, edited by S. Deneulin and L. Shahani, 240–43. London: Earthscan.

Walker, M. and M. McLean. 2013. *Professional Education, capabilities and the Public Good*. London: Routledge.

Part II

5 Higher education policies from a human development perspective

In previous chapters, we considered how the university is understood in contemporary development debates and how human development and the capability approach offer us generative approaches to assess and imagine university activities. In this chapter, we want to focus on universities policies, understanding policies in two senses: as texts produced by different actors (policy-makers, experts), and as processes in which different groups are negotiating, contesting and struggling, creating policies outside the formal machinery of official policy-making. Moreover, policy and policy-making is to be found everywhere in education, not just at the level of central government (Ozga 2000), but also at the 'street level' of bureaucrats who in implementing policy can also change it, among NGOs, at the level of the university, in local and regional government and influential funders. We argue that human development and the capability approach can be useful for analysing policies at multiple levels in the realm of higher education as a counter to the present global drivers of higher education policy – competitive growth supported by a highly skilled workforce (as we saw in Chapter 2).

At the same time, not all policy proposals for higher education are equally directed only at human capital and economic growth. The South African framework (DHET 2013) explored later in the chapter may be imperfect but has strong concerns with social justice, and while Ashwin *et al.*'s (2013) consideration of representations of quality in undergraduate English higher education policy documents concedes a dominant market discourse, it also points to an alternative. Nonetheless, the alternative view is characterised as 'fractured' and 'was less coherently expressed' (Ashwin *et al.* 2013: 619). The point holds, however, that we should not homogenize all higher education policy in all countries, notwithstanding global drivers, such as the World Bank (as we discussed in Chapter 2). There are certainly significant challenges, but this makes it more rather than less important to 'see' and claim the spaces where policy is articulated differently.

In this chapter, we therefore present examples of policy analysis with regard to universities using an explicitly normative approach of the human development and capability approach; the first two cases studies are examples of texts that shape policies in Europe, and the third looks at South Africa. We begin with a text on the new agenda on Responsible Research and Innovation (RRI) driven by the European Union (EU) in recent years, which is already having an impact on research agendas, and will have more in the future. We analyse a report made by the Group of Experts on Policy Indicators for Responsible Research and Innovation (Strand *et al.* 2015). We have selected this text because it is, to date, the clearest definition of what RRI policy looks like at European and national level. Our second example looks specifically at the Bologna Process and unpicks how power works in implementing the European Higher Education Area at the local level of a new degree programme in Spain. Third, we also analyse the South African government *White Paper for Post-School Education and Training* (DHET 2013) from the specific perspective of how quality is represented in the section on universities.

Making policy

In Chapter 3, we analysed how all development theories are based on normative approaches. As Alkire and Deneulin (2009: 4) point out, development policies or public policies are normative or ethical, based on value judgements; they clarify how groups ought to behave in order to create improvements. This normative approach can be complemented with two other approaches: positive and predictive. The first one deals with learning from past experiences and analysing data. The second one allows policy-makers to predict how a situation could change in certain ways. We are interested in the normative analysis, which sits behind predictive and positive analysis, which in themselves are not inherently normative. Such normative analysis is able to disentangle value judgements that are behind any selection of relevant information. As Sen reminds us, evaluative approaches utilise their own informational basis to make judgements about problem X or problem Y, and which will include and exclude certain information from the evaluation. In that regard, Alkire and Deneulin (2009: 5) give examples of how normative selections can affect policy decisions and outcomes:

> They shape the data that we collect; they influence our analysis; they give certain topics greater or less political salience; they feed or hinder social movements; they may motivate professionals for moral or ethical reasons and they can be more or less philosophically credible.

As we have indicated, we use human development and the capability approach as our evaluative framework to analyse university-related policies and justice-based judgements. The core values of the approach (efficiency, equity, participation, sustainability) and the main elements (capabilities, functionings and agency) are deployed. Public deliberation also has paramount importance as a principle for defining policies; we agree with Robert Salais (2009) that collective agreements on relevant social facts (such as higher education policies), in which everyone should take part, raise crucial questions about democratic deliberation. He alerts us that we need to be aware of strategies to select and manipulate information for policy judgements in order to establish the basis of the judgement of justice in public policies. He poses examples of employment policies promoted by the EU that use the notion of a 'job' in different ways from that which was promised in the model of full employment. This model included the level and guarantee of remuneration, security in the face of unforeseeable events, and social and economic rights. We would expect that increased insecurity in life and work should prompt an enrichment of the informational basis in order to improve the quality of employment. In practice, the policy-making of European authorities (and others) is altering the informational basis of justice, moving it in the other direction, away from decent work:

> In this interpretation, any work task, even one without any guarantees or any future, is called "employment". Far from enriching the informational basis, the European authorities downgrade it to the level of a scorecard (like those one can find among firms' management tools) and drastically reformulate it as a set of performance indicators, selected without any real democratic deliberation.
>
> (Salais 2009: 10)

Another example is that of measures of graduate unemployment, which may not show the constraints and unfreedoms that women graduate job-seekers face in fields such as engineering; individual women may then be blamed for lacking the 'right' attitudes or ambition. If policy information focuses only on amounts of human capital each person has, it will over-look diversity, for example how men are advantaged in the labour market in patriarchal societies, or how migrants or other marginalised groups may have very high qualifications but cannot get jobs appropriate to their level of human capital. We therefore need to ask whose voices are privileged in policy-making, and who participates in policy-making processes. Salais (2009) concludes that it is important not only to argue in favour of an informational basis of capabilities, but even more, that such an approach should identify the political channels to make itself heard and to influence the content and methods of policy-making at various levels. The import-ance of a political analysis of the forces that shape public policy is also highlighted by Spence and Deneulin (2009), who point out that a detailed analysis of power relations is essential. According to this, the success of policies should be assessed according to whether they promote not only people's freedoms but also their agency.

In our approach to two examples of policy texts (RRI in Europe and quality in South Africa), we consider the values and assumptions that are implicit and explicit in the texts and we confront these with the main values and assumptions of the human development and the capability approach. We are aware that our analysis could be expanded using other approaches to policy analysis (see Gasper 2000 or Gasper *et al.* 2013 for more detailed approaches to discourse analysis). Nonetheless, our aim is to try and explore the presence, absence and potentialities of the human development approach in challenging dominant or official discourses on higher education to show how powerful concepts and values that are a substantive part of the human development approach may lose their transformative potential when captured by other, often hidden, interests. The second case is a slightly different example of policy analysis which focuses more on the process of creating policy than on texts. From previous research conducted in 2009 and 2010, we discuss how the European Higher Education Area was adapted in a new degree at the Universitat Politècnica de Valéncia (Technical University of Valencia) in Spain. Our focus is to reveal power imbalances and participation processes that took place in the process of defining this new degree.

Policy: a focus on responsible research and innovation (RRI) in Europe

The European Commission, EU Member States and associated countries have launched various initiatives and activities under the name of RRI, a term that had found its way from academic literature into research and innovation (R&I) policy by 2011 (Strand *et al.* 2015). RRI has acquired prominence by its status as a 'cross-cutting issue' of the EU framework programme for R&I, Horizon 2020,[1] as well as its central place among the objectives of the 'Science with and for Society' programme within Horizon 2020. The goal of RRI is defined as follows:

> To achieve a better alignment of R&I programmes and agendas with societal needs and concerns. As with any other policy, it is part of good governance to monitor and assess the impacts that may result from the RRI initiatives and activities. The specificity of the purpose of RRI, however, warrants attention and care in the choice of methods for the monitoring and assessment of RRI impacts.
>
> (Strand *et al.* 2015: 9)

The report also proposes the following definition of RRI based on Von Schomberg (2011: 10):

> a transparent, interactive process by which societal actors and innovators become mutually responsive to each other with a view on the

(ethical) acceptability, sustainability and societal desirability of the innovation process and its marketable products'.... RRI is a matter of outcomes as well as characteristics of the processes that lead to the outcomes, and so we are considering indicators both for outcomes and for processes.

Taking inspiration from Ozga (2000: 98) in her policy analysis on social inclusion or exclusion in educational settings, we explore this report bearing in mind the following questions: (1) What is the main narrative of the text? How is it being presented? (2) What are the problems that are emerging? (3) What categories and ideas are presented in the text regarding human development values?

Three main narratives emerge through the text: (1) alignments of R&I activities with societal and ethical needs and concerns; (2) responsibility understood as the interaction of societal actors and innovators; (3) RRI as part of the good governance agenda which includes monitoring and assessing, both for outcomes and processes, the impacts that may result from RRI activities. It is this specific interest in the good governance agenda that led the European Commission appointed in 2014 to appoint an expert group to identify and propose indicators. The report analysed is the result of the work of the expert group and is structured around key elements: (1) governance; (2) public engagement; (3) gender equality; (4) science education; (5) open access/open science; (6) ethics; (7) sustainability; and (8) social justice/inclusion. Assuming that RRI is based on the three premises mentioned above, three questions emerge: Which are the societal and ethical needs and concerns considered? How is responsibility understood? What are the characteristics of a good governance agenda? We now explore these three questions in detail.

Societal and ethical needs and concerns

To identify societal and ethical needs in a European context, the expert group refers to two main texts, the *Charter of Fundamental Rights of the European Union*, and the *Europe 2020 Strategy*. Surprisingly, no further references to the *Human Rights Charter* appear; on the contrary, the *Europe 2020 Strategy* provides the rationale for the definition of societal and ethical needs. In brief, Europe 2020 is the EU's ten-year jobs and growth strategy. It was launched in 2010 to create the conditions for 'smart, sustainable and inclusive growth' and to move beyond the financial crisis to create the conditions for a more competitive economy with higher employment. The *Europe 2020 Strategy* is about delivering growth that is: (1) smart, through more effective investments in education, research and innovation; (2) sustainable, thanks to a decisive move towards a low-carbon economy; and (3) inclusive, with a strong emphasis on job creation and poverty reduction.

An analysis of the concepts of sustainability and social justice included in the report of the Expert Group and using the lens of the human development approach follows. In this report, sustainability (as above) is defined as 'smart, inclusive and sustainable growth'. No further conceptual clarification is provided, although the section devoted to sustainability indicators gives us more clues to the meaning they attribute to this concept. Here are some examples: stocks of natural resources; how these stocks are being used and how are they being regenerated; labour and technology and how they influence stock-flow interactions; and monitoring of ecosystem services and their effects on human well-being. As far as it is presented, this approach to sustainability follows the approach of environmental economics which, based on a neo-classical economic paradigm, brings environmental concerns into economic analysis, positioning itself as value neutral but nonetheless conducting economic analysis with a particular view of human nature and social relationships (Redclift 2000). It presupposes that the degree of substitutability between renewable and non-renewable resources and between man-made and natural capital will always suffice to realise the required utility we attribute to the use of natural resources. It barely recognises the finite limits of stocks of natural resources (Deblonde 2015). However, as we have seen in Chapter 3, there are other approaches to sustainability. These visions, in which we include the human development perspective, take absolute limits of earthly natural capital as a starting point (Dedeurwaerdere 2013), and take social, ethical and values dimensions into account (Froger *et al.* 2004), which we do not see in the Europe 2020 narrative, so that we need to ask: smart according to whom, inclusive of whom, and sustainable of what? We cannot take for granted that these 'buzzwords' will take us in the direction of human development in the absence of normative content.

The second concept that defines societal needs is social justice, which is defined as 'an ideal condition in which all individual citizens have equal rights, equality of opportunity, and equal access to social resources' (Maschi and Youdin 2012, quoted in Strand *et al.* 2015: 38). However, when social justice is contextualised in R&I activities, this right and equity-based definition is transformed into a relational approach between researchers and the research 'subjects' and participation of social groups in benefits arising from research. The relational perspective belongs to the field of research ethics, which is important for research processes, but in itself hardly counts as an expansive reading of social justice. The indicators proposed are related only to research integrity and good research practice: for example, plagiarism, fabrication, fraud, authorship and intellectual property, and citation/acknowledgement practices, scientific neutrality, conflicts of interest in peer review and scientific advice, etc. The second perspective – equal participation of social groups in benefits arising from research – looks more promising but when it is transformed into proposals for indicators it ends up with examples such as: (1) Process indicators measuring if research institutions have procedures that encourage/oblige researchers to consider the impact of their research on social justice/inclusion, or if research institutions have mechanisms that assist researchers in the recruitment of research participants from socially excluded groups. (2) Outcome indicators presented in two ways: first, research projects that modify their methodology to improve their impact on social justice (e.g. including research participants from a wider social groups to address broader perspectives/needs) and second, percentage of a research project across the six dimensions of a Social Justice Index developed by the Bertelsmann Stiftung Foundation (2011). These are: poverty prevention, access to education, labour market inclusion, social cohesion and non-discrimination, health and intergenerational justice.

An analysis of the social justice category from a human development approach throws lights and shadows. The positive point is, at least in one of the indicators proposed (referring to the Social Justice Index) there are elements that incorporate a capability dimension. The negative point is the absence of a clear normative direction which is at the core of the social justice category. The Report avoids expanding the informational basis of justice related to social justice in the *European Charter of Rights*. This evokes for us, as noted earlier by Sen and Salais: the importance of paying attention to what information is excluded from the informational basis of justice of a policy. We have seen two examples so far: an understanding of sustainability based on the economic utility of the environment, and a social justice comprehension which avoids specific references to human rights. An analysis of this social justice category from a human development perspective reminds us of the danger that Salais (2009) remarked on. Instead of enriching the informational basis of a category called 'social justice', which as the first quote points out, is rooted in the guarantee of rights and the equality of opportunities, the Report reformulates it as a set of performance indicators which transform a powerful (and political) category into new technical and institutional practices. This is captured in a potential checklist that invokes (without any further clarification and discussion) a list of strong concepts elaborated by the OECD, and the possibility of 'modifying' research methodology to include a wider range of participants.

Responsibility

Although the core of the agenda is 'responsible' R&I, references to responsibility are nonetheless extremely vague compared with the sustainability and social justice categories. 'Being responsible'; 'being seen to be responsible'; 'responsibility is linguistically and substantively an attribute of R&I' are statements found in the Report. Thus, it seems clear that the Report avoids defining more precisely what responsibility means. However, from our point of view, responsibility is a value with a long tradition in the technological field and deserves attention in the definition of a RRI. Hans Jonas (1985) has a far more robust account of the meaning of responsibility in an age of technological change; acting on the basis of scientific insights and technological know-how is acting in an ethically sensitive way (Jonas 1985). Cortina (1994) and Lozano *et al.* (2006) have expanded Jonas' definition to include insights from the capability approach. When we attribute ethical responsibility to a person, Lozano *et al.* (2006) suggest that we assume that a person can control their behaviour through having developed four crucial capabilities: (1) *freedom of choice*; (2) *reflection*: the capability to rationally assess the reasons for its action; (3) *anticipation*: the capability to consider the likely consequences of any action; and (4) *sense of justice*: the capability to distinguish between right and wrong. Moreover, usually, responsibility is exercised in an unequal relation, for example, responsibility from parents with children, teachers with students, but the goal should always be that each person can develop their capability to assume their own responsibilities. The greater the power (or capability) a person has, the greater is also their responsibility. In addition, to some degree, we are all also jointly responsible for the consequences of collective action, for example, pollution of the environment, and we must all do our part to contribute in solving common problems. From our perspective, definitions such as these provide a more relevant grounding to think about and thicken the rather thin notion of responsibility in the RRI agenda.

The good governance agenda

We now approach the third element of the RII proposal: the good governance principle, defined as an 'overarching principle for formal and informal R&I networks' (Strand *et al.* 2015: 5), where indicators play a key role. But, consistent with the principle of good governance, the Group of Experts recommends that the use of the indicators should be open to participation through a network approach rather than a linear, top-down chain of command. However, we notice that participation is limited to the use of indicators, not to their production. In the text, there are references to indicators that could be created through the participation of local stakeholders, but for the most part, the indicators presented are proposed by the Group of Experts, without any process of public deliberation. Important questions on whose knowledge counts then arise (explored in more detail in Chapters 6 and 7). The good governance agenda is linked also with the participation of stakeholders in the use of the indicators; the Group of Experts identifies groups of participants that come from academia, industry, public organisations and society at large, and that are part of innovation networks. Indicators proposed to track the activity of those networks measuring the number of joint technology initiatives or the numbers of joint research programmes between groups. However, the Report does acknowledge that qualitative information is needed and recommends narrative and case studies to describe network activities. We may expect though that qualitative narratives will be overtaken by the emphasis and power of the numbers and, while 'nice to have', will also make little impact.

Considerations of participation are also developed in the public engagement part of the Report in which we note two levels of participation: (1) participation in debates around R&I; (2) deeper forms of engagement in science and technology, where citizens are peers in the knowledge production, assessment and governance processes. Examples of indicators proposed for level 1 of participation are: level of public engagement funding as a percentage of national R&I budget; perception indicators measuring public expectations; science events (e.g. science museums, interactive science centres, mobile exhibition spaces, etc.). For level 2, proposed indicators are the activities of crowd-funded science using social media. These activities are particularly relevant in a context of declining public funding. There is only one reference to a deeper involvement of citizens in knowledge production named as 'citizen science', that is a form of engagement in which citizens participate in knowledge production by being involved in data collection or/and actual research. Does it mean that citizen engagement is restricted to data collection? What does 'actual research' mean? Once again, not surprisingly, despite the discourse that recalls the importance of public engagement in science, making a deeper democratic agenda of R&I activities seems rather remote, given the indicators proposed.

The participation aspect is also addressed in the open science section of the Report. Promisingly, a strong quote defines open science as follows:

> Open science is a practice in which the scientific process is shared completely and in real time. It offers the potential to support information flow, collaboration and dialogue among professional and non-professional participants.
>
> (Grand *et al.* 2014: 32)

But again, when the proposal for indicators is advanced, collaboration and dialogue end-up captured within an extensive repertoire of virtual environments: blogs, movies, video channels, uploading of experimental dataset to project websites, online laboratory notebooks, wiki-discussion between researchers, partners and collaborators. These are significant in current times but should be complemented by non-virtual spaces to collaborate and for dialogue; yet these are not considered suitable apparently for the 'open access' agenda.

The last comment is on the gender equality section of the agenda. At least from a conceptual point of view, this section is the most human development and capability friendly part of the Report, possibly explained by extensive European research and reports over many years on matters of gender equality, and strong feminist voices and lobbying. Clear social conversion factors have been identified as causes that hide the unconscious bias against women in the assessment of excellence, or in institutional practices and organisational culture. However, as changes in the organisational culture are difficult to capture with numerical indicators, the Group of Experts propose using the representation of women in various positions and levels of decision-making inside the university, both as indicators of a desirable outcome and as a proxy for processes of institutional change. Although the Report does not elaborate further, examples of these indicators could be the proportion of R&I projects led by women, or the proportion of female academics occupying senior positions in scientific research. Finally, to measure the width and breadth penetration of gender perspectives in research content, the Report recommends following qualitative judgements about what qualifies as a gender dimension, arguing that such procedures are opportunities for reflection and responsibility. We note with some surprise that such a proposal follows a different rationale than the previous indicators on which we have commented, and it is not clear in the Report why this is. An analysis of the conditions of production of this text needs to be undertaken to capture these different criteria, which we tentatively have suggested relate to a long history of feminist activism in the academy and in policy arenas to secure more gender equality. In other words there is a richer alternative policy–political narrative available with which to think about gender dimensions, what these should be, and who should decide.

Another way

What we have been discussing in this chapter could be considered as an example of a 'technology of governance model' (Fukuda-Parr *et al*. 2014: 106), in which indicators exert influence in two ways: by setting the performance standards against which progress can be monitored, rewarded or penalised, and by creating a 'knowledge effect' where the indicators intended to reflect a concept effectively redefine the concept. We see how powerful categories such as good governance and a rights-based approach to social justice lose their political characteristics. We have also considered how key values, such as sustainability and participation, are being interpreted in a very weak and thin way, losing their transformative potential. Also, we have seen how the first 'R' of RRI, the 'Responsible R' is underspecified, thereby setting aside a long ethical tradition that has addressed responsibility in technological changes. On the other hand, we also see how the strong category of 'gender' retains its political power and transformative potential, and we need to better understand what is different and how or if activism over time makes this difference, generating hope for change rather than hopelessness.

Policy: a focus on power in the definition of a new degree in Europe

The European Higher Education Area (EHEA), also known as the Bologna Process, has required a significant transformation for Spanish degree programmes. We want therefore to explore how a top-down higher education policy has been translated into a local context – namely the Technical University of Valencia (UPV in its Spanish acronyms) – and the decision-making process in defining the curriculum of an EHEA-adapted degree, specifically the Industrial Design and Product Development Engineering degree, which started in the academic year 2009/10 and was the first UPV degree to be EHEA-adapted. In the analysis of the decision-making processes around policy, we want to focus on the power dynamics and how those shaped participation. Because we think processes of power are integral to all levels of policy-making and adoption, we use the analytical tool of the power cube developed by John Gaventa (2005, 2006). The cube (presented in Figure 5.1) proposes three dimensions to address power issues and imbalances: how power is shaped (its forms), where it is located

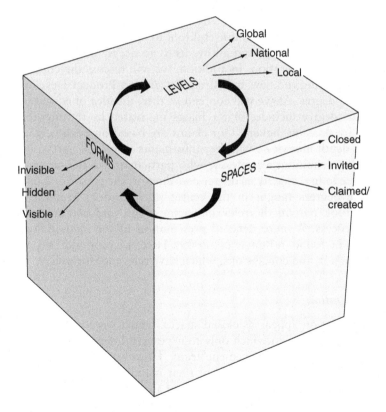

Figure 5.1 The power cube (adapted from Gaventa 2006).

(local, national and global places) and which are the spaces for participation (closed, invited and claimed).

Considering the form of power, political studies have traditionally been concerned with one form, the visible. However, Lukes' (2005) work has shown how this one-dimensional vision of power is limited; it has to be complemented with a broader conception. This leads to identifying three different forms of effective power: (1) *Visible power*, consisting of observable decision-making processes, where contestation over interests are visibly negotiated in the public sphere with established rules (Miller *et al.* 2006). (2) *Hidden power*, or the influence on who gets to the decision-making table and what gets on the agenda, that is to say being able to set the political agenda and exclude issues and actors from the arena. (3) *Invisible power*, which shapes the psychological and ideological approach of people to problems. It refers to social and political culture and an individual realm of meanings, and the way people's values and preferences are shaped through socialisation, culture and ideology, so that inequalities may be perpetuated by the definition of what is normal, 'true' or acceptable because, 'significant problems and ideas are not only kept from the decision-making table, but also from the minds and consciousness of the people involved, even those directly affected by the problem' (Miller *et al.* 2006: 9).

The power cube is a complex and useful tool to analyse power issues in the process of decision-making, and allows us to go deeply into participation and democratic deliberation. In addition, we will discuss the concept of education underlying the new Industrial Design and Product Development Engineering degree. As we will contend further, the idea of education proposed in this degree includes major biases motivated by the invisible power exerted by decision-makers. Our claims are based on documentary analysis and in-depth interviews with key informants who took part in the process of degree definition: a professor who participated in the preparation of the degree in his capacity as degree coordinator; the person responsible for all the degrees taught in the centre (the Head of Studies); a professor who took part in the relevant commissions; and two students linked to the process. A more detailed presentation of the methodology and findings can be found in Boni *et al.* (2009). Here, we only address part of the final discussion and conclusions, which have relevance for policy.

Spaces of participation

Spaces for participation appear as closed spaces, which were restricted to an Academic Commission, to which only four powerful departments were invited, together with the management team. However, except for the more critical students who complained of their inability to take part, the rest of the informants agreed with this way of making decisions for the new degree. The lack of claimed spaces is clear in this process, for example 'it has always been this way', underlined by the urgency to adopt measures, and blaming the bureaucracy are recurrent expressions from informants to justify the lack of debate and discussion. The lack of a democratic culture allows for closed spaces, where the voices of key stakeholders are excluded from the design of the university degree, with potentially damaging effects for its quality and the possibility of introducing teaching innovations. Additionally, the absence of invited and claimed spaces limits the opportunity for interacting with the social environment. As a result, the degree was designed according to perspectives only of the four departments involved, with no wider involvement or even claim to involvement.

Types of power

Concerning the types of power, we highlight here the presence of hidden and invisible power, which may hamper important discussion on relevant issues that ought to be taken into consideration in the process of creating a new degree. The educational goals, the student profiles, the curriculum content, the learning methodologies or the assessment system are all questions which were not fully addressed. The underlying ideology of efficiency, competence, employability and business orientation was rather the driving force of discussions for defining curriculum content. In particular, it was remarkable how many times 'the sake of the student' was mentioned to justify decisions. However, the analysis shows that such 'sake of the student' becomes a 'buzzword' to justify what it is really at stake, which was the distribution of course credits among the four departments involved. This is clearly a case of decision-making based on the philosophy of sharing out and getting a piece of the degree pie while appearing to take everyone into account and satisfy everyone, according to what one of our informants called 'coffee for all'. To this end, the clear presence of hidden power in the role of the head of the school was crucial in order to remove negotiations out of the public arena of all staff and all students.

Levels of power

With regard to different levels where power operates, we would like to underline the consequences in the local arena of a policy reform such as that proposed by the EHEA, of a top-down nature but nonetheless, with considerable policy decision-making power at a local level. The framework agreements are European ones (Bologna Agreements and other Declarations), but the state level is limited to providing technical guidelines and to assessing the quality of the decisions made at a local level (through the National Agency for Quality Assessment and Accreditation of Spain, ANECA), while the curriculum is shaped at a local level within universities. However, as we have explained, this university process becomes a negotiation for the distribution of credits among the most powerful departments involved and a bureaucratic technical exercise intended to justify that the proposals put forward meet the requirements issued in Madrid. What occurred was the influence of university managerialism and privileged academic elites who make decisions based on their frameworks of thinking about education, from their realities and from their theoretical comprehension, as to how the university curricula should be. As this case shows, the lack of transparency at European level was complemented with a truly opaque procedure at national level, culminating in a closed power and policy dynamic at the university level.

Power and participation

We consider it essential to open spaces for participation of all university stakeholders (professors, students, administrative support staff), but also of external stakeholders (businesses, government, civil society organisations). As we discussed in Chapter 4 and elaborate on here, Sen (1999: 38–40) identifies five 'instrumental freedoms' that contribute to the general capability of a person to live more freely: (1) *political freedoms*; (2) *economic facilities*; (3) *social opportunities*; (4) *transparency guarantees*; (5) *protective security*. With regard to the policy process we have discussed in this section, we are most concerned about political freedoms and transparency guarantees. In their absence, or their rather reduced form as in the development of the degree programme, it becomes hard to see how capabilities can be advanced, and indeed human development was not the intention of the programme leaders. But what this policy process reminds us of is that taking into account the informational basis of judgement in justice requires also that we attend to instrumental freedoms for policy-making that is human-development friendly.

Thus, for a real exercise in democratic deliberation, policy spaces ought – ideally – to be inclusive and open. Of course the policy process is messy, often incoherent and not linear (Trowler 2002). Nonetheless, if opportunities for participation are opened, better accountability is also fostered. A top-down managerial approach at university is, from our point of view, misguided. By increasing the emphasis on 'technical' procedures, asking for reports, generating files, and so on, we do not ensure that universities are necessarily more accountable towards society. On the contrary, we believe the nub of the matter lies in creating spaces for deliberation and decision-making, which are participative and accountable towards university citizens and the general citizenship. As stated in a report by the Spanish Ombudsman (2009), the EHEA adaptation in Spain will pass into history as an example of secretive and limited accountably in policy development on the ground. We are also concerned with how we change the power dynamics that hamper the materialisation of our deliberative proposal. No doubt in creating critical reflection processes between students, professors and administrative staff, power issues will emerge. This is therefore a complex, long-term strategy which in a managerial environment may face resistance, including resistance to using language which is an alternative to that of knowledge as a commodity, 'business', 'price' and 'value' applied to university degrees. But, if the university is to play a role of critical actor and challenge public and private interests in the pursuit of a common good, this task should at the least be tackled.

Policy: a focus on universities and quality

The background

In this last section, we look at a government policy text. Because space does not allow for a comprehensive analysis of the South African *White Paper for Post-School Education and Training* (DHET 2013), we focus on the policy vision and aims with particular reference to the section on universities and quality in teaching and undergraduate education. We are interested in how quality in undergraduate education is represented and how close or far from human development and multidimensional capabilities expansion this version of quality is. The *White Paper* includes public universities but is much wider in addressing all post-school provision. It follows a *Green Paper* in 2012, and claims to take into account nearly 200 responses from educational institutions, training authorities, employer groupings, trade unions, other organisations and individuals, as well as further reflection within the Department of Higher Education and Training (DHET) on the challenges facing the sector. The Minister writes in his Preface that 'all enriched our deliberations' (DHET 2013: vii). Thus, there appears to have been a form of consultation, if not shared deliberation. We are also told the names of the main authors, led by the Minister's former advisor and someone with a history of educational activism, so there is some measure of transparency insofar as we may be aware of the values and perspectives of some or all of the contributors. We can therefore assume looking at the authors of the *White Paper* and the range of respondents that the policy will not be only human–capital focused.

Vision and some contradictions

The vision is ambitious and full of good intentions:

> The *White Paper* will empower us as we strive to build a post-school education and training system that is able to contribute to eradicating the legacy of apartheid. It will assist us to build a non-racial, non-sexist and prosperous South Africa characterised by progressive narrowing of the gap between the rich and the poor. Access to quality post-school education is a major driver in fighting poverty and inequality in any society.
>
> (DHET 2013: viii)

Moreover, while jobs are important:

> the education and training system should not only provide knowledge and skills required by the economy. It should also contribute to developing thinking citizens, who can function effectively, creatively and ethically as part of a democratic society. They should have an understanding of their society, and be able to participate fully in its political, social and cultural life.
>
> (DHET 2013: 3)

This seems to locate the policy framework beyond human capital and the assumption that more and better education will solve problems of (youth) unemployment. On the other hand, the *White Paper* notes the practical reality of a stuttering economy and it claims that: 'few can argue with the need to improve the performance of the economy, to expand employment and to equip people to achieve sustainable livelihoods' (DHET 2013: 3). It explains that the social and economic challenges facing South Africa have shifted national priorities in the face of structural challenges associated with unemployment, poverty and inequality so that economic development has been prioritised, together with the role of education and training as a contributor to such development. Thus, the first policy aim takes social justice to mean education as a way out of poverty, and expanded opportunities which looks as if *White Paper*, whatever its broader claims, has prioritised employment so that social justice could become rather faint in practice. Again, seeming to prioritise employment, albeit for its social impact and benefits as well, the *White Paper* further notes that: 'Education will not guarantee economic growth, but without it economic growth is not possible and society will not fulfil its potential with regard to social and cultural development' (DHET 2013: 5). But this more nuanced message is not evident in the *White Paper* as a whole. If we look at word counts as a rough indicator of emphasis we find: quality 207; diversity 96; equity 14; social justice seven; empowerment 0; agency in the form of 'social agency' one; poor students three; poor five; access 89; transformation 11; throughput rates ten. But we also have: skills 215; economy/development/developmental state 233 (together more mentions than anything else); employment 25; efficiency and efficient nine; so that economic development, led by the state, is emphasised. Moreover, as Motala and Vally (2014: 7) argue, whatever view is taken of the economy – either business focused or state-led and developmental – the assumption is still of a causal relationship between education and skills through education and development, which does not problematise demand-side failures. Education cannot 'fix' this in the absence of complementary policy to secure social and economic conversion factors, including more economic justice, more equal social power and hence real opportunities for capabilities expansion. Yet, there is a policy optimism about how post-school education will lead to jobs and economic productivity regardless of the shape and state of the labour market. Given the economic problems South Africa currently faces, does not necessarily mean that a broader view of quality does not matter, or that the education sector should be overlooked while attempts are made to deal with the economy. There is an argument to be made for building the universities today for a better society tomorrow, even while we recognise that universities or post-school education alone are not the solution, however good the quality (although a bedrock of high quality undergraduate education may go some way to improving lives and economic chances).

Quality

We can begin to extrapolate how 'quality' is presented with regard to university education, mostly by looking at the wider policy aims, although there is no explicit definition of what 'quality' is or looks like. Quality is asserted but not directly described: 'institutions must provide education of a high quality' (DHET 2013: vii); 'ensure a wide range of high quality options' (DHET 2013: xiii); 'expanded access, improved quality and increased diversity of provision' (DHET 2013: 2); 'All universities in South Africa must offer high-quality undergraduate education. This should be the first step to overcoming historical injustices inherited from apartheid' (DHET 2013: 30). There is an implicit recognition of the link between poverty and quality: 'Most black people are still poor; they are still served by lower-quality public services and institutions (including public educational institutions) than the well-off' (DHET 2013: 4). Much is expected of quality, despite it being underspecified: 'The achievement of greater social justice is closely dependent on equitable access by all sections of the population to quality education' (DHET 2013: 5). Thus, quality takes its meaning in part from concerns with social justice, equity, access, diversity but also, it must be said, from the emphasis on skills, the economy and development. In the latter focus, quality could mean more graduates getting jobs (of any kind, full-time or part-time, secure or not) or becoming self-employed.

Nonetheless, 'quality' education is presented as an important 'right' in the *White Paper*, one 'which plays a vital role in relation to a person's health, quality of life, self-esteem, and the ability of citizens to be actively engaged and empowered' (DHET 2013: 3); access is also presented as a right, and of course access, quality and equity are, or should all be, interwoven. Thereafter, the rights discourse in relation to access and quality disappears. Although the *White Paper* invokes the core moral values in the South African Constitution (RSA 1996) (but mentioned only four times) and says that these will continue 'to inspire' education and training, as Motala and Vally (2014) point out, an aspirational Constitution on its own cannot resolve the economic contradictions in post-apartheid South Africa, or deal with serious power imbalances.

At the same time, in order to be fair in our judgement, we are careful to locate quality in relation to other discourses in the policy, from which quality partly takes it meaning. For example, in the absence of any mention of social justice and a lot of mentions of quality, we might reasonably assume that quality is not really about social justice – a high-quality and narrow – or exclusive-access university would still count as meeting quality criteria. This is not the case for the *White Paper*; indeed we have chosen quality because the policy is strong on concerns for access to university, participation and success, including but not confined to, contributions to the labour market and economic development.

However, quality is not discussed in relation to improving student access, success and throughput rates although these are noted as a very serious challenge for the university sector and a priority focus. Rather, the main focus and solution for these challenges is skills – the 'development of the scarce and critical skills needed for South Africa's economic development' (DHET 2013: 33). Knowledge, which ought to be fundamental to the university education project, hardly appears at all and is not presented as the basis of quality undergraduate education. We do find this brief mention: 'For much education and training, a combination of both theoretical knowledge and practical experience is important, indeed essential. Theory provides knowledge of general principles and laws, which allows additional learning and adaptation to new technologies and circumstance' (DHET 2013: 9), and we find a concern with reducing staff–student ratios, with teacher development, with tutor development and with differentiation but not embedding stratification based on uneven resources. Knowledge is implicit in the mention of: 'Curriculum development initiatives that will contribute to improved success and graduation rates must be explored and supported' (DHET 2013: 33). Specific mention is made of the need for knowledge of African languages but for the purposes of teachers being able to teach in mother-tongue languages. For the most part, knowledge is located in research and innovation for development so that 'knowledge production must increase if South Africa's developmental goals are to be achieved' (DHET 2013: 34). This is not dissimilar to Ashwin *et al.*'s (2013) study on quality in undergraduate education policy documents, which found in the case of England that the dominant marketised discourse did not provide a sense of the knowledge that students should gain access to and rather stressed forming flexible identities able to respond to the employment market. Even the fainter alternative discourse neglected knowledge, claim Ashwin and colleagues, in favour of student dispositions to equip them for the labour market. This is problematic they argue, because 'knowledge is central to an understanding of quality' (Ashwin *et al.* 2013: 611); quality is defined in terms of 'the kinds of knowledge students will have access to and the identities this produces' (Ashwin *et al.* 2013: 612). Similarly, as we have shown, knowledge is not integral to the way quality is presented in the *White Paper*. By neglecting the place of knowledge and especially knowledge, which is coherent with human development, it will then follow that assessing knowledge of this kind will not feature, or will not feature strongly, in the informational basis of judgement of quality for undergraduate education in South African policy. Knowledge will then be disassociated from quality undergraduate teaching and learning making for a rather thin understanding of a quality university education.

Moreover, while the *White Paper* offers a strong vision for post-school education, together with concerns for poor students and inequality, we are still not told what the informational basis will be of monitoring and evaluating implementation of the policy. This is crucial because South Africa has a history of producing strong policy frameworks with very weak implementation. In the case of universities, there have been real advances in expanding access, especially to disadvantaged students and to women, as the *White Paper* points out, but much remains to be done. We must assume that 'success' will be measured on the basis of the numbers data mentioned in some places in the policy, and collected routinely and efficiently from universities, and that quality will then mean access numbers, participation rates, and throughput numbers. These numbers are very important for access and redress concerns but they are not enough on their own; we need to be clear that they do not tell us much about quality contextually, experientially, or about access to higher and powerful knowledge. The bald numbers suffer even more limits than the indicators (which are not reduced just to numbers) discussed with regard to research and innovation policy earlier in the chapter.

But even more importantly, as Ashwin *et al.* (2013: 620) argue, only if universities emphasise the academic knowledge acquired through engagement in university education can we 'highlight the continuing importance of universities as critical and autonomous institutions'. While they emphasise this role in the face of the march of marketisation, which we also need to pay attention to in South Africa, there is the further urgent need for universities to develop the high-quality pedagogical processes through which knowledge is acquired and capabilities expanded, together with nuanced indicators in which the informational basis of judgement in justice can capture capabilities expansion and human development. Knowledge as quality, pedagogy as quality, transformed student identities – this is what would constitute quality higher education. We need much more careful attention to Sen's informational basis of judgement in justice if quality is to have a thick rather than thin meaning, to impact on young people's opportunities, achievements and agency, and if universities are going to expand rather than constrict democratic life and spaces.

Concluding thoughts

Utilising the capability approach as the informational basis of our judgements would require that we assess policies for their impact in terms of functionings and capabilities as well as agency (Sen 1999). We would make the development of capabilities the objective of higher education policy, putting in place conditions for the development of capabilities so that all students have genuine choices in choosing the life each has reason to value. Sen calls for an enriched 'informational basis of judgment in justice', because the 'bite' of a theory of justice can be 'understood from its informational base: what information is – or is not – taken to be directly relevant' (Sen 1999: 57). This has significant implications for how we design any policy in higher education, in local, national and global domains.

Could the human development and capability approach then generate new policy narratives for universities? One of the main contributions of human development thinking has indeed been to construct new narratives in the field of development policy (Deneulin 2014), showing that a potential for change does exist even if, at the present time, human development policies could be considered as contra-hegemonic policies compared to mainstream approaches. A good or quality university tends to be assessed through the accomplishment of standard benchmarking and rankings (Hazelkorn 2007) which, at the end, drive universities towards status competition. As we have seen through this chapter, 'indicators as a technology of governance' (Fukuda-Parr *et al.* 2014) are powerful tools that create new concepts, obscure others, and create incentives for policy-makers, opinion-makers, civil society groups, business and the public. Notwithstanding the power of numbers that they point to, Fukuda-Parr *et al.* (2014) also acknowledge the need for measurement of some aspects of development, but at stake is which criteria are selected for quantitative targets and indicators: human capital, human rights, human development or something else. They emphasise that:

> A transformative future development agenda requires a qualitative statement of objectives, visionary norms and priority action to achieve the objectives, including legal, policy and global institutional considerations. Quantitative targets are useful but must serve the broader development objectives of advancing human dignity and capabilities, within a narrative that is tethered to the international human rights framework.
>
> (Fukuda-Parr *et al.* 2014: 115–16)

Of course the same argument would apply also to qualitative targets, which equally should be underpinned by visionary norms.

Human development and capability thinking offers such visionary norms by adopting a multidimensional and policy responsive view of what a good university could look like, embracing the public good, social justice and sustainability in any definition of a policy narrative. The challenge is operationalising this rather more complex approach in the form of policy guidelines. We are aware that the three examples briefly sketched above offer normative frameworks rather than clear policy guidelines for human development norms to enhance macro-government policy. We can and should work at all levels, including the micro and the local, but at some point we have also to engage with power at the state level and to gain national legitimacy for a human development informational basis for judgement. Ibrahim (2014: 20) captures the challenge well when she says that:

> the operationalization of the capability approach is difficult but not impossible. There are some tough choices that need to be made to render the capability approach more "policy-friendly", but the real challenge lies in doing so without foregoing its conceptual richness.

Finally, Spence and Deneulin (2009) remind us that policy-making happens across many moments, in a web of many decisions, and as a process, but also shaped by power so that a political analysis is also required to understand which forces are influencing policy. Moreover, the boundary between making and implementation is blurred – can a policy be said to be 'made' until it is taken up on the ground? In the end, however, we need an analysis that considers if people's freedoms policy works to expand or reduce.

Note

1 This programme is the biggest EU R&I programme ever, with nearly €80 billion of funding available over seven years (2014–2020). By coupling research and innovation, Horizon 2020 emphasises excellent science, industrial leadership and tackling societal challenges. The goal is to ensure Europe produces world-class science, removes barriers to innovation and makes it easier for the public and private sectors to work together in delivering innovation. (For more information, see http://ec.europa.eu/programmes/horizon2020/en/what-horizon-2020).

References

Alkire, S. and S. Deneulin. 2009. 'A normative framework for development'. In *An Introduction to the Human Development and Capability Approach*, edited by S. Deneulin and L. Shahani, 3–23. London: Earthscan.

Ashwin, P., A. Abbas and M. Mclean. 2013. 'Representations of a high quality system of undergraduate education in English higher education policy documents', *Studies in Higher Education* 40(4): 610–23.

Bertelsmann Stiftung Foundation. 2011. *Social Justice in the OECD – How Do the Member States Compare? Sustainable Governance Indicators 2011*. Gütersloh: Bertelsmann Stiftung.

Boni, A., J. Peris, E. López and A. Hueso. 2009. 'Scrutinising the process of adaptation to the European higher education area in a Spanish University degree using power analysis', *Power and Education* 1(3): 319–332.

Cortina, A. 1994. *La Ética de la Sociedad Civil*. (Ethics of Civil Society) Madrid: Anaya.

Deblonde, M. 2015. 'Responsible research and innovation: building knowledge arenas for global sustainability research', *Journal of Responsible Innovation* 2(1): 20–38.

Dedeurwaerdere, T. 2013. *Sustainability Science for Strong Sustainability*. Lovaine: Université Catholique de Louvain and Fonds National de la Recherche Scientifique.

Deneulin, S. 2014. 'Constructing new policy narratives. The capability approach as normative language'. In *Towards Human Development. New Approaches to Macroeconomic and Inequality*, edited by G. A. Cornia and F. Stewart, 45–65. Oxford: Oxford University Press.

DHET (Department of Higher Education and Training). 2013. *White Paper on Post-School Education and Training*. Pretoria: DHET.

Froger, G., P. Meral and V. Herimandimby. 2004. 'The expansion of participatory governance in the environmental policies of developing countries: the example of Madagascar', *International Journal of Sustainable Development* 7(2): 164–84.

Fukuda-Parr, S., A. E. Yamin and J. Greenstein. 2014. 'The power of numbers: a critical review of Millennium Development Goals and targets', *Journal of Human Development and Capabilities* 15(2–3): 105–17.

Gasper, D. 2000. 'Structures and meanings. A way to introduce argument analysis in policies studies education', *ISS Working Paper* 317.

Gasper, D., A. V. Portocarrero and A. L. St. Clair. 2013. 'The framing of climate change and development: a comparative analysis of the Human Development Report 2007/8 and the World Development Report 2010', *Global Environmental Change* 23: 28–39.

Gaventa, J. 2005. 'Reflections on the uses of the power cube approach for analyzing the spaces, places and dynamics of civil society participation and engagement'. *Prepared for Assessing Civil Society Participation as Supported In-Country by Cordaid, Hivos, Novib and Plan Netherlands 1999–2004*. The Netherlands: MFP Breed.

Gaventa, J. 2006. 'Finding spaces for change. A power analysis', *IDS Bulletin* 37(6): 23–33.

Grand, A., C. Wilkinson, K. Bultitude and A. F. Winfield. 2014. 'Mapping the hinterland: Data issues in open science', *Public Understanding of Science* DOI 0963662514530374.

Hazelkorn, E. 2007. 'The impact of league tables and ranking systems on higher education decision making', *Higher Education Management and Policy* 19(2): 1–24.

Ibrahim, S. 2014. 'Introduction'. In *The Capability Approach. From Theory to Practice*, edited by S. Ibrahim and M. Tiwari, 1–28. Houndmills: Palgrave Macmillan.

Jonas, H. 1985. *The Imperative of Responsibility: In Search of an Ethics for the Technological Age*. Chicago: The University of Chicago Press.

Lozano, J. F., A. Boni and J. C. Suirana. 2006. 'Los valores morales y la universidad' [Moral Values and University]. In *La Educación en Valores en la Universidad. Los Dilemas Morales como Herramienta de Trabajo en Los Estudios Científico-Técnicos* [Moral Education at University. Moral Dilemmas as a Working Tool in Technical and Scientific Studies], edited by A. Boni and J. F. Lozano, 9–18. Valencia: Editorial UPV.

Lukes, S. 2005. *Power: A Radical View*. 2nd edition. London: Palgrave.

Miller, V., L. Veneklasen, M. Reilly and C. Clarck. 2006. 'Making change happen: power. Concepts for revisioning power for justice, equality and peace', *Making Change Happen* 3. Washington: Just Associates.

Motala, E. and S. Vally. 2014. ' "No-one to blame but themselves": rethinking the relationship between education, skills and employment'. In *Education, Economy and Society*, edited by S. Vally and E. Motala, 1–25. Pretoria: Unisa Press.

Nussbaum, M. 2000. *Women and Human Development: The Capabilities Approach*. Cambridge: Cambridge University Press.

Ozga, J. 2000. *Policy Research in Educational Settings. Contested Terrain*. Buckingham: Open University Press.

Redclift, M. 2000. 'El desarrollo sostenible: necesidades, valores y derechos' [Sustainable development: needs, values and rights]. In *Desarrollo Sostenible: Un Concepto Polémico* [Sustainable Development: A Contentious Concept], edited by I. Bárcena, P. Ibarra and M. Zubiaga, 17–38. Bilbao: Servicio Editorial Universidad del País Vasco.

RSA. 1996. *The Constitution of the Republic of South Africa, Act No 108 of 1996*. Pretoria: Government Printer.

Salais, R. 2009. 'Deliberative Democracy and its Informational Basis: What Lessons from the Capability Approach'. SASE (Society for the Advancement of Socio-Economics) Conference, Paris, France, July. halshs-00429574.

Sen, A. 1999. *Development as Freedom*. New York: Knopf.

Spanish Ombudsman. 2009. *Annual Report*. [Accessed 28 September 2015]. www.defensordelpueblo.es/informe-anual/informe-anual-2009/.

Spence, R. and S. Deneulin. 2009. 'Human development policy analysis'. In *An Introduction to the Human Development and Capability Approach*, edited by S. Deneulin and L. Shahani, 275–99. London: Earthscan.

Strand, R., J. Spaapen, M. W. Bauer, E. Hogan, G. Revuelta, S. Stagl, L. Paula and A. Guimarães-Pereira. 2015. Indicators for Promoting and Monitoring Responsible Research and Innovation. Report from the Expert Group on Policy Indicators for Responsible Research and Innovation. Brussels: European Commission. [Accessed 28 September 2015]. http://ec.europa.eu/research/swafs/index.cfm?pg=library&lib=rri.

Trowler, P. 2002. 'Introduction'. In *Higher Education Policy and Institutional Change*, edited by P. Trowler, 1–23. Buckingham: Open University Press and McGraw Hill.

Von Schomberg, R. 2011. 'Prospects for technology assessment in a framework of responsible research and innovation'. In *Technikfolgen Abschätzen Lehren: Bildungspotenziale Transdisziplinärer Methoden*, edited by M. Dusseldorp and R. Beecroft, 39–61. Wiesbaden: Springer VS.

6 University knowledge contributions and human development

One of the key functions of a university is to produce new knowledge (and through its teaching function, to disseminate this knowledge to students). Given the inequalities noted in Chapter 2, it raises the question of how universities through their research and knowledge function seek to re-imagine the university, engaging with these inequalities, understanding themselves as sharing knowledge across boundaries both academic and social, and see themselves playing a role in social development. As Bangladesh economist Anisur Rahman (quoted in Gaventa and Bivens 2014: 70) explains, 'The gap between those who have social power over the process of knowledge generation – and those who have not – has reached dimensions no less formidable than the gap in access to means of physical production'. Appadurai (2006) thus proposes that doing research is a right 'of a special kind', by which he means the right to the tools through which any citizen can systematically contribute to knowledge and to their claims as citizens; research expands the horizons of one's knowledge and develops the capabilities to inquire, analyze and communicate; it is 'an essential capacity for democratic citizenship' (Appadurai 2006: 6). Moreover, Appadurai (2006) links this to his cultural capacity to aspire, which he describes as being able to plan, hope, desire and achieve socially valuable goals so that the capacity to aspire and the capacity for research are 'necessarily and intimately connected'. Similarly Freire (1997: xi) argues that people who are the focus of research have the right to participate in knowledge production: 'In this process, people rupture their existing attitudes of silence, accommodation and passivity, and gain confidence and abilities to alter unjust conditions and structures'. Finally, at its second world conference on higher education in 2009, UNESCO (2009) noted the social responsibility of higher education with regard to knowledge production in the face of complex current and future global challenges, so that higher education has the social responsibility to advance understanding of these multifaceted issues (UNESCO 2009). This combined language of social responsibility and rights offers a challenging justice-oriented lens for thinking about the knowledge contributions of universities.

In this chapter, we therefore consider the knowledge and research contributions to human development that are possible by universities if attention is paid to whose knowledge, for whose benefit, for whose capability expansion and how research is conducted. We consider two kinds of knowledge contributions: (1) what counts as knowledge, and (2) research processes through which knowledge is produced by universities, together with examples of human development knowledge production.

Two challenges

Two challenges are now addressed in this chapter. What and who counts in legitimate knowledge formation as a matter of 'epistemic injustice' (Fricker 2007) and 'epistemological equity' (Dei 2008) is one; the second is the research practices in universities that produce knowledge and determine what counts as new knowledge (Gibbons 1997). For both (related) issues, material, power and social relations underlie research and knowledge making, and the ends to which research is oriented, whether or not the knowledge or the research is directly 'about' human development. Indeed, all kinds of knowledge being produced in universities should be contributing in different ways, not just specific human development projects, although it is these the chapter concentrates on. Nonetheless, we note that medical research, for example, should not be about making drug companies richer or devising yet more screening for already healthy and wealthy people but should also be attending to diseases of poverty and making generic drugs, such as those for HIV/AIDS, cheaply available without requiring protracted struggles to enable this.

Epistemic challenges

For both knowledge and knowledge-making through research practices, Fricker's (2007) argument about epistemic injustice and systemic power relations can hold. She explores the ethical dimensions of knowledge, and two kinds of injustice that individuals may suffer in their capacity as knowers – testimonial (person to person) and hermeneutic (social order). Testimonial injustice occurs when a speaker is granted less credibility than he or she might otherwise be accorded, or less respect as a knower. Fricker uses the example from *To Kill a Mockingbird* of a white jury not even entertaining that the testimony of the black accused may be more trustworthy than the evidence of his white accuser. A similar example might be that communities outside the academy are not credible makers of knowledge. A hermeneutical injustice would occur if we lack the language to describe a social phenomenon, for example research, which speaks for all students but in which only male students are interviewed as happened in Perry's (1970) Harvard study of student's moral development; in which case both men and women are harmed and our full educational experience is made unintelligible to others and even ourselves. Fricker (2007: 5) argues that people 'are prevented from becoming who they are' through these injustices. Using capabilities language, we could argue that social arrangements deny people the opportunity to be admitted into an epistemic community, people are not recognised as knowers, and are not able to develop the combined capability to be knowledgeable persons; in this, people are not treated as fully human knowers, which directly contravenes the philosophical basis of capabilities.

Post-colonial theorists, such as Thuwai Smith (2012: 2), argue more specifically that research is a site of significant (epistemic) struggle 'between the interests and ways of knowing of the West and the interests and ways of knowing of the other'. While we can generally claim that research aims to add value to and benefit society (and we have many good examples of this), research also 'exists within a system of power' (Smith 2012: 226), and in contemporary times, within globalisation flows and neo-liberal higher education policies. This requires knowledge-making through research 'talk back to and talk up to power' in order to get the story right and tell the story well (Smith 2012: 226). Adding to this, Barr (1999) argues from her own research on women's perceptions of science that the development of science and its application to social problems (including, health, the environment, technology, etc.), 'is more likely to be advanced in proportion to its democratic inclusiveness, that is, the closer it gets to the articulation and examination of all points of view' (Barr 1999: 144).

The point to be made is that knowledge, scholarship and research are not neutral projects but are shaped by history and the societies (more or less epistemically inclusive), in which the work is undertaken, and in which the researcher is shaped and positioned. Knowledge is constructed and produced in social and political contexts, and spaces of in/equity. Dei (2008: 8) explains:

> The question of how to create spaces where multiple knowledges can co-exist in the Western academy is central; especially so since Eurocentric knowledge subsumes and appropriates other knowledges without crediting sources. At issue is the search for epistemological equity.

If we want to get the story right, tell the story well and locate research in a human development frame, we first need to attend to the epistemic challenges of inclusion and equity regarding whose knowledge counts and who can be a knower. De Sousa Santos (2006) proposes that different ways of knowing have been neglected globally and that this is a matter of 'cognitive injustice' in which dominant knowledges have failed to recognise different ways of knowing. From his perspective, there can be no global social democracy if there is no democracy between forms of knowledge. The university, he argues, could contribute towards cognitive justice by recognising and valuing epistemological diversity, recognising the multiplicity of social practices and experiences of the world. This requires re-thinking traditional views of scientific knowledge characterised by hierarchies and singular disciplines. By way of contrast, De Sousa Santos (2014) proposes a 'pluri-universitary knowledge', which is contextual, practical, and whose results have been agreed between researchers and users. It is transdisciplinary, and due to its contextual character, is always in dialogue with other types of knowledge.

Knowledge, he argues (2009), exists *only* as a plurality of ways of knowing. The possibilities and limits of understanding and action of each way of knowing can only be grasped to the extent that each way of knowing offers a comparison with other ways of knowing. The comparison is difficult because the relations among ways of knowing are haunted by an asymmetry, which is not only epistemological but also political. De Sousa Santos (2009: 116) therefore proposes a transformatory ecology of knowledge, which is contrary to the 'epistemological fascism that amounts to violent destruction or concealment of other ways of knowing'. This involves exploration of alternative scientific practices that have become visible mainly through feminist and post-colonial epistemologies. Second, it involves promoting interaction and interdependence between scientific knowledge and other 'unscientific' knowledges. Third, rather than subscribing to a single, universal and abstract hierarchy of knowledge, an ecology of knowledge establishes hierarchies in accordance with the context and in the light of specific outcomes intended or achieved by different knowledges. Fourth, since there are real-world interventions that can, in principle, be carried out by different knowledge systems, the specific choice of forms of knowledge must give preference to those that maximise the participation of social groups involved in the design, execution, control and enjoyment of the intervention. The ecology of knowledge thus looks for a solidarity reorientation of the relationship between university and society. It offers a wide range of action informed by scientific and practical knowledge considered useful and shared by researchers, students and citizen groups and where citizens and social groups can intervene without being exclusively learners or the objects of research.

Relating this specifically to human development and capabilities, Salais (2009) considers knowledge in relation to the informational basis of judgement, that is, the information on which judgement (including research analysis and interpretation) is directly dependent and which determines social choice (as we discussed in Chapter 5). As Salais shows, what data or information is used, for example, to calculate rates of employment (full-time work, part-time work, 1 hour of work a week counted as employment, etc.), has a justice effect. He relates this to the socially constructed nature of knowledge and in our case, the frameworks which select what is an important problem to be researched. In other words, problem-posing and information selection is not neutral. Salais further seeks to connect capabilities to deliberative democracy and we think also to social research as integral to the democratic project): 'Without their [community] participation, it is impossible to bring out the internal and external characteristics of the situation that enables real possibility to emerge' (Salais 2009: 9). From a research point of view, if universities are involved in research on poverty, or on inclusive development, or in researching sustainable cities, with a view to informing or influencing policy and action, this would then require the broader participation of those affected by the substantive focus of the research. This could be done via various methods including surveys and interviews, but people would need to be not only informants and objects of research, they would need to contribute in some way to shaping the problem and the research questions. Not to proceed in this way for Salais, would be inconsistent with the principle of a capabilities-based 'common good' because it leaves the shaping and analysis of the problem only in the hands of the experts (university researchers).

Developing the argument further, in a way especially relevant to knowledge production and research, he asks under what circumstances citizens do or do not participate (for us, in the research process), and if they do, how are they involved in 'developing cognitive frameworks that are adequate to what they consider a fair handling of the problems'? (Salais 2009: 9). The key point he emphasises is that, 'Knowing and achieving the common good thus become the two sides of a single social process rooted in a situation' (Salais 2009: 16). To achieve the common good we would need to include the perspectives of multiple actors, including how to frame the problem. Social inquiry in its process could then expand people's capabilities through participation and deliberation. Kamanzi (2014–15: 8) puts the case with clarity: 'we must open up channels to engage with members of society that are not part of the university structures in ways that go beyond ... who has been traditionally allowed to claim authoritative knowledge'.

Knowledge inclusively conceived could build capabilities; indeed if social inquiry is to be aligned with human development it would be ethically required to have capabilities expansion as an aim. On the other hand, this is a demanding approach, and there is a great deal of research, including under the human development and capability approach umbrella, which does not proceed in this perfectly dialogical and participatory way and still yields valuable knowledge. The important point is less one of method but rather one of principles and values, which underpin any research process that aspires to contribute to human development and the public-good. In messy real-life contexts, things may be more muddled and we may need therefore to think about participation along a values-based continuum, with a view always to research using a variety of methods, but which seek to make knowledge for more, rather than less, justice.

Research processes

Turning now from epistemic injustices, to elaborate on the research process, Favish (2015) points out that engagement beyond the university shares a number of common principles: valuing local epistemologies; joint discussion around the research questions and methodology; discussion around expectations of the roles and responsibilities of those involved; highlighting community partner voices; and providing feedback to all partners on the research. Bearing these common principles in mind, and that in this chapter we are primarily concerned with development-oriented, engaged research, we think that 'Mode 2 research' (Nowotny *et al.* 2003) can provide a useful framework for thinking about research practices. Nowotny and her colleagues distinguish 'Mode 1 knowledge', which they describe as 'the old paradigm of scientific discovery' (2003: 180) and Mode 2, which is 'socially distributed, application-oriented, trans-disciplinary and subject to multiple accountabilities', so that the validity of knowledge is no longer determined predominantly by 'narrowly circumscribed scientific communities' (2003: 191). They further introduce the idea of the *agora*, comprising both the political arena and the marketplace but going beyond both, to conceptualise the space in which the contextualisation of knowledge production takes place, populated by experts, organisations, institutions and publics, rather like Sen's (2009) public reasoning. It becomes, they argue, 'a domain of primary knowledge production – through which people enter the research process, and where Mode 2 knowledge is embodied in people and projects' (2003: 192). The context of application of knowledge should not be understood as hierarchical or linear but as reaching out and anticipating reflexively the implications of research processes.

On the other hand, Marginson (2006) argues that universities have neglected dialogical exchanges, even though they now have the technologies and discursive resources for global conversations, for example via mobile phone and computer technology. But to deploy the communicative resources of the university beyond advancing hierarchies of power would require valuing wider contributions to public debate and policy formation, and having socially communicative faculty rather than 'a self-referencing city of the intellect' (Marginson 2006: 10). If such research dialogue across epistemic communities is important, as we argue it is, how do we foster the agora? Linda Alcoff (2002) proposes publicly engaged intellectuals who would spend a significant portion of their time engaged with the non-academic public, taking on the role of a public theorist who recognises that theory building is not located solely in the academy but in and through wider public arenas, where ideas can be tested dialogically to produce better, more rigorous knowledge. Such public-based theorising is democratic in intent and practice:

> Publicly engaged work is actually one of the best sites from which to engage in at least certain kinds of intellectual work, not because one is

merely applying and testing theory developed in the academy to the public domain, nor because one can simply gather raw data from which to build theory, but rather because the public domain is sometimes the best or the only place in which to alter one's thoughts ... and thus to engage in intellectual work.

(Alcoff 2002: 533)

The public domain is then a place for reciprocity, conversations, debates and mutual respect and also for better theorising and better knowledge-making. Calhoun (2007: 12) similarly argues that confrontation between different perspectives inside but also outside the academy, advances social science, while Burawoy (2005) also proposes the need for a reflexive science, able to deploy multiple dialogues to reach explanations of empirical phenomena, and able to engage multiple perspectives from diverse groups of stakeholders.

Others point out too that research processes that engage with citizens need not compromise academic scholarship or the development of advanced codified knowledge, nor diminish, reduce or replace the work of experts in the academy (Hall 2009). Hall (2009) calls for greater cross-discourse work by what he calls 'Science Discourse' located inside the academy and claiming sole scientific expertise, and 'Memory Work' located in the community and potentially as disciplined as anything science has to offer. He concludes that if they were to align the interest of science with those of the memory community, the creation of new knowledge could be enhanced considerably. These discourses need not be in conflict but could produce vibrant, mutually rewarding hybrid forms of knowledge. Nonetheless, Hall (2007: 3) is also clear that universities are highly relevant as key sites for producing knowledge, writing that, 'the academic obsession with evidence, argument, peer review, publication and refutations are the essence of knowledge creation'. Using the significant example of understanding poverty and its causes in South Africa, requires, Hall says, complex and specialist intellectual skills, including sophisticated research methods and the arguments which most robustly and rigorously explain the problem. Importantly, then, universities 'are specialized sites where knowledge is formed and reformed on the merits of theory and evidence, rather than according to the emergencies of immediate and short term interests' (Hall 2007: 5). But this need not be at the exclusion of other forms of knowledge, which can enrich how we define and approach human development challenges in society.

Salais (2009) has his own response to academic scepticism about expansive knowledge production. For Salais (2009: 18), the reason for inviting wider social criticism 'lies in the real value of the knowledge arising from social practice that citizens possess'; democratic social inquiry 'calls into question the strict separation and established hierarchy between scientific knowledge (intended to develop general categories) and practical knowledge (reduced to the local everyday level and consequently assumed to be prone to erroneous judgments)'. Indeed, to separate abstract social science knowledge from citizens' practical knowledge, allows technologies of governance that exclude some voices and position people only as consumers not producers of knowledge, or at least not of scientifically legitimate knowledge. This would be a matter of cognitive injustice. For Salais, it is ethically necessary to transpose scientific methodology to the field of deliberative democracy so that social inquiry would:

> enable a constituted public to enter into public deliberation facing the political authorities, armed with an achievable alternative way of being and doing and supported by objectively grounded, legitimate knowledge that cannot be disregarded.... Common knowledge constructed through deliberation is not a mere sum of sentiments, opinions or subjective, empirical assessments, nor is it a diktat out of the blue. It organises and weighs; it creates the facts and thus provides an incentive, in certain configurations, to reformulate the issues and choose other ways to solve the problems. It gives the weight of truth for criticizing the 'facts' rationally fabricated by authorities in search of justification. It gradually adds something to the deliberation that was not there in the beginning.
>
> (Salais 2009: 25)

The point is the possibility, the significance, and the usefulness of involving research partners in knowledge production, not least in research which challenges official constructions of what the problem is taken to be and what evidence counts in researching the problem.

However, as we noted earlier, this may not be easy in practice. This does not mean we do not strive towards this ideal, but nor should we fall into the trap of rather romantic views on participation. Recently, there have been disagreements publicly aired in the national press in South Africa regarding who has the right to speak on behalf of whom, who owns knowledge about civil society structures, whose knowledge is to be counted as 'rigorous', and what counts as truth. In this case, the disagreement concerned a shack dwellers' association (*Abahlali baseMjondolo*). In a public rejoinder by Bandile Mdlalose to a critical account by Huchzermeyer (*Mail and Guardian*, 17–24 July 2015), an academic, of her article published in a local journal, Mdlalose describes how the association worked with the academics (whom they called their 'trees'). The 'trees' would write academic articles or letters to newspapers supporting the organisation, talk to funders, go on overseas trips, write and edit speeches and press statements. She writes, 'as a young person from the township who never went to university, I was amazed and impressed by them' (Mdlalose 2015: 31). Mdlalose also claims that the academics knew that there were problems in the organisation, yet these never found their way into their papers and articles, she claims. Over time, she came to question if their influence was more about control; when everyone agreed then things went well, when too many questions were asked of the 'trees', the people asking questions were described as ill-disciplined and divisive. Mdlalose (2015: 31) writes further: 'What I wonder is how, when the tall trees were writing about *Abahlali* for all those long years, saying only good things, how was it this qualified as knowledge when what I say [now] does not'. She accuses Huchzermeyer of using the organisation as evidence for her own academic theory that 'good middle-class academics like her can work well with shack-dweller movements' (Mdlalose 2015: 31). The rejoinder is written, Mdlalose says, not to embarrass the academics, but to learn how rigorous academic research is done. The issue here is not to pass judgement on the rights and wrongs of this particular situation (and indeed the contested interpretations continue in the press; see the letters page in the *Mail and Guardian* 14 August 2015). Rather, the issue is that how academics work with civil structures is hard – harder than Salais perhaps allows – and there are no pre-written rules to guide such arrangements. Bourdieu (1998) thus calls on social scientists to be above all, reflexive. 'We would like', he writes, 'to invent new forms of expression that make it possible to communicate the most advanced findings of research', but he further adds that this 'also presupposes a change of language and outlook on the part of the researchers' (Bourdieu 1998: 58).

This is further complicated under neo-liberal conditions and the commodification of academic knowledge and the nature of the university. We need to engage honestly with whether academics in universities are willing to engage in these inclusive research processes and to produce knowledge as a public-good, not least if career rewards pull in a different direction in universities as they now are. While the problems may have intensified, the university context has for many years required researchers to package their knowledge and to focus on the right kind of scientific knowledge published in books and journals and presenting conferences papers to other university scholars. Deliberation and participation beyond the university are rather harder to package and market in building an academic career, but this is not new. In 1977, Hall wrote:

> For a person working in a university or research institution, knowledge is effectively a commodity. In the narrowest sense researchers gather or 'mine' ideas and information in order to survive and advance economically.... The need to serve the people from whom the information has been gathered ... is indirect and by necessity a low priority. These groups will not buy the results (and perhaps didn't want the research in the first place.
>
> (Hall 1977: 23)

Overall, we recognise the tensions and challenges in universities as they are now, but nonetheless propose working for more epistemic justice and more inclusion in research processes. We do not argue for perfection or think perfection is possible but advocate for Sen's (2009) redressable injustices.

Public-value knowledge

Related to our two challenges, we further think that we need to keep alive the argument that university-produced knowledge ought to be a public-good (Stiglitz 2003), even if in practice it is increasingly what Nowotny *et al.* (2003: 185) describe as 'intellectual property, which is produced, accumulated, and traded like other goods and services'. Supporting our position, Brewer (2013) advances a compelling case for the public value of the social sciences as researched and taught in universities. A public-value social science would be engaged, he argues, with the future of humanity, while also committed to the scientific project. More than ever, Brewer suggests, in the face of intractable problems we need social science 'with a new sense of its public value' (Brewer 2013: 4). He argues that public value constitutes an alternative vocabulary, which enables a new imaginary for research and its impact, and fosters common conversations nationally and internationally, offering 'the best prospect of restating for the twenty first century the principles on which social science can justify itself against the neoliberal push towards economic impact as the sole measure of effectiveness' (Brewer 2013: 132). Brewer further argues that social science should nurture 'a moral sentiment' and 'shared responsibility for the future of humankind', directed to understanding and ameliorating unfair social conditions (2013: 151). He argues that social science develops and disseminates public values (trust, empathy, social solidarity, etc.) that support the betterment of society. Crucially, the public good cannot be secured through market mechanisms or individual efforts only (important though the latter may be); it requires public action, agency and a different stance on the part of academics and students to fight for what is valuable about universities and their public-good contributions.

Brewer explains that this requires critical knowledge, which in turn gains from dialogue with professional and policy knowledge in a kind of virtuous knowledge-producing circle. Such social science has normative public value, 'making people aware of themselves as comprising a society, developing and disseminating social values that make and sustain good societies', so that 'social science is a public good in its own right' (Brewer 2013: 151). At its best, public social science would create, persuade, and move publics to become committed to civic action in order to impact on our human future, providing a language in which we might imagine how the university ought to be – for the public-good, for contributions to making diverse people's lives go better, and to more just and democratic societies. Moreover, the economic impact of research could be evaluated in the direction of redistribution and not necessarily in the direction of consolidating private benefits.

Spaces for human development research

With all this in mind, we now turn to examples of social research that inflect in the direction of human development. We try to understand human development-oriented research along a continuum of participation, rather than an impossible deliberative ideal, which may fall apart when confronted with messy realities and pressures of universities, funders, and so on. Here Sen's (2009) idea of comparative assessments of justice is helpful in that we can ask: is this approach to research more or less just in the problems addressed, the processes and the outcomes? Moreover, it is not easy to judge the impact of social research 'in the moment'. It may take time, even years, before the effects of knowledge produced on human development becomes clearer. We have a good example in Sen's own work, where it was some years before the public-good value of the capability approach could be fully realised in the form of the human development index, and this fundamentally required the timely intervention of Mahbub Ul Haq as a policy broker (see Chapter 4).

There are many examples we can point to of research we have ourselves been involved in, while a glance at the website of the Human Development and Capability Association (www.hd-ca.org/) will produce a rich picture of human development-oriented research. Here we focus on just two examples.

A large EU-funded project

SOCIETY is a large EU-funded project (see www.society-youth.eu/) which, using the capability approach as a framework, seeks to develop a broad knowledge base to foster socially innovative policy-making. Using a mixed-methods approach, which includes quantitative, qualitative and participatory methods, SOCIETY builds knowledge in three aspects: (1) how existing policies and social practices of networks of social support tackle the problems faced by disadvantaged young people; (2) how far, and in what ways, young people's ideas, experiences, aspirations and voices can be included in policy-making; and (3) and how social innovation can link these two issues, leading to social inclusion and to smart, sustainable and inclusive growth. The capability approach provided the theoretical framework to accomplish these goals. The 13 partners that compose the consortia of SOCIETY belong to 11 European countries and to different disciplines. In each of those countries, similar research was conducted to explore different layers of policy-making (national and local, and, in some countries, even regional), as well as to what extent young people's voices, ideas, aspirations are being heard, combining qualitative, quantitative and participatory research. In Chapter 8, we provide a more detailed account of the participatory research methodology; in this chapter we want to focus on the results of the participatory research conducted in the 11 countries based on the same research question: to what extent and in what way do social policies and practices take the perspectives of (disadvantaged) young people seriously? Although not specifically on higher education, the process of knowledge-making and the question are very relevant, and we think we can learn from both.

The methods used in the 11 cases were different; in some countries, the research team chose an audio-visual approach using photo-voice or participatory video. In other cases, the research option was to use a biographical approach using participatory biographical research or an ethnography. In other examples, methods were more conventional – focus groups or collective interviews. Giving voice to youth and making them part of the research process were the common elements. We now outline the main findings of the participatory projects and highlight some of the recommendations made by SOCIETY with the aim of inspiring a socially innovative way of understanding policy-making and influencing European policy-makers at multiple levels, and one which, we argue, brings the voices of youth into policy-making in a socially innovative way. As we have discussed in Chapter 5, the understanding of the policy-making realm is wide and includes processes in which different groups negotiate, contest and struggle, creating policies outside the formal machinery of official policy-making.

With regard to social exclusion and disadvantage among young people, the research found that policy actions identify social exclusion with not being entered into the labour market, and formal education is presented as the means to provide employment. Thus, education is meant to 'solve' the problems of the economy but the economy is to stay the same. Moreover, social exclusion and youth disadvantage is often attributed to individual actions and responsibilities (i.e. early school leaving) or attributes linked to the individual (i.e. family, area of living, deficiencies). However, in many of the research partner countries, SOCIETY's participatory studies show that young people feel that they are being undermined by not being given the opportunity to be listened to and, at the same time, they feel that policy-makers are out of touch with young people. In some cases, organisations give young people a voice in their programme delivery or ask for feedback and suggestions for the design of actions (Scotland, Spain, Switzerland), but these seem to be isolated cases. Moreover, they focus on 'soft policies' (e.g. leisure) and never involve young people in the design of 'hard' policies for the labour market and employment. While in policy documents, participation of youth is presented as relevant, only on a very few occasions does it entail really taking the voice of young people seriously. Therefore, participation remains rather superficial.

Certainly, taking the voices of young people seriously or enhancing their participation is not an easy task. Having a voice entails a degree of awareness of what is at stake in policy concerning youth, and having a sense that policy could be helpful in some way. Both social awareness and policy awareness do not seem very clear among the young people who are targeted by youth policies. In addition, social and policy awareness need to be aligned with a notion of one's agency to change or contribute to policy. This is not always self-evident, especially among young people whose early stages in life have proved difficult, and who have not often been granted chances – or even incentives – to exercise policy-directed agency. In addition, considering the voices of young people seriously would entail that the informational basis, which informs youth policy-making and policy implementation, takes far more account of the aspirations of young people, as well as their capability to aspire.

SOCIETY's research findings also show that, during the economic crisis in Europe, in some countries (mainly Spain, Italy, France) young people have been particularly affected. For many of the countries, the fact of being a young person is in itself a barrier to formulate a life-plan. Thus, youth (with only a few exceptions) becomes a category of disadvantage; to be young is to be at a disadvantage in society and the economy. Social exclusion is seen as a cumulative process, while young people feel that, as young people, they are vulnerable because they are not able to push their views or ideas forward.

The findings of the participatory research projects highlight the concept of participation and the value attached to it. Using the capability approach, participation is seen not as a forced outcome but rather as a capability or genuine opportunity that each individual can make use of (or not). In theory, in many cases, participation is available as an opportunity. But in practice, due to the lack of trust in public institutions and other factors, participation is not a valuable or trusted option for young people. If young people do not participate, they are held to be at fault, rather than the conditions that enable or constrain. However, participation cannot simply be promoted in policy without being considered in relation to other social and personal conversion factors and to the set of opportunities that can be generated during the process of being a participant. Hence, trust in public institutions is not something which comes before participation. Additionally, different (pre)forms of participation need to be promoted, which entails the democratisation of institutions as well. Institutionalised arenas, where young people are allowed and empowered to voice their concerns and wishes, and professionals working with young people who are obliged to take account of these, should still be at the core of deliberative policies and democratic social services.

Beyond the expansion of valuable opportunities of participation in employment and education, the research proposes that spaces should be offered to young people, so that they can develop and design those areas of well-being relevant for them. For example, in the Spanish participatory video project, one group decided to conduct the video project on youth opportunities in the labour market and entrepreneurship to 'show that young people have ideas but not enough opportunities and that there is something to be done about it' (M. quoted in López-Fogues *et al.* 2015: 120). Another group focused its video on educational law reforms, political parties, religion, segregation. As M. (in López-Fogues *et al.* 2015: 120) explains: 'They change the law all the time they want, and ask for more money and for more years, and we cannot do anything about it'. The third group decided to focus on youth participation, volunteering, leisure time, to show 'the good and the bad things of being a volunteer' (L. quoted in López-Fogues *et al.* 2015: 120).

The different methodologies used in the participatory case studies reveal the potential of social media and innovative methods to capture the interest of young people and to foster their aspirations. The core aim of participatory research in SOCIETY has been to change the informational basis of judgements and to include the perspectives of those who are the focus of research, because they have the right to participate in knowledge production (Appadurai 2006). In the different case studies and methods used, the results are that participatory research contributes to knowledge through deliberation and through shifting the role of young people from the objects of study to the subjects of the study. The use of bottom-up methods, which encourage discussion and dialogue, such as biographical research (Belgium), photo-voice (Romania and Scotland), participatory video (Spain), focus groups (Italy) or sociological intervention (Switzerland), have shown that all young people – even ones who at first sight seemed unmotivated and even apathetic – aspire and have a critical perception of their own social condition and lives. Through the participatory research, young people have generally highlighted that existing policies are not innovative and that they would favour experimental policies which will contest those structures in which they as young people could contribute to defining the means to tackle employment and vocational training courses, educational plans, democratic procedures and, most generally, disadvantage.

A South African project

A second example of a human development research project set out to select 'public-good professional capabilities', which could be developed through professional education in South African universities (Walker and McLean 2013). This selection is open to public scrutiny and revision and has the potential to be taken up for systematic analysis, evaluation and adjustment in a range of contexts; while the project's participatory and iterative research process in which groups interested in professional education came to agreements, could be replicated elsewhere. Further, as Sen (2009) explains, while the exercise of freedom is mediated by values (public-good values in this case), these values are influenced by public discussions (in professional associations, professionals working alongside civil society, and so forth). The professional capabilities list process is intended to capture these connections between values, discussion and freedom.

The project focused on five professional departments in three South African universities (law, engineering, public health, social work and theology) in a context in which professionals are urgently needed to address the multidimensional problems associated with poverty and to contribute to social transformation in a highly unequal society. The project developed a methodology that allowed us to draw up a set of professional capabilities that were agreed on by professional education interest groups in South Africa; for the purposes of this chapter, we focus on this process as a dialogic knowledge-making process. The set or list developed was a combination of ideal theorising (what a public-good professional ought to do and be in conditions of inequality) and pragmatic grounding in people's contextual everyday lives (what could a public-good professional actually do to reduce poverty). Although each professional-field interview dataset is not homogenous, including as it does, lecturers, students, alumni, NGOs, professional bodies and university leaders, we found each subset to be sufficient for our analysis and the saturation of the capability dimensions which emerged. We assumed that all interviewees were competent to comment in their specific area (e.g. student experiences, curriculum, professional practice, etc.), and each group was asked a similar set of questions. Lecturers, students, alumni and practitioners in all fields were involved at each stage in negotiating what became the final set of professional capabilities. We did not speak directly to people living in poverty; but we did use the perspectives of professionals working with people living in conditions of poverty as an imperfect proxy. The respectful and convincing accounts of these professionals about their clients gave us indirect access to the stories of individuals and communities living in poverty.

We first identified a list of 'comprehensive' capabilities required for a fully human life, and then posed the further question: which of these capabilities and functionings should inform what professionals ought to be and do to work for social transformation and hence, which should be the goals of public-good professionalism to enable the expansion of the human capabilities of others? Our first iteration of professional capabilities was not data- or dialogue-driven. We conceptualised professional education theoretically as enabling students to clarify their own conception of the good and to form justice-enhancing relationships with others. The data collection that followed aimed to test and operationalise the theoretical ideas to establish more precisely: which professional capabilities were valued and why; dialogue with research working groups at each participating university; debate in public seminars in South Africa; and internationally provided formative feedback. We used the feedback to refine the emerging list and to inform continuing questioning about the usefulness of the capabilities approach. A complex account emerged in which the capabilities are potentially widely applicable as long as they remain 'vague' and 'thick', while the functionings from the data are contextual and specific and will vary according to profession.

For the second iteration of professional capabilities, we brought theory into play with dialogue and practice, drafting two core capabilities – the capability to be a change agent and the capability for affiliation – which had emerged from our early discussions. For the third iteration, we moved from fieldwork to producing a case record by selective editing of the case data. We initially selected 'social work' as a critical case of a profession working directly at the interface of vulnerable lives, so if an emergent list of public-good capabilities focusing on poverty reduction was not valid in this case, it was unlikely it would be valid in professions further removed from working with the people living in poverty. We generated four central professional capabilities, which were extrapolated from the functionings that emerged from the Social Work data. We described these as: vision, professional agency, affiliation and resilience. We began to build case studies of each profession working from these initial four empirical capabilities. Working systematically across our interview datasets, we organised data from lecturers, students and alumni and NGOs and professional bodies, under three analytic categories of: *Professional capabilities* (e.g. 'making a difference'); *Educational contributions* (e.g. not enough practical education; curriculum); and *Constraints* (e.g. changing student values; failures of the law). We compared and contrasted diverse groups in each profession, and then across different professions. We continued to generate capabilities until the data was exhausted and used new capabilities to revisit previously coded data. Variation within and across case sites and informant groups was looked for, as well as any negative cases (a capability, which did not appear in a profession). This yielded evidence-based tables organised around three key categories of: human development professional capabilities; educational arrangements (including institutional conditions); and, socio-historic constraints for each case study.

Eventually, a list of eight professional capabilities emerged, which we thought could realistically be developed through professional education in universities:

1 *Informed vision*: being able to imagine alternative futures and improved social arrangements; commitment to economic development and equitable economic opportunities; environmental awareness. This functioning is based on an understanding of how the profession is shaped by historical and current socioeconomic, political context national and globally; understanding how structures shape individual lives;

2 *affiliation*: accepting obligations to others; care and respect for diverse people; understanding the lives of the poor and vulnerable; developing relationships and rapport across social groups and status hierarchies; critical respect for different cultures; communicating professional knowledge in an accessible way/courtesy and patience;

3   *social and collective struggle*: community empowerment approach/promoting human rights; contributing to policy formulation and implementation; identifying spaces for change/leading and managing social change to reduce injustice; working in professional and inter-professional teams; participating in public reasoning/listening to all voices in the 'conversation'; building and sustaining strategic relationships and networks with organisations and government;

4   *integrity and courage*: acting ethically; being responsible and accountable to communities and colleagues; being honest; striving to provide high-quality service;

5   *knowledge and skills*: having a firm, critical grounding in disciplinary, academic knowledge; valuing indigenous and community knowledges; having a multidisciplinary/multiperspectival stance; being enquiring, critical, evaluative, imaginative, creative and flexible; integrating theory and practice; problem-solving; open-minded;

6   *resilience*: perseverance in difficult circumstances; recognising the need for professional boundaries; fostering hope; having a sense of career security;

7   *emotional reflexivity*: empathy/narrative imagination; compassion; personal growth; self-care; integrating rationality and emotions; being emotionally reflexive about power and privilege;

8   *assurance and confidence:* expressing and asserting own professional priorities; contributing to policy; having confidence in the worth-whileness of one's professional work; having confidence to act for change.

The public-good functionings (actually being and doing professionally in a public-good way), which were transversal to all the professional capabilities and derived from them were: (1) recognising the full dignity of every human being; (2) acting for social transformation and reducing injustice; (3) making sound, knowledgeable, thoughtful, imaginative professional judgements; and (4) working/acting with others to expand the comprehensive capabilities ('fully human lives') of people living in poverty. The other two elements of what we came to call the 'professional capabilities index' were educational arrangements in departments and universities, and the social and historical context.

While the project could identify professional capabilities common to all, the professions that were the focus of our study, nonetheless there were variations. As might be expected, we found a sharp distinction between high status, high-income professions of Engineering and Law on the one hand, and the lower status, lower paid professions of Theology, Social Work and Public Health, on the other. Thus from the data, departments pursued the eight public-good professional capabilities in weak and strong forms, depending on the values of the professional field. There were five major strands (inevitably more strongly expressed in some

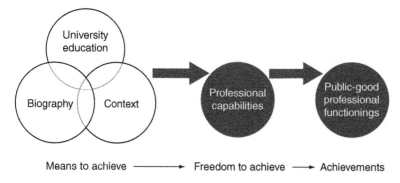

Figure 6.1 Formation of public-good functionings.

departments than others) that relate to four of the capabilities. First, in all the departments, even if in one course or module, students were expected to understand that they were entering a professional field in specific socio-historic circumstances in a country where many people are living in conditions of poverty and that they have a role to play in addressing the problem (informed vision). Second, in all departments there were attempts to inculcate respectful relationships (affiliation). Third, knowledge and skills were seen as vital to make some form of contribution to a society that is in need of a great deal from its professionals, whatever the field. Fourth, the messages were strong in teaching that professionals must display integrity. Fifth, we observed students gaining confidence and assurance as they were being educated. The other three capabilities were not evident strongly across all professions but did appear, even if weakly. Social and collective struggle made almost no direct appearance in the curriculum or pedagogy in Engineering or directly in Law but could be extrapolated nonetheless. In Theology, there was a strong focus on bringing black and white people and churches together; this could be understood as a form of social and collective struggle. In Social Work and Public Health, social and collective struggle appeared as encouragement for advocacy, leadership and policy contributions. In Public Health, appreciating and acting on the necessity of services and systems working together to promote the health of people living in poverty was a central value.

Both Theology and Social Work education stressed emotional reflexivity, albeit differently so that Theology saw emotional reflexivity as making personal transformations through discussion, prayer and thought, whereas, in Social Work it related to the clinical placements students had experienced during which they had come face-to-face with the harrowing realities of extreme poverty. The relatively light emphasis on practical, concrete experiences in real communities in Theology might also explain the absence of discussion about resilience (except from the alumni), which is in contrast with Social Work for which it was a central capability. Public health appeared to assume resilience on the part of their working health professional students. And there were small hints of the need for both emotional reflexivity and resilience in Engineering and Law, insofar as students and alumni saw themselves as working directly on poverty reduction.

Overall, the participative exploration of public-good professional capabilities shed light on how capabilities can constitute a set of goals for professionalism that holds across professional fields but which require dialogue in identifying the set. The case studies also show how material conditions can constrain efforts to educate the public-good professional so that identifying capabilities through a public and inclusive process must always attend to context and to history.

The public-good professional capabilities have now been taken up in countries as diverse as the UK, South Africa, Australia and Palestine, while the list of professional capabilities remains open to adjustment.

Concluding thoughts

We have argued here for a more inclusive approach to knowledge and to knowledge-making through research, together with the potential public-good value of social science knowledge. We have also acknowledged that because knowledge and research involves power and careers, there will be sceptics in universities about broadening the knowledge base and about what kind of research is both valued and rewarded, although as we have tried to make clear the distinctive scientific base of what universities do should be brought into a wider conversation, not dismantled. 'Others' need to become 'actors, active subjects', we need to 'know' our responsibilities in the world'. We think this applies to any research project where others outside the university are involved: indigenous people, migrants, working-class communities, unemployed youth, marginalised university students, and so on. As Sanchez and Escrigas (2014: 63) reiterate:

> The current polycentric production of knowledge must consider the universities, the new centres of expertise, as well as all the agents that can and want to be involved in hybrid, horizontal and cooperative spaces of reflection and action, with the purposes of co-creating knowledge in each situation. This reflective modernization is also a promotion for equity in the spread, use and creation of knowledge.

Thus, epistemic justice, epistemological equity, cognitive justice, public deliberation would all be criteria for doing and evaluating human development-oriented social inquiry, its process and methods and outcomes.

We are neither credulous nor utopian in this aspiration. Rather, as Hannah Arendt (1958: 177) said, in politics (and we say in the politics of research), we can expect the unexpected because human beings are, when acting freely and in concert with each other, 'able to perform what is infinitely improbable'. We can be socially responsible researchers, and do this in different but principled ways; we have suggested that participatory forms and attention generally to who participates, need to be considered seriously as one approach. Moreover, the dialogue that ensues is itself constitutive of development (Sen 2009). As we explained in Chapter 4, Sen (2009: 392) makes the case for the crucial importance of public reasoning and rational scrutiny to democratic life. He does not argue for complete agreements on every issue, but rather for reasoned scrutiny and for better reasoning. It is then up to us as a community of researchers to think through how his broadly framed emphasis on public reasoning and open impartiality would work in our specific situation, and a context of higher education's contributions to equity, justice and democratic life. Moreover, such participatory dialogue about research, about knowledge and about theories, is a way to name the world and in naming it, to change it (Freire 1972).

What also matters is how, or if, we bridge the inequity gap between developed and developing countries to foster genuine North–South and South–South cooperation to promote the exchange of resources, innovative ideas and experiences, while allowing for collective reflection and co-production of knowledge regarding innovation, relevance and responsibility (GUNI 2014). We would also need to problematise the gaps between universities in developed countries and those primarily in developing countries in order to foster genuine collaboration, rather than extractive funding and fieldwork relationships, which work in favour of careers, knowledge ownership and publication in and by universities from the North (as we mentioned in Chapter 1). Such unequal relationships will also not be consistent with human development and richly collaborative research partnerships.

References

Alcoff, L. 2002. 'Does the public intellectual have intellectual integrity?' *Metaphilosophy* 33(5): 521–34.

Appadurai, A. 2006. 'The right to research', *Globalisation, Societies and Education* 4(2): 167–77.

Arendt, H. 1958. *The Human Condition.* Chicago: University of Chicago Press.

Barr, J. 1999. *Liberating Knowledge.* Leicester: NIACE.

Bourdieu, P. 1998. *Acts of Resistance.* (Translated by Richard Nice). Oxford: Polity Press.

Brewer, J. 2013. *The Public Value of the Social Sciences.* London: Bloomsbury.

Burawoy, M. 2005. 'Response: public sociology: populist fad or path to renewal?' *British Journal of Sociology* 56(3): 417–32.

Calhoun, C. 2007. *Social Science for Public Knowledge.* Brooklyn: Social Science Research Council.

Dei, G. J. S. 2008. 'Indigenous knowledge studies and the next generation: pedagogical possibilities for anti-colonial education', *Australian Journal of Indigenous Education* 37(Suppl.): 5–13.

De Sousa Santos, B. 2006. *The Rise of the Global Left: The World Social Forum and Beyond*. London: Zed Books.

De Sousa Santos, B. 2009. 'A non-occidentalist West? Learned ignorance and ecology of knowledge', *Theory, Culture & Society* 26(7–8): 103–25.

De Sousa Santos, B. 2014. *Epistemologies of the South: Justice Against Epistemicide*. London: Paradigm.

Favish, J. 2015. 'Research and engagement'. Briefing paper prepared for the second national Higher Education Transformation Summit, Durban, South Africa, 15–17 October 2015.

Freire, P. 1972. *The Pedagogy of the Oppressed*. New York: Herder and Herder.

Freire, P. 1997. *Pedagogy of the Heart*. New York: Continuum.

Fricker, M. 2007. *Epistemic Injustice: Power and the ethics of knowing*. Oxford: Oxford University Press.

Gaventa, J. and F. Bivens 2014. 'Knowledge democracy, cognitive justice and the role of universities'. In *Higher Education in the World 5: Knowledge, Engagement and Higher Education Contributing to Social Change*, edited by Global University Network for Innovation, pp. 69–73.

Gibbons, M. 1997. 'What kind of university? Research and teaching in the 21st century'. Beanland lecture, Victoria University of Technology. [Accessed 16 July 2015]. www.uws.edu.au/__data/.../Gibbons_What_Kind_of_University.pdf

GUNI. 2014. *Higher Education in the World 5*. Houndmills: Palgrave MacMillan.

Hall, B. 1977. 'Participatory research: expanding the base of analysis', *International Development Review/Focus*: 23–8.

Hall, M. 2007. 'Poverty, inequality and the university: poorest of the poor'. Paper presented to Institute for the Humanities, University of Michigan, February.

Hall, M. 2009. 'New knowledge and the university', *Anthropology Southern Africa* 32(1&2): 69–76.

Kamanzi, B. 2014–2015. 'Decolonising social responsiveness in the university', *University of Cape Town Social Responsiveness Report 2014–2015*. Cape Town: University of Cape Town.

López-Fogués, A., A. Boni, V. Edgell and H. Graham. 2015. Young people voices: the use of participatory video in Quart de Poblet, Valencia; 11 case study outcomes on the regional case studies. SOCIETY Project, pp. 99–125. [Accessed 29 September 2015]. www.society-youth.eu/publications/wp5/141-wp5-11-case-studies.

Marginson, S. 2006. 'Putting "public" back into the public university', *Thesis Eleven* 84: 44–59.

Mdlalose, B. 2015. 'Who produces this "rigorous knowledge"?' *Mail and Guardian*, 24 July.

Nowotny, H., P. Scott and M. Gibbons. 2003. 'Mode 2 revisited: the new production of knowledge', *Minerva* 41: 179–194.

Perry, W. G. 1970. *Forms of Intellectual and Ethical Development in the College Years: A Scheme*. New York: Holt, Rinehart, and Winston.

Salais, R. 2009. 'Deliberative Democracy and its Informational Basis: What Lesson From the Capability Approach?' SASE Conference Panel on Social Rights and Capabilities, Paris, 16–18 July.

Sanchez, J. G. and C. Escrigas. 2014. 'The Challenges of knowledge in a knowledge democracy'. In *Higher Education in the World 5*, edited by GUNI, 60–5. Houndmills: Palgrave Macmillan.

Sen, A. 2009. *The Idea of Justice*. London: Allen Lane.

Smith, T. 2012. *Decolonizing Methodologies*. 2nd edition. London: Zed Books.

Stiglitz, J. E. 2003. 'Knowledge as a global public good'. In *Global Public Goods: International Cooperation in the 21st Century*, edited by I. Kaul, I. Grunberg and M. Stern. Oxford: Oxford University Press.

UNESCO. 2009 *World Conference on Higher Education: Final Report*. Paris: UNESCO

Walker, M. and M. McLean. 2013. *Professional Education, Capabilities and Contributions to the Public Good: The Role of Universities in Promoting Human Development*. London: Routledge.

7 Democratising research
Expanding capabilities through participatory action research

In the previous chapters, we have made the case for a university that promotes the public good through its teaching and research activities. We have also examined what kind of knowledge needs to be fostered for this purpose and have argued for the importance of 'cognitive justice' (De Sousa Santos 2006) that recognises and values epistemological diversity in making knowledge. Cognitive justice could deepen democracy, as De Sousa Santos points out. If there is a way of conducting research that is aligned with these principles of cognitive justice, we think it is Participatory Action Research (PAR). We do not suggest that all research activity in universities should use PAR or that this is the only way towards cognitive justice. As we noted in Chapter 6, universities are likely to be involved in a mix of basic, applied and 'blue skies' research, and will have more or less PAR projects and a greater or lesser degree of public or citizen participation. However, we do suggest that, whatever the research activity or methodology, the aims and principles outlined – especially those in Chapter 6, and the human development paradigm that informs the whole book – should be taken into account in informing what is researched, who does the research and who potentially benefits; even if this may not be immediate or direct. The point is to have a principled awareness of research beneficiaries and to have, as Alkire and Ritchie (2008) argue, 'ideas waiting in the wings' for a different kind of university. For this chapter, we want a focus on PAR to explore its potential as a knowledge-generating process, but also as a way to generate some shared principles or ideas that could be common to all research activity that is concerned with advancing human development and the public-good function of the university. Moreover, our particular interest is in social science research (including education) and it is primarily to social scientists that we address our arguments in outlining the case for PAR.

However, this way of conducting research is not straightforward, as we have found in our own work, and as we also explored in Chapter 6. If we agree with Cahill and Torre (2007) that PAR researchers who are serious about social change must think through how they provoke action through research that engages, that frames social issues theoretically, that 'nudges' those in power, that contributes to social justice campaigns, and that motivates people to change both the way they think and how they act in the world, the challenges for PAR researchers are considerable. How, in a democratic way, can we develop research action that is engaging for participants and, at the same time, reframe knowledge that could motivate wider audiences to change their way of thinking and acting? The intrinsic political understanding of PAR and the diversity of actors engaged make this way of conducting research challenging.

We now make the case why PAR is relevant for universities today and its alignment with the vision of the university for the public-good we explored in Chapter 2. We then outline the main characteristics of PAR and, subsequently, explore the relations between PAR and participatory approaches of human development and the capability approach. We develop our own theoretical framework to analyse and inform PAR processes from a human development and capability perspective. We have named it the 'participatory research capability cube' due to its tridimensional perspective: (1) the expansion of the capabilities and agency of co-researchers; (2) the characteristics of the knowledge produced; (3) the democratic processes that PAR could enable during and beyond the research process. We then apply this framework to understand a PAR process in Spain in 2014. We have selected this example because it combines research and teaching and demonstrates an innovative approach to PAR methods based on participatory digital technologies. Also, different participants from all across Europe took part in this case study of an interesting multicultural exchange. Our aim is not to conduct an exhaustive evaluation of the research process; rather, we want to explore the different potentialities that this understanding of PAR could bring.

PAR and universities

Putting PAR into practice in a university environment represents a challenge, taking into account the current tendencies of universities that push research and teaching in different directions. Levin and Greenwood (2011) in analysing those tendencies consider how PAR offers a different understanding of research and teaching aligned with what we have called a 'public-good university' (see Chapter 2). They argue that many university-based social scientists lack a clear understanding of the context in which knowledge is generated and communicated. Many factors contribute to this, as they point out: disciplinary specialisation, isolation, a university management system that prioritises 'excellent' research measured by publication in highly ranked journals and that takes strategic decisions possibly with limited involvement of the academic community and external stakeholders, while favouring the interests of more 'traditional' players (see Chapter 5 for an example of university policy that illustrates this). Levin and Greenwood make the case for the crucial role PAR could play to challenge this kind of situation. They name it 'the balancing act' which is a:

> radical and transformative vision of the future of social science and of universities because it creates new points of encounters as everyone involved moves away from their former positions and institutional bunkers, taking on new theoretical, methodological and institutional positions.
>
> (Levin and Greenwood 2011: 31)

PAR is founded on a *multidisciplinary perspective* of co-generation of knowledge, which includes not only different disciplines but also local and contextual knowledge. PAR also considers *methodological diversity* and challenges the traditional division between qualitative and quantitative methods, which has proved unhelpful in understanding more complex and multidimensional problems. PAR is *inclusive* and creates mutual learning opportunities between universities and non-academic stakeholders without reducing expectations of theoretical and methodological rigour. PAR is also able to integrate and foreground the importance of *social science teaching*. In an environment where teaching is less valued than research, PAR could be viewed as a learning opportunity 'built on real-life problems where theory and methods are challenged and also used to broaden understanding' (Levin and Greenwood 2011: 28).

An emancipatory and democratic vision of PAR

Orlando Fals Borda, a Colombian sociologist, was the first person to use the term 'participatory action research' in the late 1970s (Hall 2005). Fals Borda and many of his colleagues in Colombia and elsewhere in Latin America had made the decision to use their intellectual skills and connections to strengthen political movements associated with revolution and democracy at that time (Hall 2005). An additional important influence for PAR was Paulo Freire and his understanding of the research process. In his *Pedagogy of the Oppressed* (1970, 2005), Freire proposed investigating 'generative themes', which are relevant for people's lives:

> To investigate the generative theme is to investigate people's thinking about reality and people's action upon reality, which is their praxis. For precisely this reason, the methodology proposed requires that the investigators and the people (who would normally be considered objects of that investigation) should act as co-investigators.
>
> (Freire 1970: 106)

The methodology of *conscientização* (similar but more political than problematisation) is crucial to co-research these generative themes and 'introduces or begins to introduce women and men to a critical form of thinking about their world' (Freire 1970, 2005: 104). Paulo Freire's central message is that one can *know* only to the extent that one 'problematizes the natural, cultural and historical reality in which both the individual and the collective are immersed' (Vandekinderen and Roose 2014: 9). Freire, Fals Borda and other Southern thinkers have been influential in developing an emancipatory rather than a domesticated understanding of PAR. Starting from these traditions, we can highlight the dimensions that characterise an emancipatory and democratic understanding of PAR.

First, PAR involves *action*. PAR aims to alter the initial situation of the group, organisation, or community in the direction of a more self-managing, liberated, and sustainable state (Greenwood and Levin 2007). What is defined as a liberated state varies from one practitioner to another. For example, Reason and Bradbury (2008: 4) propose the pursuit of 'practical solutions to issues of pressing concern to people, and more generally the flourishing of individual persons and their communities' as a goal of PAR. For others, PAR could be aligned with revolutionary praxis. However, we agree with Greenwood and Levin (2007) that, by and large, PAR practitioners are democratic reformers rather than revolutionaries.

Second, PAR involves *research* (building knowledge, theories, models, methods, analysis).

What this research tradition provides is a shared commitment to fundamentally disrupt conventional hierarchies of knowledge production: who decides on the questions to ask, how to ask them, and how to theorise the world (Pratt *et al.* 2007).

Third, PAR means *participation*, placing a strong value on democracy and control over one's own life situation. PAR often involves trained social researchers who serve as facilitators and teachers of members of local communities or organisations. Because these people work together to establish the PAR agenda, generate the knowledge necessary to transform the situation, and put the results to work, PAR is a participatory process in which everyone involved takes some responsibility, and in which all are co-learners (Greenwood and Levin 2007).

Nevertheless, without diminishing the transformative potential of the participatory production of knowledge, Gaventa and Cornwall (2008) refer to critiques made of PAR and propose a way to overcome them. These criticisms include the view that PAR entails the danger of perceiving knowledge that comes from the community or from 'the people' as good per se, without knowing if this knowledge obscures differences inside groups, whether it may have been built on a false consensus, or if it reinforces local power dynamics. The solution, they argue, comes from the intrinsic nature of PAR, which has the power to create a different kind of knowledge built through cycles of reflection and action. Participants should find spaces for self-critical investigation and analysis of their own reality, in order to gain more authentic knowledge as a basis for action and responsibility of others. 'By involving people in gathering information, knowledge production itself may become a form of mobilization, new solutions and actions are identified, tested and tried again' (Gaventa and Cornwall 2008: 75–6).

Thus, the fourth dimension of PAR is this *cyclical component* (cycles of analysis-reflection and action), which is another essential element of the approach for its potential in generating emancipatory knowledge and because it can generate powerful learning for participants. As Somekh (2006) stresses, PAR involves powerful personal-professional learning for the participant-researchers about the impact of their own assumptions and practices. Gaventa and Cornwall (2008) named this learning component *awareness building*, which is fostered among the participants through self-critical investigation and analysis of their own reality. They argue that the combination of the co-production of different areas of knowledge through cycles of reflection and action, with processes of critical reflection and learning, makes PAR an empowering methodology.

The capability approach and participatory research practices

PAR and participatory approaches to capabilities formation share similar characteristics, highlighted by Alkire (2002), who argues that both approaches pay attention to the inclusiveness of the process, and the importance of obtaining outcomes that people value, while also empowering participants. However, both participatory approaches and capabilities have distinct features that can reinforce understanding of PAR. As we have discussed in Chapter 3, participation discourses provide an interesting contribution to the capability approach, offering an expanded idea of citizen's participation and deepening democratic practices for a deeper engagement of citizens in public policies. As we will see, this is a relevant subject for our analysis of PAR. Another essential contribution is the power analysis they introduce for scrutinising participatory practices. We have seen a practical example of how an understanding of power (using Gaventa's power cube, 2006a) has been helpful in analysing the local implementation of a higher education policy at the local level (see Chapter 5). The analysis of power is essential for PAR, as we have seen in the previous section. Taking into account not only 'visible' power dynamics that occur among the participants, but also manifestations of the 'invisible' power, which shapes the psychological and ideological approach of people to problems (Gaventa 2006a), is paramount for understanding participatory dynamics. If Gaventa's invisible power is rooted in our imagination, beliefs and assumptions, the experience of participatory approaches demonstrates how creating conditions of freedom and equality for a democratic deliberative process is not only a question of developing cognitive and communicative abilities or overcoming social or economic difficulties, but also of incorporating critical and reflective practices that enable people to question beliefs and previous assumptions to remove tacitly imposed restrictions (Frediani *et al.* 2015).

Biggeri and Ferrannini (2014) illustrate the marriage of capability ideas with a multiplicity of methods and instruments for project planning and evaluation, especially from the participatory research repertoire. One of the methods they outline is the opportunity-gap matrix that provides an analysis of a current situation, identifying capability dimensions and various determinants of conversion factors. Fernández-Baldor *et al.* (2014) show how the use of participatory methods to analyse the impacts of technological inputs, such as the energy delivered through four electrification projects in Peruvian rural communities, differ between men and women. So human diversity is stressed in the approach by an explicit focus on personal and socio-environmental factors that affect the conversion of resources into functionings, and on the social, institutional, and environmental contexts that affect the conversion factors and the capability set directly (Frediani *et al.* 2014).

Alex Frediani (2015) has developed a comprehensive framework to link capability with participatory methods in action-learning processes. He has called this *participatory capabilities*, and defines it as:

> people's choices, abilities and opportunities to engage in a process of participation that is driven by a goal of deepening democratic practices as well as individual/collective critical awareness. Participation through such perspective is recognised as both a means and an end.
>
> (Frediani 2015: 10)

'Choices' are the available strategies people have at their disposal to expand their well-being aspirations. 'Abilities' refer to the set of skills and capacities individuals and groups have access to which would mediate the achievement of a particular dimension of well-being. Meanwhile, 'opportunities' are the structural elements conditioning the availability and use of abilities and choices. A capability analysis would require a dynamic assessment of the relationship between choices, abilities and opportunities to achieve well-being outcomes (Frediani and Hansen 2015). They argue that participatory practices need a preliminary stage for the discussion of values. This stage of unpacking values is crucial to generate the collaborative learning process, and to re-framing the diagnosis of the problem. Additionally, the capability approach proposes reasoned deliberation as an explicit and valuable method for evaluating and making policy (see Chapter 4). Finally, such collective discussion can also facilitate the resolution of conflicts; understanding about the nature of disagreements can be a starting point in finding spaces of agreement.

The last contribution we want to mention comes from Vandekinderen and Roose (2014), who propose a common framework for participative research in youth policies in the SOCIETY project (see Chapter 6), inspired by the capability approach. Their first proposal is that participative research can deepen and broaden the informational basis of judgement for social policy. As we have discussed previously (see Chapters 5 and 6), the information that is included and excluded matters when designing and evaluating policy (Sen 2009). Thus, PAR could contribute to an 'alternative' information basis, by giving voice to invisible actors, privileging a situated appraisal of living conditions, identity constructions, and opportunities for meaningful participation, in socially unequally structured settings (Vandekinderen and Roose 2014). Participatory research can contribute to knowledge constructed through deliberation: 'it organizes and weighs, it creates the facts and thus provides an incentive, in certain configurations, to reformulate the issues and choose other ways to [address] the problems' (Salais 2009: 26).

A capability and human development framework proposal for interpreting PAR in higher education

Based on our emancipatory and democratic understanding of PAR, which is oriented to social justice goals, we have highlighted the transformative potential of a kind of knowledge co-created through cycles of action and reflection and the importance of the *awareness-building* component to promote self-critical investigation and analysis of their own reality among participants. We have also pointed out that reasoned deliberation among participants is a way to construct knowledge that can be relevant for the informational basis to design and evaluate policies. Moreover, we have highlighted other relevant elements of the capability approach that can be useful for PAR processes: the abilities, choices and opportunities spaces, or the relevance of personal and social conversion factors as elements that can explain differences among human beings in those three spaces of abilities, choices and opportunities.

With all these insights in mind, we propose a framework to understand PAR processes in higher education. We have named this the 'participatory capability research cube' (PARC) taking inspiration from Frediani's (2015) and Gaventa's (2006a) work. We imagine the three axes of PARC being the: (1) participatory axis; (2) knowledge axis; and (3) public deliberation axis, as depicted in Figure 7.1.

The *participation axis* encompasses the expansion of capabilities and agency among the participants directly involved in the PAR during the participatory process, in other words, all the co-researchers. Identifying which abilities, capabilities and agency have been expanded could be another cycle in the PAR process. As we have pointed out previously, questions related to power among participants should also be considered in the expansion of capabilities and agency. A draft list of capabilities that have specifically been thought out for higher education domains could be useful

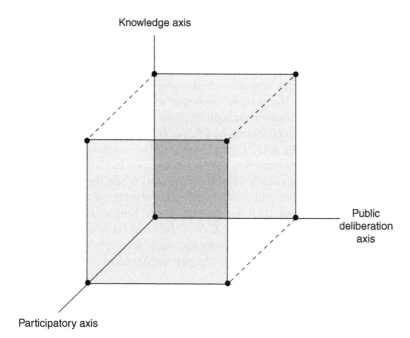

Figure 7.1 The Participatory Capability Research Cube (PARC) framework.

to kick-start the discussion; Walker's (2006) or Wilson-Strydom's (2015) lists are two interesting contributions. Nussbaum's (2006) three capabilities for democratic citizenship, or the attributes of global citizenship (Boni *et al.* 2013) could also be used as normative frameworks to analyse the specific dimension of participation. Whatever frame is used, two capabilities appear fundamental in the participation axis of PARC in higher education: one is the awareness capability that includes being able to carry out self-critical investigation and analysis of our own reality, for example of gender inequality. The second is the capacity to aspire (Appadurai 2004), which encompasses the capability to envision a desired future and a way to achieve it, at least in part, through research processes (Frediani 2015); for example aspiring to a more gender-fair university.

The *knowledge axis* considers the transformative characteristics of experiential, practical and propositional knowledge. We assume that, in order to be transformative, this knowledge has to be aligned with some of the following characteristics: a concern with human development values (participation, equity, sustainability, diversity, human security, etc.); a multidimensional and plural vision of well-being; an understanding of the interdependencies between the local and the global, between micro- and macro-politics; a consideration of the structural conditions that hinder the expansions of capabilities and an historical analysis of these conditions.

As with the *participation axis*, a power analysis should be undertaken. In the knowledge production dimension, it is important that excluded voices, or voices with fewer opportunities to be heard, be included in the knowledge base.

The last axis of our PARC framework is *public deliberation*. Here, the main question is: what kind of public deliberation spaces is it possible to open up during and after the research process? Public deliberation is one of the core ideas of the human development and capability approach and we have seen how our understanding of PAR is fully aligned with it. Thus, we can expect that during PAR several deliberative moments can occur between the participants. However, beyond what can happen during the process (insofar as we can clearly bound where and when the PAR ends), can we expect influence beyond it? Can PAR contribute to a new social justice-oriented policy? Can PAR influence a more human development-friendly vision on a particular subject? Can it shift institutional and organisational changes towards more democratic and accountable forms of organisation? Can it contribute to a deeper engagement of citizens in democracy building?

Habermas (1989) refers to the public sphere, a communicative space open to reasoned arguments and contending values (Marginson 2011). However, assuming that this communicative space is essential, we would like to aspire to a more transformative impact of PAR. The debate on the deepening democracy issue presented by Gaventa (2006b) could be useful to illustrate what we have in mind. Gaventa argues that the critical challenge for democracies nowadays is how to deepen their inclusiveness and substance, especially in terms of how citizens engage within democratic spaces to create more just and equitable states and societies. In Gaventa's view, democracy may be seen as constantly contested and under construction; the issue is not replicating one version of democracy, as a standard set of institutions and practices, but to construct and deepen democracies, which may work differently in different places, and to find the most effective entry points for doing so, based on the local contexts. At the same time, while recognising the diversity of forms of democracy, such diversity does not preclude more universal commitment to the core values of democracy as highlighted by Sen (1999). Under this perspective, a relevant contribution of a PAR process can be to facilitate the deliberative entry points Gaventa refers to, both in local and global spheres.

The idea of presenting a three-dimensional image is to highlight how knowledge, participation and deliberation are all necessary, multidimensional, and interactive. A genuinely participatory process creates spaces for public deliberation and makes the knowledge created more transformative; relevant knowledge co-created through PAR opens up spaces for democratic deliberation that can go beyond the timeline of a particular participatory research process. If we consider that the goal of a PAR is to enhance public deliberation, it can be influential in the way we want to disseminate the knowledge created and, consequently, can shape our participatory design. We will see how these interactions occur in practice in the following empirical example.

Using participatory digital technologies: a PAR teaching and research experience

The aim of this section is to describe and analyse a PAR process that took place in Castellon, Spain, in June 2014. During a Summer School of 14 days, 30 students from seven different European Master's programmes focused on the development aid field, were asked to capture powerful narratives of a neighbourhood named 'San Lorenzo' and produce short videos, which were shown in a public screening at the end of the process. We have chosen this experience because, although the core of the PAR lasts only ten days, we tried to combine research and teaching in a participatory way. Moreover, human development was a source of inspiration, both at the theoretical and practical level, and there was a range of actors from different parts of Europe, who intervened in the project in different ways to make the exchange of knowledge and experience very valuable. In the following section, we will give an outline of the context and describe the main players involved; then we explain briefly the participatory digital methodology we used and, finally, we analyse what happened during the project using our PARC framework. We will base our analysis on three main sources: the first is a participative evaluation conducted by an external organisation (INCYDE 2014). They were commissioned to look at the project from the outside to give us insights on how it worked and how it could be improved. They interviewed participants and conducted participant observations. Second, we analysed the content of the videos produced during the project (which are available at: http://globcons.uji.es/projects/global_id); third, Alejandra Boni was directly involved as a teacher and co-researcher. Her own reflections on the project form part of the analysis.[1]

The context

San Lorenzo is a neighbourhood located to the west of the city of Castellon, in Spain, with the highest levels of unemployment and marginalisation in the city. Within its boundaries, there are historically conflicting spatial issues that reinforce social divisions in the area. The first inhabitants of San Lorenzo arrived during the 1960s as migrant workers from different parts of Spain. They built their own houses, planned basic sanitation and mobility infrastructure, and built social spaces, such as the church and the school. In the mid-1980s, six blocks of social housing flats were built under a new programme implemented by the IVVSA (Valencia Housing Institute). They were aimed at housing very low- or non-income gypsy families being relocated from slums elsewhere. This process generated a dramatic divide in the area, the lack of consultation on behalf of the housing institute in San Lorenzo left residents with no other option than to accept the incomers who, as gypsies, were seen as being difficult to integrate and were regarded as 'dangerous' and 'uneducated'. In general, they were viewed as people who did not have the same ideals and status as the first wave of residents from the 1960s.

Gypsies and *Payos* – a word used by the gypsy community to describe people who do not belong to their culture – live in disagreement. Social spaces are divided and used by specific groups who have become dominant in those spaces. Because of this, in recent years, the local government of Castellon and local NGOs have channelled resources into funding programmes that seek to promote dialogue and improve communication between the divided communities. The programmes have been implemented by social workers who, as a result of the length of the programmes, have virtually become residents of the neighbourhood.

The activities developed in San Lorenzo range from teaching new skills to marginalised women and engaging with the elderly, to teaching alternative skills for youth empowerment and organising cultural and sporting events. This ongoing engagement led to the creation of *La Taula*, a representative structure that facilitates coordination among the various initiatives and aims to improve dialogue between local residents and government actors. However, the context has become particularly complex in the face of the Spanish economic crisis, combined with a housing crisis that increases threats of privatisation of social housing stock. This has meant, on the one hand, local residents constantly facing economic uncertainty and, on the other, the local government trying to reduce costs, leading to cuts to social projects.

The local university, which has collaborated in the neighbourhood for more than 15 years, has developed collaborative work with *La Taula* and conducted various research projects with students at the Master's and PhD level. One of the most relevant projects, which started in 1999, is named *Pisos Solidarios* ('Supportive Flats') and consists of providing university students with subsidised accommodation in San Lorenzo. Students pay only a small sum of money (currently €120) and in return do 4 hours a week of social work within the neighbourhood.

Another important project in the neighbourhood were the gardening courses, taught in the *Centre de Formació Ocupacional* and managed by the Catholic NGO, *Caritas Diocesana*. Currently, there are 16 youths and students of various nationalities and ethnic backgrounds involved in the project. Apart from gardening, the students learn social skills and basic competences for work. As we will see in the next section, these students played an active role during the Summer School.

The participants

As we mentioned earlier, this project was a combined teaching and research initiative. The main co-researchers were the 30 students from the seven Master's programmes related to the development and international cooperation field from the University of Pavia in Italy, University of Bath and University College London in the UK, University of Ven din Timisoara in Romania, and the University of Valencia, the Technical University of Valencia and the local University Jaume I of Castellon, all in Spain. Three academics acted as facilitators, giving support for the participatory methodologies and bringing theoretical insights on the human development approach in order to better understand the community and build the video narratives. Other lecturers were also involved in explaining theoretical contents, while local lecturers from the U. Jaume I organised contact with the local associations and were in charge of the practicalities of the Summer School, although none of them played a role as active facilitators of the process. For them, the use of English was one of the main barriers to more active involvement.

The third wave of main participants was the group of practitioners working in San Lorenzo. Two of them were especially engaged in the process and played an active role by facilitating all the research fieldwork and being involved in discussions with the students: one was the head of the Municipal Social Services in San Lorenzo and the other was the teacher of the gardening courses. She was able to involve her 16 youths and students during the Summer School: they showed the neighbourhood to the group of international students and visited the local university – some of them even performed there. Although these youngsters cannot be considered co-researchers, the interaction they had with the international students was valued as a really positive impact of the PAR.

Aims

The main aims of the Summer School were to capture powerful local narratives that could help re-imagine the future of the neighbourhood while strengthening the local identity and values of the diverse residents. Also, the narratives aim to illustrate how these values are being constructed through local practices aimed at improving the quality of life locally. Apart from that, for the main participants described in the previous section, this PAR process had specific goals, some explicit and some implicit. For the students, the Summer School aimed to familiarise them with the human development approach as a theoretical framework to understand and analyse PAR processes in real context; to acquire skills to use participatory digital technologies; and to be able to apply them in a real social context, putting into practice and developing skills and attitudes for teamwork in an interdisciplinary and multicultural context. For the practitioners, although the goals were just as explicit, the Summer School wanted to facilitate discussions and reflections on their own work in the neighbourhood and to explore a different way of collaborating with the University. For the group of three facilitators, this project was an opportunity to expand their understanding of human development and participatory digital technologies in a real multicultural and multidisciplinary context, as well as to acquire practical knowledge about the context of the research to try to give insights to the group of practitioners.

The methodology

The methodology chosen was Participatory Video (PV), which has been largely used as a tool and a process with the objective to empower communities through sharing stories and making videos depicting people's own realities, challenges and aspirations for the future (White 2003). PV can be considered as one of the many manifestations of the relationship between media and development (Scott 2014) but also as a tool under the umbrella of PAR methodology. In the context of this Summer School, we used a research-led approach to this practice, where students (researchers) aimed to gather and collect all the information, working closely with local residents and actors, and subsequently analysed this information, processed it and generated significant visual outputs that could contribute to practices and initiatives supporting social change in San Lorenzo. Figure 7.2

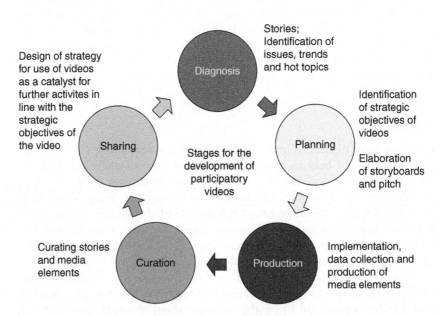

Figure 7.2 Stages for the development of participatory videos (source: Millan and Frediani 2014).

outlines the main stages through which PV evolved throughout the Summer School, from the early diagnosis stage to the final one of sharing and disseminating.

Entry points

Participants were divided into five groups; each of them had a different entry point for engagement with the residents of San Lorenzo. These entry points were used for guidance in the process of identifying stories that had the potential of being elaborated into powerful narratives for the videos, although groups were invited to remain open and flexible with their entry points in case more relevant issues were identified during the diagnosis stage of the workshop. The first group focused on the aspirations and challenges associated with housing in the neighbourhood of San Lorenzo. The *Pisos Solidarios* (Supportive Flats) programme was a visible entry point for this group. The second group engaged with public spaces in the neighbourhood and analysed their potential to bring about social inclusion and improve the quality of life in San Lorenzo. The vocational courses on gardening were the entry point. The third group focused on the livelihood opportunities and aspirations of local residents, paying special attention to how gender relations shaped livelihood opportunities and aspirations. The entry point for this group was *La Llar*, an initiative that aims to run a series of capacity-building workshops in San Lorenzo, focused on improving income-generation opportunities but also bringing about gender empowerment. The fourth group focused on education to try to capture the aspirations of young people towards education and the challenges they face in pursuing these aspirations. The entry point was an ongoing project on *absentismo* (scholar absenteeism) targeting young people. The fifth group focused on the elderly population. In San Lorenzo, there has been a series of activities to support the 'active third age', a potential entry point for the group.

There were two key cross-cutting issues, inspired by the human development approach that every group was asked to keep in mind during their research and production of PV. One was social *diversity* and its purpose was to pay attention to particular diversity issues associated with their theme, reflecting on how issues of class, age, ethnicity and abilities intersect with each other to condition residents' abilities and opportunities for a better quality of life. The second cross-cutting issue was to reveal the *aspirations* associated with the future of the neighbourhood, as well as the capacities and challenges to make them happen. These reflections on aspirations aimed to contribute towards the definition of principles that could be used to advance the communities' interests with other actors (i.e. municipality, NGOs, etc.).

The process

To give a practical example of how the Summer School proceeded in practice, the first five days were dedicated to an explanation of the main elements of human development and the PV methodology. At the same time, different techniques of diagnosis were applied to develop an in-depth idea of the neighbourhood and the specific themes of the five entry points: walks through the neighbourhood led by the group of students from the gardening courses, mapping, interviews with associations belonging to *La Taula*, etc. The 6th and 7th day were devoted to the planning stage, with the elaboration of storyboards and presentations of the video narratives. These proposals were also presented to the practitioners of San Lorenzo, with two aims: to improve and enhance the narrative and to pay attention to sensitive issues that may not have been properly understood.

The video production stage took place between days 8 and 11 (see Figures 7.3 and 7.4). Following the storyboard, with the help of the facilitators, the students recorded the voices and images of the local community.

As the previous stage ended, the curation phase started, although this was not a linear process and it so happened that participants realised that new footage was needed. In the Summer School the curation stage took three days and, before the final presentation, a preliminary version of

Figure 7.3 Example of the production stage (source: INCYDE 2014).

Figure 7.4 Example of the production stage (source: INCYDE 2014).

videos was presented to the local practitioners to get their comments and feedback. Finally, on day 13, we reached the dissemination stage with a public presentation of the five videos in the social centre at San Lorenzo. Finally, the last day was dedicated to the evaluation of the process.

Applying PARC framework

We now analyse the Summer School using our PARC framework. First, we will discuss what capabilities have been enhanced through the participatory process, considering the three main groups of co-researchers: international students, three facilitators and local practitioners. We will use some capabilities highlighted by Walker (2006) as a starting point to illustrate what happened during the process. Second, we make a more detailed analysis of the knowledge produced and evaluate to what extent it resonates with the main elements that make knowledge transformative. Third, we focus specifically on the moments of public deliberation that were regarded by the participants as especially empowering. The analysis of each axis interacts with the others; in participatory moments new knowledge was built and there were relevant moments of public deliberation. Moreover, the knowledge produced includes reference to the process and public deliberation moments. We will conclude with some considerations on this PAR process, the usefulness of our framework, and generally reflect on PAR as a methodological approach to bring human development and capability values to teaching and research.

The participatory axis

Expansion of capabilities among students

'Being able to gain knowledge of a chosen subject – disciplinary and/or professional – its form, academic enquiry and standards'. This describes one the elements of the 'knowledge and imagination capability' according to Walker (2006: 128), which was undoubtedly the capability that was most expanded among all the participants through the process. Starting with the group of international students, they explained that they gained a new understanding of what participation means in practice and the barriers to a participatory process: the importance of having a good knowledge of the context in which PAR is going to take place and having time to develop relations with the local community, were two important aspects mentioned. One of the biggest constraints of the Summer School was the limited time the students had: 'everything was too compressed and this was a barrier to understanding the context and the power dynamics at stake and to developing a different relationship with local people'. Some of the students even perceived themselves as 'landing' in San Lorenzo for a social experiment.

It is particularly interesting to confront the vision of the most critical students with perceptions of some inhabitants of San Lorenzo, who experienced their participation in a very positive way: they enjoyed being the main characters in the videos, being able to tell their story, and to convey their vision of San Lorenzo. Some local women felt more recognised and, in general, the local people interviewed acknowledged the importance of the spaces of public discussion created through the process. There was also a general agreement on valuing the attitudes of respect and responsibility of the international students toward the community. We do not have more information to explain these different perceptions further, and can only speculate about the negative perceptions of some students: too much self-criticism, frustration with the process because they expected to conduct a more participatory video process and a feeling of stress as a consequence of a very tight timeframe.

Practical knowledge acquired on aspects of participation was the importance of having a good command of the local languages. For those able to communicate in Spanish and English it was satisfactory, but others said that they experienced barriers in following theoretical explanations in English, or in acting as a translator between the local community and the rest of the group. However, there were interesting reflections from some of the students saying that this situation could be usual in a development aid context, and that this was therefore significant learning for them.

Other interesting understandings of participation were linked with teaching and learning. The majority of the students appreciated the coherent way of teaching on the part of the lecturers (who were able to create a horizontal relationship with them and encouraged and facilitated team work, identifying tensions and mediating between the groups). Some lecturers followed a 'banking' way of lecturing and this was questioned by the students. However, the students were also critical of their own capability to participate in groups and work with others to solve problems and tasks. This is part of the 'social relations and social network' capability described by Walker (2006: 128) and, for some of the students, the experience of doing PV was a way to enhance this capability because roles are defined from the beginning and this allowed smooth interactions. For others, power dynamics inside groups were barriers to good teamwork, as was the language or the excessive focus on the product (the final video), which can be an obstacle for the participatory process. Open attitudes, flexibility and inclusive leadership were seen as the ways to overcome these challenges.

Three more capabilities, not on Walker's list, were developed among the students. The first one was the 'capability to reflect and improve their understanding of their role as practitioners in the development field' (Walker 2006: 128). The Summer School had been perceived as a smaller-scale experience of what students could experience in a real context: time constraints, power dynamics, language barriers, difficulties in team work, poor diagnosis, etc. The second capability was 'to be able to express their own ideas in a different language' (Walker 2006: 128). How to work with video in participatory research led the group of students to rethink how to express ideas and concepts in a creative way, and to try to find powerful and positive narratives while being respectful of San Lorenzo's inhabitants. However, they acknowledged difficulties due to their lack of command of the audio-visual language.

Expansion of capabilities among facilitators and practitioners

Other main actors at the Summer Schools were the three lecturers who acted as facilitators of the process. All of them valued the experience, even though they acknowledge that it was really demanding. One of the most relevant capabilities developed was 'to be able to work with others to form good groups for collaborative and participatory learning' (Walker 2006: 128) which was fostered through the interaction between the three of them and with the local practitioners and the local community, while the process throughout paid attention to creating participatory and inclusive spaces for the local actors. The lecturers also shared a positive understanding of PV as a methodology that enables collaborative and participatory learning. As one said, 'PV offers an affordable technology that is appealing for people and opens communication possibilities at a more global scale'. They valued

PV for its potential to integrate many people at different stages of the process: the students experimented and enhanced their creativity using PV; the local practitioners gave their opinion through the process and the local community transmitted their stories and points of view. However, the lecturers acknowledge that, for some students, technology could be a barrier that blocked their learning process.

Another key capability developed was 'to gain new knowledge on several topics relevant for their own professional practice' (Walker 2006: 128). Some examples are: a new understanding of the relationships between human development and participatory methods and digital technologies; knowledge of the reality of the gypsy community and the importance of deconstructing stigmas; understanding the links between the local and the global that digital technologies can open and how theoretical knowledge can be informed by practice, and vice versa.

From the local practitioners side, there was a positive evaluation of the Summer School. They acknowledged an enhancement of their capability to 'participate in a group for learning, working with others to solve problems and tasks and form effective or good groups for collaborative and participatory learning' (Walker 2006: 128), especially in their interactions with the group of students and the facilitators. They learned another more participative way of interacting with university actors. Also, the use of video was perceived positively because it is respectful of the messages people wanted to transmit.

One capability they consider to have been enhanced among the community was 'being able to have respect for oneself and for and from others, being treated with dignity, not being diminished or devalued because of one's gender, social class, religion or race, valuing other languages, other religions and spiritual practices and human diversity' (Walker 2006: 128). In the interactions with the local community, and with the group of youths and students of gardening, the international students showed a positive and respectful attitude (i.e. not demonstrating sexist behaviour), while the locals had the opportunity to have their own space and to be in the spotlight. They consider that the Summer School was exceptional for the San Lorenzo's people as they had the opportunity to see other faces, languages and other realities that could enable openness, respect for the differences, commitment and a will to contribute to change.

Finally, we argue that the awareness capability (that includes being able to carry out self-critical investigation and analysis of our own reality) we indicated as one of the most relevant capabilities in a PAR process, was expanded among some of the local practitioners. One of them acknowledged that the PAR process made her re-think her narrative on gypsies and non-gypsies, questioning her own reflections on diversity. Practitioners recognised that this experience enabled an exchange of knowledge of a different kind, between people belonging to the university, the local community and themselves as practitioners. This understanding of the benefits of the Summer School was also shared by the three facilitators; for them there was also an expansion of the awareness capability in relation as their role as teachers, researchers and facilitators of PAR processes.

The knowledge axis

Five videos were produced during the Summer School: *Ven a vivir a mi barrio* ('Come to live in my neighbourhood'); *Sembrando* ('Sowing seeds'); *Aspiraciones de las mujeres* ('Women's aspirations'); *Aprendiendo del pasado* ('Learning from the past') and *Voces de juventud en San Lorenzo* ('Voices of the youth in San Lorenzo'). Even though each video has a different narrative and technical features, all of them are extremely respectful of the voices of local people (mainly gypsies) and of the practitioners and educators who worked in San Lorenzo. They try to offer a positive view of the neighbourhood, highlighting that San Lorenzo is a good place to live because of the friendship, collaboration, social relations, etc., counteracting the outside view, which sees San Lorenzo as a violent and dangerous place. Local conflicts that had occurred in the past were not shown in any of the videos so that a vision of unity and cohesion among the inhabitants of the neighbourhood was predominant. We think that this is the vision that the local community, including practitioners, wanted to offer to the world, with one exception being the director of the local school, who felt that divisions in the neighbourhood were still present.

Nonetheless, there is a feeling that social divisions are a thing of the past and now efforts should be focused on finding a job, which is one of the main concerns for the youth. There is a general concern among boys that they are discriminated against in their opportunity to get a job due to their ethnic identity; among girls, there is a will to get a university degree and, in some cases, an aspiration to escape from an early marriage and child bearing. Furthermore, the practitioners who worked in the neighbourhood expressed a general acknowledgement that education is a way to increase professional opportunities and gain self-esteem, confidence and discipline. The teacher in the gardening project proclaimed this view especially strongly. The young gypsies felt proud of their cultural identity and of their ability to play, dance and sing, however, the words of the songs describe gypsies as drunk and violent people, which is, according to their complaints, the general image non-gypsies have of them: 'nobody is expecting anything from gypsies' said one of the main characters of one video.

We believe these videos include at least some features of transformative knowledge: first, because the voices most heard are those of people with less opportunity to speak up. There is also a multidimensional understanding of what quality of life means for young people in San Lorenzo. Probably some voices are missing, as well as a more critical approach to structural constrains that limit the opportunities of youth, while the historical perspective has not really been tackled.

Public deliberation axis

As we have seen, the participatory process created spaces where different arguments were contrasted and discussed. The teaching moments between the international students and the facilitators were useful for reflecting on human development in practice; the assemblies and the collective interviews with the practitioners and the local community produced interesting exchanges with the university group on the needs and aspirations of the local people; the interviews conducted for the videos were also a fruitful interaction, as well as many other informal moments that happened during the process. However, one of the most important moments of the Summer School was not the reasoned deliberation, but the symbolic power of the public screening, which was particularly compelling. As one of the practitioners said, for the first time in their lives some members of the gypsy community attended a public event in a non-gypsy space. And, what is more important, through the videos, their voices were being listened to by local policy-makers and students and scholars from around the world. This moment was also important for the practitioners who, after working in San Lorenzo for many years, obtained public acknowledgement of what they have being doing. In a very emotive way, one of them commented:

> It was a dream. I've been working in San Lorenzo for more than twenty years ... what San Lorenzo was at that time ... remembering those images and seeing San Lorenzo now.... I was really happy to see my students and neighborhood participate ... really exciting to see this with so many people from outside ... it gives you life and energy ... we miss you.

However, despite this positive appreciation of the Summer School, we need to be critical of one of the aspects concerning public deliberation. Apart from the videos, policy and practical recommendations from evidence collected in the Summer School, and endorsed by the universities participating in the project, could have been helpful for opening spaces of discussion with the local authorities. That was the commitment the Summer School made but, unfortunately, more than a year later, nothing has been implemented. This is, in our opinion, a missed opportunity to open new spaces of public deliberation towards democratic practices, in the way that Gaventa (2006a) outlines. What we have learnt from our experience is that a long-standing commitment to local actors is essential, even though we also understand that this may not always be possible. Of course this may not be enough either, as many factors can be influential in changing policy, but it is a crucial ingredient towards social transformation.

Reflections on the use of PARC

The use of PARC allows us a more comprehensive understanding of the different processes that happen in a participatory research process and to value them as having the same importance. The expansion of capabilities and agency of co-researchers (although the former did not happen in our example) should be one of the goals of PAR. In PAR-processes using digital technologies it may be the case that the outcome (the edition of the video in our case) diverts attention from the participatory process that, apart from the expansion of capabilities and agency, could generate transformative knowledge. In our example, we have seen how the process generated experiential, practical and propositional knowledge among the participants, which is more transformative than the videos could capture. The videos were able to present the voices of the community and of the local practitioners, which is important. However, if we analyse the knowledge produced through the participatory process, we find a more transformative knowledge: new understandings of participation, reflections on the links between theory and practice, limits and potentialities of digital technologies to bring about change, etc.

We do not want to say that videos cannot capture transformative knowledge. Our experience has limitations. It is almost impossible for the international students who made the videos, in such a short period of time, without previous knowledge of the neighbourhood, to try to capture transformative elements. Access to people to be interviewed was also restricted and was arranged through the local practitioners who had access mainly to groups who attended their projects (the gypsy community). Moreover, as we have discussed in the previous section, there was not enough time to develop more in-depth relations with the local community. Part of those constraints could be addressed by the planning of the Summer School, but others are inherent in a PAR such as this.

Applying PARC has allowed us to face another limitation of our experience. As we have discussed, apart from the public deliberation moments that were created through the participatory process (which were so valuable in terms of expanding capabilities and creating a transformative knowledge) we were unable to open new spaces for more democratic practices. The absence of a long standing commitment of the main co-researchers to the local practitioners, together with the fact that the main group of co-researchers were the international students with no particular need to change the situation of the local community, could explain the limitation of a PAR experience such as this, designed to be an academic activity and not primarily to bring about change for the local community.

Concluding thoughts

In this chapter we tried to show how PAR is a valuable approach to teaching and research in a democratic way, foregrounding important issues from a human development and capability perspective. We also tried to show some similarities and complementarities between PAR and the capability approach and have developed an original framework to analyse PAR processes. This framework revealed an interesting analysis in its application in a teaching and research experience conducted in Spain and based on participatory video methodologies. Its consideration of three dimensions (participation, knowledge and public deliberation) offers a different perspective to understand PAR experiences that can be complemented with other approaches sketched in this chapter (Frediani 2015; Gaventa and Cornwall 2008).

We find PAR to be coherent with the vision of a public-good university that we have argued for throughout the book. PAR could contribute to an 'alternative' information basis, by giving voice to invisible actors, privileging a situated appraisal of living conditions, identity constructions and opportunities for meaningful participation, in socially unequally structured settings. Additionally, in a university environment, PAR could contribute to a knowledge and critical thinking project in universities, with multidimensional goals for the academic community, and engagement with wider communities as a way to practice engaged scholarship and provide effective support for stakeholder actions, organisations and/or communities in their processes of self-determining social change.

Note

1 We also have contrasted our ideas with one of the members of the project core group, Gynna Millan, and with a colleague who is an expert on participatory methodologies, Maria J. Cascant. We are grateful to them both for their comments and suggestions.

References

Alkire, S. 2002. *Valuing Freedoms*. Oxford: Oxford University Press.

Alkire, S. and A. Ritchie. 2008. 'Winning ideas: lessons from free market economics', *Working Paper No 6*, Oxford: OPHI. [Accessed 25 June 2012]. www.ophi.org.uk/wp-content/uploads/OPHI-wp06.pdf.

Appadurai, A. 2004. 'The capacity to aspire: culture and the terms of recognition'. In *Culture and Public Action*, edited by V. Rao and M. Walton, 179–95. California: Stanford University Press.

Biggeri, M. and A. Ferrannini. 2014. *Sustainable Human Development 2014. A New Territorial and People-Centred Perspective*. London: Palgrave.

Boni, A, E. López and R. Barahona. 2013. 'Approaching quality of global education practices through action research. A non-governmental development organization–university collaborative experience', *International Journal of Development Education and Global Learning* 5(2): 31–46.

Cahill, C. and M. Torre. 2007. 'Beyond the journal article: representations, audience, and the presentation of participatory action research'. In *Connecting People, Participation and Place: Participatory Action Research Approaches and Methods*, edited by S. Kindon, R. Pain and M. Kesby, 196–206. London: Routledge.

De Sousa Santos, B. 2006. *The Rise of the Global Left: The World Social Forum and Beyond*. London: Zed Books.

Fernández-Baldor, A, A. Boni, P. Lillo and A. Hueso. 2014. 'Are technological projects reducing social inequalities and improving people's well-being? A capability approach analysis of renewable energy-based electrification projects in Cajamarca, Peru', *Journal of Human Development and Capabilities* 15(1): 13–27.

Frediani, A. A. 2015. 'Participatory capabilities in development practice'. *DPU Working Paper 178*. [Accessed 28 September 2015]. www.bartlett.ucl.ac.uk/dpu/latest/publications/dpu-working-papers/WP178.pdf.

Frediani, A. A., A. Boni and D. Gasper. 2014. 'Approaching development projects from a human development and capability perspective', *Journal of Human Development and Capabilities* 15(1): 1–12.

Frediani A. A. and J. Hansen. 2015. 'Introduction: The Capability Approach in development planning and urban design', *DPU Working Paper* Special Issue 3–10. [Accessed 27 September 2015]. www.bartlett.ucl.ac.uk/dpu/latest/publications/special-issues/capability-approach.

Frediani, A. A., J. Peris and A. Boni. 2015. 'Notions of empowerment and participation: the contribution of the Capability Approach'. In *The Capability Approach, Empowerment and Participation*, (forthcoming), edited by D. Clark, M. Biggeri and A. A. Frediani. Basingstoke: Palgrave.

Freire, P. 1970 and 2005. *Pedagogy of the Oppressed*, London: Continuum.

Gaventa, J. 2006a. 'Finding spaces for change. A power analysis', *IDS Bulletin* 37(6): 23–33.

Gaventa, J. 2006b. 'Triumph, deficit or contestation? Deepening the 'deepening democracy' debate', *IDS Working Paper* 264.

Gaventa, J. and A. Cornwall. 2008. 'Power and knowledge'. In *Sage Handbook of Action Research: Participative Inquiry and Practice*, 2nd edition, edited by P Reason and H. Bradbury, 71–81. London: Sage.

Greenwood, D. J. and M. Levin. 2007. *Introduction to AR: Social Research for Social Change*. Thousand Oaks, CA: Sage.

Habermas, J. 1989. *The Structural Transformation of the Public Sphere: An Inquiry into a Category of Bourgeois Society*. Translated by T. Burger, with the assistance of F. Lawrence. Cambridge, MA: The MIT Press.

Hall, B. 2005 'Reflections on participatory research from 1970–2005', *Convergence* 38(1): 5–24.

INCYDE. 2014. *Evaluación 'Global Identity through Human Development: Summer School on Participatory Research Video'*. Bilbao: INCYDE.

Levin, M. and D. Greenwood. 2011. 'Revitalizing universities by reinventing the social sciences. Bildung and Action Research'. In *The Sage Handbook of Qualitative Research*, edited by N. K. Denzin and Y. S. Lincoln, 27–42. London: Sage.

Marginson, S. 2011. 'Higher education and the public good', *Higher Education Quarterly* 65(4): 411–33.

Millan, G. F. and A. A. Frediani. 2014. *Terms of Reference of the Summer School.* Castellon: UJI.

Nussbaum, M. 2006. 'Education and democratic citizenship: capabilities and quality education', *Journal of Human Development* 7(3): 385–95.

Pratt, G. in collaboration with the Philippine Women Centre of BC and Ugnayan Kabataany Pilipino sa Canada/Filipino-Canadian Youth Alliance. 2007. [Accessed 27 September 2015]. https://participaction.wordpress.com/whatpar/defining-par/.

Reason, P. and H. Bradbury, eds. 2008. *Sage Handbook of Action Research: Participative Inquiry and Practice.* 2nd edition. London: Sage.

Salais, R. 2009. 'Deliberative democracy and its informational basis: what lesson from The Capability Approach?' SASE Conference Panel on Social Rights and Capabilities, Paris, 16–18 July.

Scott, M. 2014. *Media and Development.* London: Zed Books.

Sen, A. 1999. *Development as Freedom.* New York: Knopf.

Sen, A. 2009. *The Idea of Justice.* London: Allen Lane Penguin Books.

Somekh, B. 2006. *Action Research a Methodology for Change and Development.* Maidenhead and New York: Open University Press.

Wilson-Strydom, M. 2015. *University Access and Success. Capabilities, Diversity and Social Justice.* London: Routledge.

Vandekinderen, E. and R. Roose. 2014. *Conceptual Guide for the Participative Research: A Common Framework for Participative Research in Local Youth Policy from a Capability Perspective.* SOCIETY Project. [Accessed 27 September 2015]. www.society-youth.eu/.

Walker, M. 2006. *Higher Education Pedagogies.* Berkshire: Society for Research into Higher Education and Open University Press.

White, S. A., ed. 2003. *Participatory Video: Images that Transform and Empower.* London: Sage.

8 Student learning opportunities and outcomes

In this chapter, we turn to the specific education function of the university and focus on student learning opportunities and outcomes to explore whether or how human development is operationalised in university spaces and diverse students' multidimensional capabilities expanded. Our primary concern in this chapter is with micro-data at the level of how students are doing and what they are experiencing, with what effect for their capability expansion. This is not obviously connected to global development; however, the operationalisation of human development principles and capabilities shows how the micro-space of learning conditions is shaped by wider circumstances of inequalities in society but not over-determined by the macro-global political economy. We see this most sharply in the formation of the new student movement in South Africa (Naidoo 2015) and the call to 'decolonise' the university and transform curriculum and pedagogy.

We draw also on other theories, as we have done in earlier chapters. Indeed, we have found that in examining processes of transforming education that there are other more powerful 'activist' languages offered, for example, by a humanising critical pedagogy (Freire 1972) in which we learn our reality in order to transform it, and learn this through a 'co-intentional' education of reflection, action and construction of knowledge (Freire 1972: 56). It is not that the language of human development and capabilities is not a call action (here Sen's 1999 instrumental freedoms are strong); it is that we do not find human development called on when activist student movements, such as that in South Africa, struggle for a different kind of university. Students turn to political language, in South Africa drawing on among others Paulo Freire (1972), Franz Fanon (1965) and the black consciousness activist Steve Biko (1987). As Forst (2014) reminded us in Chapter 4, power is the first question of justice so that being recognised as a political being is essential for freedoms. On the other hand, as we noted in Chapter 4, Sen (1999: 38) does outline five instrumental freedoms including two which we could describe as directly political and which we repeat here: (1) political freedoms, e.g. democracy, the freedom to scrutinise and criticise authorities, to enjoy a free press and multi-party elections; (2) transparency guarantees, e.g. the ability to trust others and to know that the information one receives is clear and honestly disclosed. This could add to or be part of the more explicitly political language we see the South African students drawing on in their education struggles. At any rate, we think, a political strengthening of human development is required, in that political struggles may be needed to move a university and a university system in a fairer and more just direction (and this point would hold also for the previous chapters). While Nussbaum (2013) argues rightly for the cultivation of 'political' emotions that support justice as fundamental to a democratic society, the South African students claim and do the politics of emotions and affect in practice and make clear the collective political struggle needed to transform political emotions into educational and social change. Freire (1972) was always clear that education is inherently political. In the sphere of education processes, as in development (Chapter 3) and research (Chapters 6 and 7), we therefore need other discourses to connect the implicit dots as it were, including in policy analysis as the example of the power cube in Chapter 5 shows, and advance democratic shifts away from inequalities towards greater political and personal freedoms.

In this, we acknowledge the real tensions between higher education as a space to reproduce injustices and a space to imagine and make a decent society. Bernstein reminds us powerfully that:

> Education is central to the knowledge base of society, groups and individuals. Yet, education, also, like health is a public institution, central to the production and reproduction of distributive injustices. Biases in the form of content, access and opportunities of education have consequences not only for the economic; these biases can reach down to drain the very springs of affirmation, motivation and imagination. In this way such biases can become, and often are, an economic and cultural threat to democracy.
>
> (Bernstein 2000: xix)

According to Bernstein (2001: 23), the university is a place where, 'consciousness, dispositions and desire are shaped and distributed through norms of communication which relay and legitimate a distribution of power and cultural categories'. Bourdieu and Passeron (1977) have pointed out how university education is middle-class in its assumptions and pedagogical practices, tacitly requiring students to work with and through middle-class language codes and the socially constituted dispositions and codes which students are assumed to already have when they enter the university. Not only are the codes middle-class, this is not made explicit or taught in a systematic way. The exclusionary experience of university appears as the 'natural order' of things and working class or disadvantaged students, Bourdieu argues, accept their subordinate positioning as a response to the 'logics' of power; both middle- and working-class students come to form particular identities as more or less successful learners. In this way, universities reproduce inequalities and privilege as a kind of a 'racism of intelligence' (Bourdieu 1994: 177). Thus, learning, and by association, teaching, curriculum and pedagogy involves the formation of identities and the way one learns to see oneself in relation to one's peers and lecturers and to the world; Bernstein and Bourdieu warn how this may be disabling and constraining while appearing to be 'fair'. The challenge is that learning processes are suffused with the exercise of power and control, and knowledge is mediated and acquired through often invisible processes in which not all are accorded equal power, recognition and esteem.

On the other hand, we also find evidence of transformatory learning, which can happen in different spaces both shaped by the formal curriculum and also outside it. Take as an example of a formal learning space, that of Paula (Walker 2008: 43), at the time a history student at a UK university, who exemplifies, we think, opportunities and outcomes enabled by a critical curriculum and quality teaching: knowledge and critical thinking, reflexive practical reasoning about her life and goals and the aspiration to make a difference in society. She described how learning history had fostered her deeper understanding of people. Learning to undertake a close and critical reading enabled her to 'take texts beyond face value' and she now recognised how language works in forming critical reasoning, 'just the certain words you use to describe something, certain metaphors you draw, the way how you write about something can tell you something about yourself'. She comes from 'a very white middle-class background', from an English town where there is no racial tension because of its homogeneity, 'so it's very easy to make assumptions or hold views that you never have to test because you are only surrounded by sort of the same kind of people as you'. While debating had been strongly encouraged at her school, 'everyone held the same opinion'. However, her history curriculum and the lecturer's way of teaching had enabled her to 'reassess my prejudices because your prejudices characterize the way you deal with the world and deal with people, read things, interpret things, things like that and having to look at that and be challenged'. History was contributing to her 'quality of life', both because she enjoyed it and found it intrinsically interesting; she felt history had broadened her opinions and made her 'think outside my small world', making her more aware of the way she understands society, so that she now thinks that this knowledge and understanding 'is something that could, you know, if you choose the right [work], I don't know, maybe make a difference'.

Despite its reproductive role, we thus understand higher education as intrinsically valuable and a potentially significant capability multiplier in the impact it can have on strengthening other freedoms. Education which expands capabilities and agency freedoms supports and advances other capabilities both for the individual but also of others in the contributions graduates can make in society. We try to capture the intersections and enablements and constraints of opportunity (capabilities), choice (agency, including obligations to others), and freedoms (well-being) in students' lives, and what difference education interventions can make. The education field as we understand it includes the context, the formal teaching and learning in courses and classes, extra-curricular opportunities, and social interactions inside and outside of classes. Learning is influenced by student diversity across dimensions of social class, gender, race, disability, age, nationality, and so on. It will also be influenced by public policy as we discussed in Chapter 5, in ways which contribute to or constrain development as freedom. We understand curriculum and pedagogy as conversion factors constituting the educational arrangements through which the capability for critical knowledge is acquired or denied, shaping learning opportunities and outcomes in deep and often lifelong ways.

We now turn to examples of how human development might work out in university spaces, focusing on challenges of curriculum, citizenship and (social) capital and refracted through valuable and worthwhile functionings that are observable, as well as how education arrangements can act to constrain well-being freedoms, agency and choices. In different ways, in all three cases curriculum and pedagogy are included, although the focus may be more or less direct. We now sketch some features that can make each issue helpful for seeing the difference a human development and capabilities lens can offer, and then consider the issue of values formation in and through education with some implications for selecting worthwhile education capabilities.

Curriculum: knowledge opportunities

Curriculum foregrounds knowledge, how it is selected and how it is mediated pedagogically and acquired by learners. Put simply, curriculum determines the selection of what counts as valid knowledge; curriculum questions relevant to a human development approach might include: (1) Are global North knowledge resources appropriate for Africa? (2) Should curricula respond to the demands of business and the marketplace for 'flexible', 'employable' graduates; or prepare critical thinkers? (3) Should curricula advance disciplinary knowledge or also foster interdisciplinarity? (4) Should a 'development aid' programme include humanities-based courses? There are many more questions we could ask. As Apple (1979) explains, educational institutions such as universities help control meaning by distributing culturally legitimate knowledge, and this is related to power relations in the larger political and economic arena, so that, Apple argues, economic power and control is interconnected with cultural power and control. Statements about what should be included in a curriculum exemplify what things powerful groups (government, pharmaceutical corporations, religious groups, etc.) in a society think students should learn and value, so that curriculum knowledge can entrench or transform power relations, identities and agents and inflect towards or away from 'epistemological transformation' (Shay 2011). Curriculum debates are thus cultural, social and political, turning on knowledge (what is worthwhile, what to put in, what to leave out, how to structure and sequence a programme, to whom it is distributed, who decides, etc.), and directly affects learning opportunities. Curriculum has wider consequences for how knowledge carried by individual graduates is distributed in society and has an instrumental role in making society, for example one which values the humanities or sees them as irrelevant to economic growth. Thus, a curriculum encapsulates value judgements about what sorts of knowledge are considered important: neoclassical economics or alternative theories; the ethical dimensions of biotechnology advances; understanding or ignoring poverty and inequality; the exposure to arts and science knowledge for all students; or which literatures are studied. As such, curriculum is a statement of intent, although there may be practical gaps between what is intended by those constructing the curriculum, implementing it in action, and what is actually learned by the students who experience the curriculum.

Rather crucially, a focus on curriculum change offers the possibility of more sustainable shifts than only a focus on teaching and learning where much rests on the individual teachers. In curriculum reform, we find a more powerful combination of curriculum structures (which are institutionally embedded and persist over time) and individual efforts aligned with these and evaluated against them. Thus, attention to curriculum as a university-wide project holds considerable – and sustainable – transformative potential in the direction of a public culture, which nurtures lively knowledge-based communities able to challenge injustice, corruption and power. This is significant for human well-being and social change.

To illustrate this more concretely, we draw on a student-led curriculum developed as an aspect of the 2015 new student movement in South Africa (see: https://en.wikipedia.org/wiki/Rhodes_Must_Fall), in which the idea of 'decolonisation' has become a rallying cry for those trying to undo the racist legacies of the past. Citing Ngugi wa Thiongo, Achille Mbembe (2015: 2) explains that decolonisation is an ongoing process of 'seeing ourselves clearly', 'emerging out of a state of either blindness or dazziness'. Decolonisation, he writes, is a struggle over what is to be taught, and about the terms under which we should be teaching. To this end, the Rhodes Must fall (RMF) student movement calls for a curriculum which critically centres Africa and the subaltern, treating African discourses as the point of departure through addressing not only content, but languages and methodologies of education and learning, and only examining western traditions in so far as they are relevant to their own African experiences. In the light of student activism, Mbembe (2015: 6) calls for a transformative shift:

In order to set our institutions firmly on the path of future knowledges, we need to reinvent a classroom without walls in which we are all co-learners; a university that is capable of convening various publics in new forms of assemblies that become points of convergence of and platforms for the redistribution of different kinds of knowledges.

In effect, he echoes our call in Chapters 6 and 7, one which applies across the global South and North but manifests especially starkly at this historical moment in South Africa.

Mbembe is responding to curriculum events in informal university learning space emerging from and shaped by student activism in South Africa. Naidoo (2015) writes more specifically about the curriculum and pedagogy practices of the RMF student movement at the University of Cape Town (UCT), pointing in particular to the three-week 'occupation' by the students of the main administration building renamed 'Azania House' by the students (Azania being the name used by the black Africans fighting the apartheid regime). Students embarked, she says, on an education programme that offered public evening seminar programmes, open to anyone willing to engage and 'think through a new way of fighting oppressive white supremacy, which remains largely intact in South Africa, and especially Cape Town'. She refers back to earlier black consciousness (Biko 1987) struggles in which students were encouraged by older activists who 'understood that you [students] had the kind of consciousness needed to lead the movement'. She calls on these former activists to acknowledge the importance of a student-led curriculum and pedagogy, and here we quote her fully in her pleas to former student activists to enable her [student] voice to be heard:

> show solidarity and engage from the vantage point of being willing to listen and learn rather than knowing better than them [students]; then you would be able to start seeing the amazingness of these young students – mostly undergraduates and honours students. They don't have all the answers as they grapple with competing oppressions and urgent issues. They are working with concepts like "intersectionality" that bring in to focus the multiple oppressions that occur in addition to the race/class lenses of the past. The movement and its public or popular education programme has created a space that has allowed for people with varying privileges and their corresponding blind spots, to be part of the conversation. This is radical dialogue ... [which includes] black female voices and black transsexual voices in the conversation.
>
> (Naidoo 2015: 4)

She compares these education struggles to earlier struggles of black consciousness activist in the 1960s and 1970s who were also:

responding bravely to a context that was untenable [apartheid oppression] and you therefore committed to creating a space to find your voice by centring black experience and black pain, and then building solidarity from there. I am seeing similar things happening at Azania House now. Young students thinking and acting beyond their years and in spite of their [middle] class aspiration. It was Biko himself who said that students are a 'wishy-washy group' until they find themselves in a context that wakes them up.... These students are playing a very serious role in redeveloping relevant philosophies and figuring out a decolonised consciousness ... to engage the question of what is a decolonised university and society.

(Naidoo 2015: 4)

The students, Naidoo says, are playing a serious role in redeveloping relevant philosophies and figuring out a decolonised consciousness, and a platform to engage the task of what is a decolonised university and society, in other words they are working to shape a new curriculum and pedagogical practice which refuses the practices of receiving, storing and filing of banking education and domination (Freire 1972) in favour of knowledge as inquiry with each other and with the world.

Another (unnamed) commentator describes the process of curriculum and education at Azania House:

Tuesday evening's gathering invited a number of black UCT faculty members to address students.... This was not a normal lecture though. The entire space was not only packed to the brim but lacked any hint of the traditional patriarchal classroom structure. There was no head of the room, no centre, no spatial hierarchy. The discussion spoke to the theme: what would a transformed university would look like? Lecturers, sitting amongst the crowd rather than in front of an old-fashioned seminar room, stood up and addressed the need to transform curricula, hire and promote more black, female and queer professors, and build a different kind of classroom based on co-learning. 'Students are not empty vessels', exclaimed one faculty speaker.... The most pointed response of the evening was by Adam Haupt, Associate Professor of Media Studies, who indicated that the occupation itself was the best example of educational transformation. Sitting through almost three hours of talks by teachers who acknowledged their presence as also a learning experience and students who demanded recognition of their ability to teach, I was inspired and also a bit jealous ... at no time during my [own university] education can I confidently say that the actual structure of the university classroom was challenged at all ... many people do not realise is that there is nothing more scholastic and empowering than what these students have created inside Azania House: an inclusive, transformative and democratic space were everyone's voice matters and no form of oppression is left unchallenged.... Let us hope it spreads further.... We could all use a real education.

(see: www.facebook.com/RhodesMustFall/posts/1560246894250803)

From a transformative perspective, for education to be 'a practice of freedom', Freire (1976) proposes that it have three features: learners should be active participants and co-constructors of knowledge, learning should be meaningful, and learning should be critical. These can be understood as significant well-being freedoms and agency freedoms so that students are acting in the world of the university. We see all these features in the curriculum and pedagogy developed by the students in Azania House. Freire (1972) is also helpful in challenging us to critique the deadening effect of oppressive 'banking education', power relations, and undemocratic practices, always with a view to change through action and reflection (*praxis*), as we see in the students pedagogical practice in Azania House.

A human development aligned formal curriculum and pedagogy would challenge us to recognise, engage and critique education practices which assume the homogenous middle-class student (probably also male and white), and knowledge practices which assume whose and which knowledge counts. A capabilities-friendly approach would critique not just educational hurdles to educational success and agency, but also how these barriers are shaped by social, economic and political obstacles to social justice and democracy, as the students make very clear by also connecting their efforts to wider poverty and inequality challenges and these back into the nature of the university. Their solidarity is striking and reminds us that learning is deeply social and requires inclusion, recognition, and participation. Having access to critical learning opportunities, critical voice, and critical knowledge resources emerge as crucial capabilities and functionings for student well-being and agency and for expanding the necessary space of political and cultural freedoms.

Citizenship: from local learning to global awareness

Turning now to curriculum, pedagogy and student learning in university education in Spain, we consider how expanding students' capabilities in a global world requires cosmopolitan citizenship and included in this, commitments to social change. We report on two initiatives developed at the Technical University of Valencia (UPV) in Spain, which have contributed to the creation and expansion of cosmopolitan citizenship (Boni *et al.* 2010, 2012, 2015). We discuss an example of curriculum constructed in a technical environment intended to be more reproductive than transformative, but even in such a context we can create interesting curriculum and pedagogical spaces. Moreover, we do not find the idea of cosmopolitanism explicitly in Freire's thinking discussed above but as presented here can enable a connection with transformation in both local and global realms. Nussbaum (1997) defines the cosmopolitan citizen as one who is engaged with the global community of human beings, and provides four reasons for choosing cosmopolitan citizenship as the basis for democratic education: (1) the possibility of learning more about ourselves; (2) the need to solve global problems through international cooperation; (3) the acknowledgement of moral obligations to the rest of the world; and (4) the ability to prepare a solid and coherent series of arguments based on the differences that we are prepared to defend. Sen (2006: 123) describes how we each have multiple identities, and it is here that he locates global affiliation:

> Why should women and men from one part of the world worry about the fact that people in other parts of the world are getting a raw deal if there is no sense of global belonging and no concern about global fairness? Global discontent, to which the protest gives voice ... can be seen as evidence of the existence of a sense of global identity and some concerns about global ethics.

More concretely, Delanty (2006) remarks that the development of a cosmopolitan identity emerges from the encounter between the local and the global through an analytical and reflective thinking process. Second, he proposes that a cosmopolitan project can be carried out by individuals, associations, organisations, and so on, and that it may be conducted anywhere in the world, not only in the West. Finally, the third idea is to distinguish between types of cosmopolitanism. According to Delanty (2006), a true cosmopolitanism is oriented to change and social justice. We believe this nuance to be essential to distinguish between cosmopolitism and globalisation or transnationalism, often based on ethnocentric norms. The approach is rather different from the marketing by universities of something called 'global citizenship' intended to give students, mostly from the global North but generally from elite universities, a further advantage in employment and opportunities in a neo-liberal, international world.

The first education initiative in Valencia is a formal space in which a global citizenship curriculum has been implemented offering two elective courses, one on introductory issues regarding development and another on development aid projects. The goals and contents of the curriculum and the pedagogical approach seek to foster empowerment and agency. A focus is placed on developing skills and values in order to enable students to become members of a global community of equals. The teaching-learning process is oriented to meaningful and experiential learning, where students are encouraged to apply their own previous knowledge, experiences and insight to the topics of the course, such as a historical perspective, development theories, human and sustainable development, poverty, migration, globalisation, development aid and projects, NGOs, or the role of technology. Critical reflection and questioning are encouraged so that students explore new ways of thinking, which can lead them to change their previous attitudes and actions. To achieve this, the classroom dynamics are based on dialogue, discussion and cooperative work, with the aim of developing critical thinking, effective arguing, cooperation and conflict resolution, among others. Participation is a key feature of the teaching learning process and teachers from different parts of the global South and members from non-governmental organisations (NGOs) talk about their experiences. In this way, students are faced with previously unknown realities, thus fostering their critical skills. In addition, students can engage in short-term internships in NGOs in Valencia and the surrounding area. The second experience refers to an informal space of student organisation called *Mueve* (roughly 'mover'), which emerged through informal gatherings among students with converging interests in the two courses. As a consequence, about 15 students in the Industrial Engineering Degree started a social movement at university devoted to promoting change at a local level.

Twelve interviews with students enabled an analysis as to whether both the courses on cooperation and development and the university group *Mueve* were appropriate spaces to encourage and develop a transforming global citizenship. The interviewees understood themselves to have many identities – Christian, worker, nationalist, woman, etc. However, 'cosmopolitan' identities were rarely mentioned, and those interviewees who did mention them belonged mainly to *Mueve*. Even in this case, we find it difficult to identify elements of a transforming cosmopolitism. An exception is S. who seems worried about the issue of equal rights for all and is outraged by inequality and the lack of respect for minorities. However, she then defines herself as a conformist, as she believes that 'things cannot be changed; that it is very difficult to face up to and try to change things and overcome the general inertia'. But she also recognises that her involvement in *Mueve* changed her perspective by showing her that things are gradually changing.

The interviewees in *Mueve* offered suggestive answers in relation to the tension between the local and the global sphere in the configuration of identity. The local offers support and a basis for the global aspect. Regarding this J. D. says:

> I am part of the world as I am part of my friends and my family ... but at the same time I feel "a citizen of the world". I firmly believe that I can live in another country.... Yes I consider it important to know where you come from and what your identity is and never lose sight of where you are going ... the place where you grew up and keep aware of the influences of the culture ... it is good not to give all this up ... when it has a positive influence on you, because it is important never to lose your origins, to use them as a basis for moving on.

Of the interviewees, only three both participated in *Mueve* and also took the courses. Two of them concluded that the courses provided a theoretical basis and knowledge and awakened sensitivities, whereas *Mueve* has provided a realistic dimension for opening up the possibility of changes. E. explained:

> The subjects [courses] have given me a framework to interpret the world, showing me the structural motives. They were also useful to structure what I already knew. They helped me to reflect and think about social justice.... *Mueve* had an inspirational spirit. It helped me to generate commitment and understand the changes.... The courses and *Mueve* played a complementing role. *Mueve* was more locally orientated, while the subjects had a global orientation. But we could say that they followed a logical evolution from local motives to global ones and from them to global justice. Both of them have provided me with an open mind and opened new horizons.

Focusing on the specific contribution made by each space, the interviewees involved in *Mueve* explained how the group had helped them to acquire the following abilities: working and organising themselves in groups to produce collective work; becoming aware and discovering the ability to do things and to be able to change; understanding the changes and generating a commitment; persevering and fulfilling obligations; promoting a different perspective on life; developing a range of problem-solving abilities and the capability to deal with stress; and, organising and managing ideas. The responses by the students who took the course pointed out a different set of abilities not acquired through life and group experiences but nevertheless valuable in the process of developing global citizenship: knowledge to understand the complexity of development; critical thinking; ability to participate actively and express a personal opinion; ability to listen, to be tolerant about different ideas and to be able to understand the reasons behind other's behaviour; and, awareness of the need to consider the context before taking action, particularly when facing situations that involve international cooperation.

In the final part of the interview, students were given a list of capabilities written on cards and were asked to organise them according to their relevance. The list was as follows: (1) critical thinking (the ability to reason in a logical and argumentative manner); (2) empathy (putting yourself in somebody else's shoes); (3) participation (at local, national and global level); (4) coexistence and intercultural respect; (5) reflexiveness; (6) curiosity. The cards most picked by the interviewees involved in *Mueve* were: participation, commitment, empathy and coexistence, and intercultural respect. A. says, confirming this:

> *Mueve* was a participation forum, a space to seek agreement and ideas, to produce them, to get answers, positive or not. It was never an introspective or philosophical activity.... Regarding commitment, *Mueve*

contributed to develop group responsibility .... The best proof of it, is that the group is still working. There was a real commitment to ideas.... As a working space, *Mueve* allows us to confirm that others do not always share our ideas, even in a relatively homogenous group. This allows you to identify your standpoint and to make an effort to understand the reasons behind others' ideas.... As an ideas forum we were convinced that cultural diversity added and did not subtract.

For those interviewees who took the elective courses, the most mentioned ability was critical thinking. J. comments that:

Nowadays when I read news in the papers or Internet that tries to give an excessively nice picture of certain issues, I know it is not like that. Of course, in this respect critical thinking has changed us, as you have provided us with information that allows us to say: No, it's not like that ... we did not do that before.

The rest of the cards were also valued positively but without reaching the level of consensus achieved among the students involved in *Mueve*. However, the importance of the courses in a technical context is recognised. For example, C. says:

The university should be a place to develop culturally and not only scientifically.... Here the teachers [in other courses] provide us with material but they are not particularly interested in checking whether we put it to good or bad use or indeed if we make any use of it at all.

In a similar vein, J. says in relation to the engineering curriculum:

It is important that not everything is economically orientated ... after all we are going to become professionals with a certain level of power in our hands to take important decisions ... this year I am becoming aware that most of this degree is economically orientated.... We are only exposed to different criteria in this [elective] subject.

Three new abilities were proposed by the interviewees. E. suggests *self-awareness* as an essential ability, adding a nuance to reflexiveness:

Being self-aware of the direction you want to take in life stops you from seeing yourself as a person who goes with the flow and changes you into an active agent. This awareness to be able to change or not is generated from critical thought and participation.

Another two interviewees, who were involved in *Mueve*, mentioned the following abilities promoted by this space. J. D. adds the *ability to surprise* and *respect*: 'The ability to surprise ... to give presents, not to buy them but to make them ... to be excited about doing something for others and to know that it will make them very happy'. And, 'respect ... avoid judging prematurely ... respect somebody else's decisions in their circumstances ... we have experienced personal conflicts and the group has always behaved in a respectful way'. D. C. emphasises initiative and lack of fear of change:

> If you are socially committed, you want to participate in society and you can identify your role in it; all of these generate an initiative.... Lack of fear of change or of challenge. At the beginning we had a strong pyramidal vision of the university organization so we convinced ourselves that a group of ants could do as much as a single person at the top of the pyramid.

This data allows us to venture some ideas regarding the potential of the university space for developing plural functionings for agency in the direction of a transforming cosmopolitan citizenship. *Mueve* appears as a space with great potential. The interviewees agreed that they acquired new abilities related to organisation and relationship skills (group work, problem-solving, structuring ideas). Moreover, it was a platform for generating opportunities for practical actions to bring about change, thus challenging the preconception that changes are almost impossible to achieve. On the other hand, the elective courses also appeared as a highly valued space by the interviewees, who emphasised the importance of such forums in a technical environment. Unlike *Mueve* which was more experiential, the courses work towards a more reflective and conceptual cosmopolitism and the provision of relevant knowledge to understand the complexity of development, develop critical thinking, inner thinking, and considering context before taking action.

Drawing also on evidence from previous research (Boni and Pérez-Foguet 2008), we believe that both the subjects and *Mueve* are good forums to promote an ethical global citizenship, beyond marketing and instrumental neo-liberal assumptions about 'adding value' to one's individual curriculum vitae. They are also complementary spaces, which can be useful and inspirational to promote a transforming cosmopolitan citizenship at university, with critical reflection and independent thought, access to political knowledge, and allowing students to consider different perspectives. The *Mueve* group and the development courses offered at UPV demonstrate what is possible, showing how a formal space to develop citizenship identities and an informal arena for activism and change unfolded.

A capabilities lens asks us to consider cosmopolitan or even global citizenship not as an attractive but rather shallow marketing tool to 'polish' one's CV to one's individual advantage, but as a space for well-being freedoms and for agency freedoms enabled through formal pedagogical approaches and informal organisational experiences which locate students in an expansive citizenship and which universities can enable formally and informally.

Capital: a focus on conversion factors and outcomes

Drawing on a research project on employability and inclusive development (McCowan 2015), we now focus on employability. The literature on this concept both in its reductionist and its more expansive interpretations has been comprehensively reviewed (Tomlinson 2012). Suffice to note the popularity of employability in universities has developed in the light of the connections claimed between economic growth and a highly skilled workforce, together with the rapid rise in the number of university students who will enter the labour market as graduates. We also differentiate between employment – actually getting a job – and employability – being equipped by one's university education with subject knowledge and other attributes to become employed if labour market opportunities are available or if conditions allow for the creation of self-employment. Thus, we do not assume that all the responsibility for graduate jobs lies with universities, rather we are concerned to understand what aspects of having economic and allied social opportunities universities can and should address. The capability approach allows us to ask questions beyond human capital about diversity, inequalities and human development in relation to employability and what universities do. If the opportunity to develop capabilities and valued functionings for employment is uneven among students, then we look to wider educational and social arrangements to understand what is unjust and needs to be changed to enable well-being in each student's life.

In the South African case study, which includes four diverse universities (Walker 2015), we have found that unequal amounts of social and cultural capital (Bourdieu 1977) enables or constrains student opportunities, and that this especially affects working class students. To take a concrete example of how social and cultural capital is formed in South Africa: an outstanding state school to which academics and high-status professionals send their children is the key feeder school for a leading university, and provides multiple opportunities for a wide range of school activities, enabling durable connections between students and parents. The school and the parents also have deep connections to the university, as well as knowledge of what school subjects to choose and how to apply successfully to an elite university. By contrast, in a poor [black] township school, even one which may be relatively functional, teaching is of variable quality, extra-mural activities are scarce, and the teachers may have either little knowledge or understanding of the process of preparing and applying for university, including access to funding for poor students. The students' families also will not have this knowledge, nor easy access to the internet for free online applications. Indeed the means-tested student financial aid scheme form is so complicated that negotiating it requires considerable skill. Such students will be shut out from valuable social and cultural capital now and hence in the future.

We found correlations across dimensions of social capital in each university case study that make it clear that a narrow interpretation of employability as human capital obscures advantage and overlooks marginalised students. In the research, factors affecting graduate employability can be (imperfectly) divided into three overlapping dimensions: personal, university, and external factors, pointing to the overlapping intersections of individual student biographies, what the university offers, and the influence of the labour market and public policies. Some students were better placed to choose their university and their course; some students need state loans in order to study at university; some students are advantaged by the reputation of their university among employers; some students are able to choose high employment–high earning fields of study and work; some students have access to internships and networks which open up interview opportunities; and some students know how to make better use of both the university careers office and extra-curricular opportunities. It is not clear from our data the extent to which this correlates to social class; it may be that even black middle-class students in post-apartheid South Africa find that opportunities for networks are more constrained. Nonetheless, we can be certain that working-class (largely black) students do not have access to social networks that will expand their economic opportunities. In short, a capability approach enables us to see that more choices and more opportunities are available for some students and at some universities than others; employability and individual choice-making does not operate under fair educational and social conditions.

In the research, it is evident that in an historically advantaged and stratified university system such as South Africa's, an elite university confers social capital, and thereby advantages the already advantaged. Neither the elite nor the non-elite university may be aware of this conferring of advantage, or have strategies to address social capital acquisition, while students are at university. Nonetheless, social capital, if not addressed, reinforces past inequalities of race and social class so that any education 'dividend' is unevenly distributed. Nor is this a challenge confined to South Africa. There is evidence from the UK (e.g. Greenbank 2009) that working-class students have less access to employability relevant social capital. While Piketty's (2014) study confirms the importance of investments in higher education and training, the benefits of higher education accrue most to those who access elite universities, who in turn tend to come from advantaged families. One academic captured the challenge facing universities and society well:

I think that people should be given the same chance. People shouldn't be judged for where [university] they come from or what they look like, because I think that that is one of the issues that generally makes people ... fear about their employability.... I think that [negative labelling] should be removed and people should be given the same chance.

(quoted in Walker 2015: 1)

While the research acknowledges that a university cannot do everything to get jobs for its students, it does argue that a university can do a great deal in terms of resources such as teaching and learning, ethos and values, actively encouraging and promoting extra-curricular participation, and filling in social capital 'gaps' to enhance the employability of individual students, even though the labour market and public policies might be constraining. While graduate employability is affected by a wide range of factors and stakeholders, the university still has a crucial role in enhancing employability and equipping students with knowledge, skills, values and confidence to identify and make the most of opportunities to build their careers. For example, knowing – and being confident – that a lower-level entry job can be leveraged to advance one's career, as opposed to thinking that only a high-entry position should be pursued (as many working-class students do). This requires fostering student agency and confidence to choose plural valued functionings from a wide capability set.

In the project we found a misalignment of theory and practice. While, overall, students valued knowledge as the most important graduate functioning, the data show a significant concern with the limited opportunities in both the curriculum and pedagogy to integrate and apply theory to practice and work experience. If this is not enabled by the university, it particularly affects those students from poorer backgrounds who lack the social capital to find vacation work in order to apply their knowledge in a work situation and be better placed for employment. The theory–practice misalignment then has inequity effects for students who do not have networks (family and friends) with potential employers. Asked about the implications of student background and social capital in enhancing a graduate's employability, one student captured the challenge succinctly:

If you are from a poorer background and probably black or previously disadvantaged, then the likelihood of you having strong contacts is unlikely. If you are from a wealthier white or advantaged background then it's ten times easier.... Just from the people I graduated with from high school, you can just tell that certain people are set from the get go. Irrespective of what they are studying, they always land on their feet. So you may be lucky and have a contact or two in a very influential position, it's not impossible, it does happen, but the likelihood isn't strong [if you are from a disadvantaged background].

(quoted in Walker 2015: 17)

Put simply, poorer families cannot provide as many opportunities as richer families and these differences influence who is more employable. As another student said, 'if someone sees your name and they know it, or they put in a good word for you, you're in with a chance' (quoted in Walker 2015: 16).

Being situated close to a range of employers also makes a significant difference, yet historically disadvantaged (that is black) universities were all deliberately located under apartheid laws in rural areas far from industry, service and finance sectors, compared with the historically advantaged University of the Witwatersrand (Wits) in the economic heartland of the Gauteng region. As a student careers officer at the rural university reflected:

> The university cannot be compared to a university like Witwatersrand in the urban area of Gauteng.... People from industries have easy access to students, unlike us here where, when you invite a company from Gauteng, they ask you about the cost of accommodation and travel. They ask you, "where is this University of Venda? How do we get there? If we fly, is there an airport?" Such factors limit our students' access to people in industries.
>
> (quoted in Walker 2015: 27)

It is then not enough to argue for the value of internships or work experience without attention also to who gets these opportunities and who is excluded. South African students are very aware of the status differences between universities and comment on how this affects their fair chances with employers. As one commented: 'The Wits name implies you are smart ... if you have a Wits degree then you are set' (quoted in Walker 2015: 18), while another said, 'I think a student from the University of the Free State would not have the same fair advantage' (quoted in Walker 2015: 18). This reputational effect can discount even courses of good quality at less prestigious universities. As one student commented:

> Universities are ranked and unfortunately [this university] is slightly at the bottom; so if a person is looking at my degree and the degree of someone who went to Wits, looking only at the status of the University, then obviously the person from Wits has an advantage over me.... [Yet] as for the content of our degree I honestly believe that in the faculty of agriculture we are very well off.
>
> (quoted in Walker 2015: 19)

Such assumptions reinforce past inequalities. It is fair to say that historically, disadvantaged universities (set-up for black students under apartheid) and their graduates are seen to be less employable and less attractive to employers. While students in the humanities and social science say they face challenges in access to internship opportunities, as well as access to decent employment, such students from the historically advantaged universities are still much more likely to find jobs, or to be able to afford a further qualification, such as law.

Field of study is also a source of personal and social capital, especially given that not all students are equally able to access high-status fields and high-status universities. Without mathematics and science passes at matriculation some fields will be closed to students, while for engineering, medicine and allied health professions, and law much higher admission scores are needed and this will usually correlate with type of school attended. According to the IRR (2015) some 50 per cent of the cohort who begin school will make it through to year 12 (matriculation) – in 2014, this was 549,203 students. Of this group, 225,458 students took maths as a subject; 50,365 obtained more than 50 per cent and only 16,491 obtained a grade of more than 70 per cent. We can assume that the bulk of these students will come from advantaged schools. Thus, field of study is not one of equal opportunity to choose. This unfairness is then compounded by some fields of study being more employable than others, the subject knowledge is in greater demand, and students and academics indicate that particular technical skills and subject fields are key in enhancing employment outcomes. However, prospects are not as good in all fields, as one law student said of her BA degree: 'I call this degree my useless but powerful degree.... I find it useless [for employment] but powerful in the knowledge that it has' (quoted in Walker 2015: 14).

Student support services aimed at enhancing the employability of graduates have been established across the four universities. Careers services include: career guidance offices with the task of linking students to potential employers, providing opportunities for internships or work placements, as well as training final-year students in job-seeking skills such as CV writing, interviewing and work etiquette. However, overall, there is a low level of participation in activities aimed at supporting and enhancing the employment of graduates after graduation. In most of the universities, the students in their 3rd year (in one university up to 90 per cent) did not know about the careers office. Universities also offer a wide range of extra-curricular activities (ECA): student representative councils, volunteering, sports, student associations, arts and culture activities, and so on. While these were more or less wide-ranging on the different campuses, they do exist everywhere. Where students do get involved in ECA, they clearly gain immensely. In interviews, students commented on the value of ECA, for example:

> Being part of the Construction Management Student Society was one of the best experiences I've had at varsity. Because I was president of the society it allowed me the opportunity to make so many contacts with the working world. I was chatting to people that are heads of

departments in some of the big five companies. I was on speaking terms with the head of a big company here in Port Elizabeth. So it does give you a lot of contacts and it also allows you the opportunity to organise events.... I was able to deal with different departments within the university, I had to speak to a lot of people and make sure that all my relevant information and details were up to scratch.... I had to organise quite a few events so there was a lot of event planning and coordination and working with different people, which is to me, all about learning.

(quoted in Walker 2015: 14)

Nonetheless, not all of the students participate, or realise the importance of participating in ECA for their career and personal development. Indeed, students from less advantaged universities may need to make more of whatever personal capital they have (Kupfer 2011) through taking up valuable and enriching extra-curricular opportunities, and yet seem least aware of how to do this, or why this is important for their futures.

On the other hand, the study also found some universities doing well in developing 'diversity capital', which could be converted into social capital in inclusive workplaces, and which certainly seems essential for living well in South Africa and for future of peace and reconciliation. Yet students seemed not to recognise how important this is for their futures or to be helped in understanding that this would be an advantage in the workplace. Many students valued the exposure through teaching methods to collaborative learning where students from different backgrounds in a still racially divided society can be brought together in classrooms. As one student explained: 'it exposes you to a person's life. You [tend to realise], this person is not that bad. Maybe I thought white people are like this, but this guy is different. So we've learned to appreciate other people' (quoted in Walker 2015: 14). Moreover, students in all three cases committed to making contributions to improve society, and are aware of the responsibility of the university to social development. In this way, university education as a conversion factor had positive citizenship outcomes. One lecturer in the study commented that 'the most important value that we try to develop is a student who is a responsible citizen and responsibility comes with understanding your role and what society expects of you.... To be educated is something much more than having a certificate in your folder' (quoted in Walker 2015: 14). We find the same concerns in the cases of curriculum and of citizenship.

What a human development and capabilities lens enables us to do in relation to this research, is to ask whether human development values inform the university education each students has access to and to ask, again, whose capabilities are being expanded, and whose agency freedoms are being advanced. It is clear that conversion factors of university reputation, field of study, and amounts of social capital are unevenly distributed and that this correlates to historical and current disadvantage by dimensions of race and social class; this is inequitable and needs to be addressed. The lens further shows that there is something universities can do by building the social capital of all students, by systematically challenging assumptions about university reputation, and by at least engaging in dialogue about why some fields of study seem more valuable to employers than others (especially as these in turn correlate to advantage). In this way 'employability' would be neither reductionist, nor technical, nor assume that the university must do everything, but also not assume that there is nothing universities can do.

Concluding thoughts

In the three cases above, it is clear that the university is a space of direct and indirect values formation as to who one wants to be, what one wants to do and what one will contribute to society and the public good. We observe that the university could be a place where transformative knowledge is fostered, as in the Spanish example and Paula's account in the UK, and where issues of power can be brought to the surface and confronted (as in Rhodes Must Fall). From a learning perspective, the university could be a place to put into practice transformative pedagogies, even while we remain aware of the reproduction role of university in the employability example, and how social conversion factors and personal conversion factors can be powerful even beyond graduation.

As Vaughan and Walker (2012) explicate, education is a moral enterprise and hence inescapably normative in that it seeks to change us for the better, developing our powers of reasoning, criticality and reflection to form our judgements about activities and lives that are worthwhile. R. S. Peters (1966) explains that it would not make sense to say something like, 'my child has been educated but is in no way changed for the better'. Values determine and shape an individual's capability set – we prioritise and then choose functionings on the basis of what we have reason to *value*. University is then a potential place to expand this capacity to reason critically and reflexively about our values, in dialogue with knowledge and with other students and lecturers. This valuation process, as the examples above suggest, is not open-ended. We do not see university education as a space for the formation of any values, but rather values consistent with the capability approach's concern with equity, empowerment, well-being freedoms and achievements, and the values implicit in Sen's (2009) emphasis on public reasoning. Education takes a view on what is worthwhile and does not see all forms of education as equally valuable. The point is that to count as *education* as opposed to training or indoctrination, processes and outcomes ought to make each person's life 'richer with the opportunity of reflective choice', for a life 'of genuine choices with serious options' (Sen 1999: 41), 'enhancing the ability of people to help themselves and to influence the world' (Sen 1999: 18). While we cannot and should not want to prescribe the choice of functionings students make beyond university, their university education ought at least to foster the capabilities that make it possible for them to act differently and decently on the future and to renew the common good. Arendt (1993: 196) explains the challenge: 'The problem is simply to educate in such a way that a setting right [of the world] remains actually possible, even though of course it can never be assured'.

Valuation thus raises the question of which capabilities should be selected as dimensions of human development in university education. On what basis would we select or reject these or any others? In Chapter 4, we noted Nussbaum's (2000) approach of drafting a central list of ten human capabilities for a life worthy of human dignity. We further noted that Sen's (2009) process of public discussion is crucial in formulating capability lists. For education, we note that an open-ended approach may not work so well if it comes up against erroneous common sense understandings of disadvantage, for example, people might not understand that gender equity is not settled even though the overall majority of undergraduates are now women, or staff and students might not have sufficient awareness of the lives of students with disabilities, or well-off students of the lives of students who do not get enough to eat. Or there could be problems arising from persistent racial discrimination at our universities such that we want a functioning to be developed that addresses this. While Sen has an 'unshakeable' faith in human reasoning to decide on what is good (Deneulin and McGregor 2010: 513), this may not work well in the face of power inequalities in education, and the obtuseness of the advantaged.

What we have suggested elsewhere (Walker 2006) are workable agreements around at least some educationally worthwhile higher education capabilities as a yardstick to judge whether things are more or less just and fair and educationally effective, together with attention to actual functionings while students are at university. In education functionings are significant for three reasons, we think: (1) because we need information on whether students are able to exercise their well-being freedoms (not just the capability for voice but having a voice); (2) because functionings deepen the capability to make it more secure for the future; and (3) because, as Sen (1999: 131) points out, 'the valuation of actual functionings is one way of assessing how a person values the options she has', given that we cannot observe capabilities in some cases – and we think education is such a case (Walker 2006) – it might be better to concentrate on both capabilities and functionings to understand the well-being freedoms students have, how they use them to achieve or underwrite agency freedoms, realise their values in practice, and are empowered.

To conclude, we have examined in previous chapters how universities do not stand apart from inequalities at multiple levels; they have the potential to reproduce or reduce such inequalities and could work towards transformative ends, including equitable educational opportunities and achievements for human development. We understand the power of neo-liberal discourse in contemporary higher education; as we have discussed in previous chapters, this discourse crowds out other ways of imagining and understanding education and society, so that we lose the language to talk about education in a different way. Wendy Brown (2011: 39) talks about 'conversions' in the direction of academic human capital, which 'interpellate[s] the subject only as speck of human capital, making incoherent the idea of an engaged citizen, and educated public, or education for public life'. But in this book and this chapter, we are trying to reach for an aspirational narrative which is radical; we see this most dramatically, but not only, in the educational work of the student movement in South Africa.

The chapter assumes that curriculum and pedagogy (teaching and learning) both formally and informally at universities is a crucial space for making narratives and pictures of students' formation as ethical graduates, equipped with knowledge, skills and values to contribute to more equal societies. In this reading, universities would become more rather than less just spaces, and education narratives would use human development language. In this chapter, we explored how this might happen and what might get in the way using a capabilities and human development lens to demonstrate the possibilities and the challenges of university education which should inflect to the public good, which develops human development values, and which seeks to expand the capabilities which students value, in the process challenging disadvantage in many forms. While neo-liberal times may undoubtedly make life hard in universities, there are spaces to practise education differently as this chapter shows, and to be agents as students and lecturers, rather than onlookers to policy. Learning is powerful and endlessly possible; as Maxine Greene writes, it is about, 'I am who I am not yet' (quoted in William Pinar 1998: 1). The challenge is to expand learning paces and to foreground human development and capabilities as the conceptual, policy and practical lens for analysing, developing and evaluating university education as both educational and political and hence requiring the expansion of Sen's (1999) political freedom in multiple actions towards transformative change.

References

Apple, M. W. 1979. *Ideology and Curriculum*. London: Routledge.

Arendt, H. 1993. 'The crisis in education Arendt'. In *Between Past and Future: Eight Exercises in Political Thought*, edited by H. Arendt, 173–96. New York: The Viking Press.

Bernstein, B. 2000. *Pedagogy, Symbolic Control and Identity. Theory, Research, Critique*. Oxford: Rowman & Littlefield Publishers.

Bernstein, B. 2001. 'Symbolic control: issues of empirical description of agencies and agents', *International Journal of Social Research Methodology* 4(1): 21–33.

Biko, S. 1987. *I Write What I Like*. Harcourt: Heinemann.

Boni, A. and A. Pérez-Foguet. 2008. 'Introducing development education in technical universities: successful experiences in Spain'. *European Journal of Engineering Education* 33(3): 343–54.

Boni, A., J. Peris, A. Hueso, J. M. Rodilla and J. F. Lozano. 2010. 'Capabilities for a cosmopolitan citizenship in higher education: the experience of the technical University of Valencia', *Procedia-Social and Behavioral Sciences* 9: 1998–2002.

Boni, A., J. Peris, J. M. Rodilla and A. Hueso. 2012. 'Cómo cultivar la ciudadanía cosmopolita en la educación superior. El caso de la Universidad Politécnica de Valencia'. *REIFOP* 15(2): 131–9.

Boni, A., J. J. Sastre and C. Calabuig. 2015. 'Educating engineers for the public good through internships in developing countries: an exploration based on a case study at the Universitat Politècnica de València'. *Science and Engineers Ethics*, forthcoming.

Bourdieu, P. 1977. *Outline of a Theory of Practice*. Cambridge: Cambridge University Press.

Bourdieu, P. and J.-C. Passeron. 1977. *Reproduction in Education, Society and Culture*. 2nd edition. London: Sage.

Bourdieu, P. 1994. *Sociology in Question*. London: Sage.

Brown, W. 2011. 'The end of educated democracy', *Representations* 116: 19–41.

Delanty, G. 2006. 'The cosmopolitan imagination: critical cosmopolitanism and social theory', *British Journal of Sociology* 57(1): 25–47.

Deneulin, S. and J. A. McGregor. 2010. 'The capability approach and the politics of a social conception of wellbeing', *European Journal of Social Theory* 13(4): 501–19.

Fanon, F. 1965. *The Wretched of the Earth*. (Translated by Constance Farrington). New York: Grove Press.

Forst, R. 2014. *Justice, Democracy and the Right to Justification*. London: Bloomsbury.

Freire, P. 1972. *The Pedagogy of the Oppressed*. New York: Herder and Herder.

Freire, P. 1976. *Education: The Practice of Freedom*. 1st edition. New York: Writers and Readers Publishing.

Greenbank, P. 2009. 'An examination of the role of values in working-class students' career decision-making', *Journal of Further and Higher Education* 33(1): 33–44.

IRR (Institute of Race Relations). 2015. *Fast Facts*. Issue 282. February 2015.

Kupfer, A. 2011. 'Towards a theoretical framework for the comparative understanding of globalisation, higher education, the labour market and inequality', *Journal of Education and Work* 24(1): 185–207.

McCowan, T. 2015. *Policy Brief: Student Perceptions of Employability and Inclusive Development*. Manchester: British Council.

Mbembe, A. 2015. *Decolonizing Knowledge and the Question of the Archive*. [Accessed 17 October 2015]. http://wiser.wits.ac.za/content/achille-mbembe-decolonizing-knowledge-and-question-archive-12054.

Naidoo, L-A. 2015. 'Open letter to Barney Pityana, on the Rhodes Must Fall Movement', *Daily Maverick* 14 April 2015. [Accessed 18 October 2015]. www.dailymaverick.co.za/opinionista/2015-04-14-open-letter-to-barney-pityana-on-the-rhodes-must-fall-movement/#.Vma9FL-Z1Gk.

Nussbaum, M. 1997. *Cultivating Humanity. A Classical Defence of Reform in Liberal Education*. Cambridge, MA: Harvard University Press.

Nussbaum, M. 2000. *Women and Human Development*. Cambridge: Cambridge University Press.

Nussbaum, M. 2013 *Political Emotions*. Cambridge, MA: Belknap Press.

Peters, R. S. 1966. *Ethics and Education*. London: George Allen and Unwin.

Piketty, T. 2014. *Capital in the Twenty-First Century*. (Translated by Arthur Goldhammer.) Cambridge, MA: Belknap Press.

Pinar, W., ed. 1998. *The Passionate Mind of Maxine Greene*. London: Falmer Press.

Sen, A. 1999. *Development as Freedom*. Oxford: Oxford University Press.

Sen, A. 2006. *Identity and Violence. The Illusion of Destiny*. London: Penguin.

Sen, A. 2009. *The Idea of Justice*. London: Allen Lane.

Shay, S. 2011 'Curriculum formation: a case study from history', *Studies in Higher Education* 36: 315–330

Tomlinson, M. 2012. 'Graduate employability: a review of conceptual and empirical themes', *Higher Education Policy* 25: 407–31.

Vaughan, R. and M. Walker. 2012. 'Capabilities, values and education policy', *Journal of Human Development and Capabilities* 13(3): 495–512.

Walker, M. 2006. *Higher Education Pedagogies. A Capabilities Approach*. Maidenhead: Open University Press.

Walker, M. 2008. *Ontology, Identity Formation and Lifelong Learning Outcomes: Theorising the Relationship Between Discipline-Based Research and Teaching*. York: Higher Education Academy.

Walker, M. 2015. 'Employability and Diverse Student's Opportunity Sets'. Seminar paper presented at the University of Bath, 8 June.

Part III

9 The human development-friendly university

In this last chapter, we reflect on the theoretical and empirical insights based on the human development and capability approach that we have woven through the book. We propose that human development offers a global development framework that provides us with a multidimensional approach to the university oriented to social change. Following this approach, universities would be shaped by human development values in all dimensions of their core activities including research, curriculum and pedagogy and policy. Examples of the kinds of activities are presented in matrix at the end of the chapter. Furthermore, we suggest that the human development approach could be a valuable way to endow the contemporary university with a different language and alterative informational basis for justice, one which could challenge the current mainstream vision of a university based primarily on neo-liberal values.

Reflections on theoretical insights

In this book, we set out to make the case for the role the university can play in contributing to social changes in the global arena and in the national and local contexts, all of which are interconnected in development processes and all of which matter when it comes to thinking about global development and global agendas across multi-developmental pathways. Scott (2011) reminds us that it is a matter of debate as to whether the university in the twenty-first century is a less national institution than its predecessors, notwithstanding major shifts towards internationalisation: staff and student mobility, collaborative research, joint degree programmes, global rankings, and so on. On the one hand, as we discussed in Chapter 2, the higher education policy-driver of a knowledge economy, with knowledge and human capital embodied by graduates as the product of university, is now dominant; this feature appears globally throughout developed and developing countries. Various global indicators, such as rankings, pressurise universities to be more global and equate this with them being 'better' universities. On the other hand, these developments are neither hegemonic nor uniform and happen differently in relation to varying university histories and backgrounds. We also know that, increasingly, going to university can fundamentally affect your life opportunities. For example, a recent Australian study based on a group covering multiple generations, found that what matters most is simply the fact that one attends university, regardless of what or where one studies (King 2015).

The capability approach and human development provide us with the rationale to scrutinise the meaning of these social changes in relation to their contribution to the university and to problematise neo-liberal directions of change. The approach prioritises the expansion of capabilities, or the real opportunities of people from all around the world, but not without considerations. There are important limits to take into account, as well as global challenges that cannot be ignored. The expansion of real opportunities should be enabled in a sustainable, equitable and participatory way, *by people*, *for people* but not to the detriment of other species – or humans ourselves – or the environment we share. There is no genuine human development if it is not both equitable and sustainable, as we explained in Chapter 4. Moreover, the public-good university is a human development-friendly university, as we explain in more detail later in the chapter, and a university that seeks to deepen democracy through its research and teaching activities.

As we have seen in the book, neo-liberal approaches to development that advocate competitive markets (in health care, in education, etc.) as the solution to reduce poverty and inequality are not taking us towards human development for all and indeed, appear to be exacerbating existing inequalities. We have a great deal of evidence that the benefits of globalisation are very unevenly distributed, both among countries and among citizens, and this has increased inequalities and threatens a shared sustainable future. For universities, there have been some advantages: globalisation has widened access to university, especially for women (but with exceptions, such as in Africa), while internationalisation has fostered more interaction and mobility opportunities (albeit uneven to and from South and North), and these are valuable changes. However, globalisation also drives a particular understanding of the political economy of academic knowledge increasingly controlled by views from the USA, which ranks journals, and prioritises 'excellent' research measured by publication in higher-ranked, financially costly journals. Publication of dialogic research of the kind we describe in Chapter 7 is harder to publish in these journals and ends up being marginalised in low-ranking journals that specialise in action research. Moreover, the shift to 'open-access' publication requires upfront payment to the journal at a level unaffordable to scholars from the global South and early career academics everywhere. All this benefits English-language universities based in the global North, leaving scholars from the global South forced into publishing in journals that their own universities may not even be able to afford to subscribe to.

Globalisation has also pushed universities to prioritise their contributions to economic growth and national innovation systems, obscuring other valuable purposes of higher education in relation to development. We noted in Chapter 2 that globalisation has prioritised instrumental knowledge and skills and the production of knowledge to increase economic opportunities for technology-driven economic sectors. For example, the World Bank is expanding its centres of excellence to East and Southern Africa, and says that the countries involved have prioritised science, technology, engineering, agriculture, health, science technology and innovation, applied statistics and education quality (Makoni 2015), although we do not know how they arrived at these priorities or what steering role the World Bank played. Nonetheless, we recognise that the quality of education, as we also appeal for in this book, underpins the human development-friendly university – and this is a good thing – while science and technology could benefit people on the ground depending on the research problems chosen, making the knowledge produced accessible and free to all, and so on.

Critical approaches to development, however, propose another pathway for universities, as we have seen in Chapter 3: sustainable development introduces into the discussion the importance of values connected with environmental and social sustainability, local and global interdependence as well as the importance of transdisciplinarity. Gender approaches remind us that it is important to make links between the micro-politics of subjectivity and everyday life, and the macro-politics of the global political economy. Participatory views consider the importance of linking universities and communities through a more democratic approach to research and teaching.

We consider that human development offers a complete framework that, enriched by other development contributions aligned with similar values, provides us with a multidimensional and integral approach to university and university education that is oriented to social change. This includes: (1) equality of opportunities to aspire to and to access higher education, not only with regard to teaching, but also a more equal understanding of knowledge-making and the benefits of research which should reach and include citizens in some way, especially marginalised groups; (2) a broad understanding of people's well-being freedoms and achievements that includes rational, emotional, individual and social aspects and how these can be expanded and secured through quality university education; (3) a concern with fostering people's agency to bring about the (human development) goals they have reason to value; (4) consistent with human development's emphasis on participation and deliberation, meaningful involvement by all staff and students in the core activities of a university is required to enable a deep democratic way of taking decisions; and (5) sustainability which highlights local and global connections and is forward thinking.

Following this approach, universities would be shaped by human development values in all the dimensions of their core activities, two of which we address in the book, namely student learning and research, but also in the dimension of policy. A good university (by implication a university that promotes social change) would then be a university based on human development principles and values and such a university would in turn, for example, promote more justice by contributions to poverty reduction; forming particular kinds of reasoning graduates and equipping them to participate in the economy; undertaking research and producing knowledge to understand how to reduce and eradicate poverty; working with communities outside the academy to share this knowledge, also in an inclusive process of knowledge making; and making contributions to the lives of people living in poverty, for example by funding a legal-aid clinic, or supporting adult literacy, or providing free health services.

Reflections on empirical insights

The aim of the book is also to show that it is possible to practice a human development engaged scholarship. We provided several examples based on our own research and teaching experiences.

In Chapter 5, we examined the gaps in higher education policies to provide the room for manoeuvre essential in order to scale-up transformative practices. The three different policies examined – a European proposal for a policy on Responsible Research and Innovation; the implementation of the European Higher Education Area at the local level of a new degree programme in Spain; and a South African government *White Paper for Post-School Education and Training* – all have an informational basis somewhat distant from that proposed by human development, although the South African policy is nonetheless strong on good intentions and employs the language of equity and social justice, albeit rather weakly realised in relation to quality. In Chapters 6 and 7, we considered how universities could produce knowledge meaningful for social change. In Chapter 6, we considered a broadening of how university researchers engage with other forms of knowledge; even where researchers do not wish to work in this way, they need to understand that neo-liberal global pressures have not necessarily been good for science, replacing scientific curiosity as the main concern with government and funders' concerns for competitive advantage, in the process subordinating science to innovation (Hicks and Katz 2002). In Chapter 6, we also explored the challenges of participation from beyond the university and how these can enable cognitive justice and epistemological equity by including more knowledge and perspectives in the research frame but, at the same time, may not be supported or welcomed by all university researchers. We tried to show how expanding the frame of knowledge-making for wider inclusion can produce more rigorous knowledge and how participation in many forms and levels contributes substantially. In Chapter 7, in particular, we presented an example of participatory action research (PAR) as a way to illustrate the potential of this approach to contribute to a knowledge and critical-thinking project in universities, with multidimensional goals for all the academic community, and in engagement with wider communities as a way to practice engaged scholarship and provide effective support for stakeholders in their processes of self-determining social change. Based on the human development and capability approach we created an original framework to analyse PAR, which highlights the importance of participatory process for the expansion of capabilities of all the groups involved in the research process, the transformative potential of knowledge, and the possibilities of research of this kind to open up spaces for public deliberation. Our example of a research and teaching experience based on a participatory video showed a noticeable expansion of capabilities, a formation of practical knowledge, as well as the creation of several spaces for public deliberation during the process.

In the three cases of curriculum, citizenship and employability that we presented in Chapter 8, we considered how the university could be a space for the formation of direct and indirect values: as to who students want to be, what they want to do, and what they could contribute to society and the public good. We found that a university can be a place to expand the capacity to reason critically and reflexively about values, consistent with the capability approach's concern with equity, empowerment, well-being, freedoms and achievements, and public reasoning. We also saw how universities can reproduce the inequalities that prevail in society, or at the least fail to challenge them, because they may be contrary to their own interests in the ranking and status systems, or because they may not notice them. However, we also noted that while there is much that universities can do – in our case in relation to students' employability and employment – they cannot do everything and cannot compensate, at least on their own, for economic problems or the demand side of the labour markets, which in turn may be skewed by wider global patterns of development. We also noted that while universities should not prescribe the functionings students choose beyond university, their university education ought at least to foster the capabilities that make it possible for them to act differently and decently in the future and to renew the common good.

Reflections on social change

In this final section, we reflect on the prospects for the public-good university, underpinned by our view that we should not resign ourselves to universities becoming less just, to research failing to promote democratic practices or to curriculum and pedagogy that reproduces inequalities. We have found human development ideas at work in universities, so the issue is to think about some of the conditions for the development of alternative possibilities. Onora O'Neill (1996: 183) reminds us that we need to try out new actions; they may turn out to be imperfect or even defective but without trying we cannot know 'what new institutions, policies and practices can be forged'. We need to try human development in our universities.

A different language is needed

We need a strong and clear normative language to support desirable social changes. Human development and the capability approach provide us with such a language for the analysis, development and evaluation of universities. The challenge of neo-liberal times is the way the language employed changes the way we understand the purposes of the university and our own work in it: university fees become 'price', students the customers, knowledge changes into value-based units (so much for a book, so much for an article), and education into a commodity to be bought and sold. At the same time, it reduces our ability to understand our work in anything other than neo-liberal terms. As Gramsci (1997) explained, you can occupy people's heads, and their hearts and hands will follow. Nussbaum (2010: 142) powerfully reminds us just what is at stake in this global trend to educate, above all else, to achieve economically productive students:

> Democracies have great rational and imaginative powers. They are also prone to some serious flaws in reasoning [...]. Education based mainly on profitability in the global market magnifies these deficiencies, producing greedy obtuseness and technically trained docility that threatens the very life of democracy itself, and that certainly impedes the creation of a decent world culture.

Instead, human development language provides us with an advocacy language for improved policy and practices. In the powerful words of Toni Morrison (1993: 1), it offers the song, the literature, the 'poem full of vitamins ... to help us start strong'. Human development language can generate new policy narratives for universities based on deliberation, citizenship and capability expansion. Such policies would support inclusive and expansive purposes and struggles even where, at the present time, human development policies are considered to be contra-hegemonic in comparison with mainstream approaches. Human development and capability thinking offers visionary norms by adopting a multidimensional and policy-responsive view of what a good university could look like, embracing the public good, social justice and sustainability in any definition of a policy narrative.

It also means challenging the prioritisation of science and technology at the expense of the humanities. For example, research has shown that international development organisations value the role of the humanities in seeking solutions to global development challenges. A study commissioned by the British Council (2014) found that all development programmes, even the most technical, needed 'humanising', and that an education in the humanities helps develop a base of knowledge and key skills in four main areas of development: critical/analytical thinking, flexibility and tolerance for ambiguity, communication and negotiation and local knowledge. While development needs science and technology, it also needs the humanities.

Making human development

By constructing social pathways through practices of human development-friendly research and teaching, by trying out new actions and activities to push forward these alternative practices, by 'multiple tramping' of the same terrain (Cooper 2001: 129) we can make the public-good university by doing the public-good university. Focusing a lens on comparative assessments of justice could reveal the potential for change by asking which situation is more just than another, even if the situation is not perfect in all aspects of social justice. Indeed, in policy and practice, perfection is hard to come by and, in specific contexts, we settle for that which is better and takes us closer to human development. Our examples show that when research and teaching activities are performed differently, they can bring into being moments and spaces of 'another university': there are scholars, students, social organisations that want to engage in a different way to produce a different practice and to realise the potential of universities to contribute to development in the global South and the global North. The human development-friendly university would seek to expand capabilities not only in students, but also in teaching and research staff. Through the empirical chapters we explored a number of capabilities, drawing on Walker's list as a starting point, but finding other capabilities not covered by her list. Here we remind people of the capabilities from her list (Walker 2006: 128–9):

1 *Practical reason.* Being able to make well-reasoned, informed, critical, independent, and reflective choices about higher education. Being able to construct a personal life project in an uncertain world.
2 *Educational resilience.* Able to navigate study, work and life. Able to negotiate risk, to persevere academically, to be responsive to educational opportunities and adaptive to constraints. Self-reliant. Having aspirations and hopes for a good future.
3 *Knowledge and imagination.* Being able to gain knowledge of a chosen subject. Being able to use critical thinking and imagination to comprehend the perspectives of multiple others and to form impartial judgements. Being able to debate complex issues. Being able to acquire knowledge for pleasure and personal development, for career and economic opportunities, for political, cultural and social action and participation in the world. Open-mindedness.
4 *Learning disposition.* Being able to have curiosity and a desire for learning. Having confidence in one's ability to learn.

5 *Social relations and social networks.* Being able to participate in a group for learning, working with others to solve problems and tasks. Being able to work with others to form effective or good groups for collaborative and participatory learning. Being able to form networks of friendship and belonging for learning support and leisure.

6 *Respect, dignity and recognition.* Being able to have respect for oneself and for and from others, being treated with dignity, not being diminished or devalued because of one's gender, social class, religion or race, valuing other languages, other religions and spiritual practices and human diversity. Being able to show empathy, compassion, fairness and generosity, listening to and considering other persons' points of view in dialogue and debate. Having a voice to participate effectively in learning; a voice to speak out, to debate and persuade; to be able to listen. (Added from Chapter 7 to this capability: Avoid judging prematurely, respect somebody else's decisions in their circumstances, always behave in a respectful way if there are group conflicts.)

7 *Emotional integrity, emotions.* Not being subject to anxiety or fear, which diminishes learning. Being able to develop emotions for imagination, understanding, empathy, awareness and discernment.

8 *Bodily integrity.* Safety and freedom from all forms of physical and verbal harassment in the higher education environment.

In Chapters 7 and 8, we found evidence that these additional capabilities are valued:

• Being *self-aware* of the direction you want to take in life as an active and reflexive agent, generated from critical thought and participation.
• The *ability to surprise,* that is to give presents, not to buy them but to make them, to be excited about doing something for others and to know that it will make them happy.
• *The ability to reflect and improve people's understanding of their role as practitioners in the development field.*
• *To be able to express one's own ideas in a different language.*
• *To have fair and inclusive economic opportunities*, including social capital to access employment (going beyond the social relations capability above).

We could add others, such as the capability to participate in research, which would secure the right to research of each citizen. There are also others that could be chosen, but the basic principle is always that the capabilities selected have their basis in human development, and are open to public development and scrutiny. A capabilities set or list is helpful in making judgements about education, whether about quality, participation, access, success and so on, but it should always be contextual, provisional and be a product of ongoing public dialogue.

Change the informational basis of judgement in justice

We need to work on elaborating different ways to analyse, develop and evaluate university contributions to human development, and this should include a mix of numbers, quantitative and qualitative evidence related to human development values and capability expansion – this is the information on which we should base our judgements of justice, whatever the methods we choose. We think this is a challenging project, but if we want to argue for a different informational basis of judgement in justice, we need to have ideas about what we will put in the space. We suggest working on an access and equity indicator, given how university admissions globally tend to favour the better off. This might be captured through robust national data systems (e.g. in South African Higher Education and Management Information Systems – HEMIS), but would be more difficult to achieve where data systems are weak, although this shortcoming could serve as a spur to develop better systems. If underpinned by human development values, it would be understood that an equity and access number would only indicate if more women, or more marginalised students were entering higher education as a percentage of the total. Following Langford's (2012) advice, this indicator would be robust and easy to communicate and could be comparable across systems (with each country having to decide what the relevant equity dimensions are for them, be they gender, social class, race, ethnicity or language spoken). However, this alone would not tell us why students aspire to or choose higher education, which subjects and universities they choose, or what happens to them after entry.

Therefore, we also need a quality 'measure' for participation and success, but this is more difficult. One way might be to employ a set of capabilities with functioning exemplars as outlined above. This could be kept much more simple, even being limited to three core capabilities, for example: the capability for critical thinking, the capability for work and the capability to make contributions to society. The data for this may be tricky to collect and it would be important for it to not be so onerous that universities would be unwilling to try it. Nevertheless, many universities routinely collect evaluation data and these forms could be slightly adjusted to capture these three capabilities (and others), but it would also be important, we think, to include some participatory data for the core capabilities (Chapter 7). Whatever is decided, it would be important to bear in mind that this data should not take on a life of its own but be developed to constitute the informational basis for human development-friendly policies.

The human development-friendly, public-good university

Finally, we offer a matrix of the human development university adapted from Boni and Gasper (2012) but including in our example the main areas

Table 9.1 Matrix of a human development-friendly university

University activities/HD values	Teaching	Research	Policy (national and university)
Well-being freedoms (e.g. autonomy, critical thinking; reflexivity, emotions, creativity, health, etc.)	Pedagogies to foster critical thinking and reflexivity (and other valuable functionings). Professional education which attends to poverty and inequality in the society	Research ('blue skies', basic, applied) on inequalities (e.g. HIV, poverty, schooling, race)	Policy of decent grants and financial aid to students who cannot afford to attend university. Monitoring of student success using capability-based information and indicators
Participation and empowerment (includes agency, social transformation)	Participatory learning methods, including student volunteering and community-based learning	Research themes relevant for social change. Participatory research. Research impact on users of the research; public engagement events	Universities lobbying government for human development higher education policy; working with all universities in the system to this end. Participation in the definition of a university mission, strategic plans, elections, boards of governance that include internal and external actors
Equity (social justice) and diversity (learning between different cultures and identities, cultural freedoms)	Cultural and multicultural presence in curriculum. Funding for subjects which do not generate 'profit'	Benefits of research to society. Funds for research themes with low economic profits	Equitable access to university for all students (national and university policy). Diversity in the student body and staff
Sustainability (global issues; holistic perspectives; long-term perspectives; interdisciplinarity)	Global issues in the curriculum (ethics, sustainable development, peace studies). Interdisciplinary	International links, including North–South networks. Interdisciplinary research. Research themes relevant for global issues	Environmentally friendly infrastructure projects (often funded by state grants), e.g. solar geysers, solar panels and rainwater tanks for all new buildings. Greening projects and awareness campaigns

Source: adaptd from Boni and Gasper (2012).

of university activity that we have discussed in this book: policy, research and teaching (curriculum and pedagogy). The idea is that human development values would infuse all activities at the university. The teaching, research and other cells could be filled out by the university, but the values would hold across all activities and be the basis for adjudicating choices, priorities and trade-offs. We can easily perceive the connections between university activities inspired by human development values and the expansion of capabilities we describe above. A curriculum and pedagogy based on an idea of well-being (as those shown in Chapter 8) could have a multiplier effect, expanding practical reason, knowledge and imagination, or learning disposition capabilities. Research that is inspired by participation and empowerment values (as we have seen in Chapter 7) can expand the capability of knowledge and imagination, social relation and social networks, or the capability to reflect on professional work, among others. A policy that aims towards equity and diversity will have a powerful effect, expanding almost all the capabilities listed through equitable access to higher education.

As we have discussed previously, universities can develop their own proposals for valuable capabilities through public deliberation, as a way to evaluate the activities proposed and implemented in university policies inspired by human development values. It is important that those policies can achieve the essential purpose of the university, and not be confined to 'peripheral' policies. This is a danger we perceive in some of the policies that have addressed development issues (i.e. development cooperation policies or social responsibility policies), which, in the case of Spain, have been endorsed by many universities but have had no great impact. It is true that we make the path by walking it, but it is equally true that the direction of the path should be clear and this is a major contribution of the human development and capability approach.

Our hope therefore is that this book will provide both a resource and a challenge for all those people working in universities who wish courageously and imaginatively to co-create another kind of university and make it possible through their analysis, actions, human development values and their search for justice.

References

Boni, A. and D. Gasper. 2012. 'Rethinking the quality of universities – how can human development thinking contribute?' *Journal of Human Development and Capabilities* 13(3): 451–70.

British Council. 2014. *Mobilising the Humanities*. [Accessed 18 August 2015]. www.britishcouncil.org/education/ihe/knowledge-centre/challenging-systems/mobilising-humanities-development-perspective.

Cooper, D. 2001. 'Against the Current: social pathways and the pursuit of enduring change', *Feminist Legal Studies* 9: 119–48.

Gramsci, A. 1997. *Selections From the Prison Notebooks of Antonio Gramsci*. New York: International Publishers.

Hicks, D. and S. Katz. 2002. 'Science policy for a highly collaborative science system', *Science and Public Policy* 23: 39–44.

King, C. 2015. 'Education matters', *University World News* 16 August 2015. [Accessed 17 August 2015]. www.universityworldnews.com/.

Langford, M. 2012. 'The Art of the Impossible: Measurement Choices and the Post-2015 Development Agenda'. Background paper for Governance and Human Rights: Criteria and Measurement Proposals for Post-2015 Development Agenda, OHCHR/UNDP Expert Consultation, New York, 13–14 November.

Makoni, M. 2015. 'New centres of excellence for East and Southern Africa', *University World News* 16 August 2015. [Accessed 17 August 2015]. www.universityworldnews.com/.

Morrison, T. 1993. 'Nobel Prize banquet speech', 10 December 1993. [Accessed 1 August 2015]. www.nobelprize.org/nobel_prizes/literature/laureates/1993/morrison-speech.html.

Nussbaum, M. 2010. *Not for Profit*. Princeton: Princeton University Press.

O'Neill, O. 1996. *Towards Justice and Virtue*. Cambridge: Cambridge University Press.

Scott, P. 2011. 'The university as global institution'. In *Handbook on Globalization and Higher Education*, edited by R. King, S. Marginson and R. Naidoo, 59–75. Cheltenham: Edgar Elgar.

Walker, M. 2006. *Higher education pedagogies*. Berkshire: Society for Research into Higher Education and Open University Press.

Index

Page numbers in *italics* denote tables, those in **bold** denote figures.

 Taylor & Francis eBooks

Helping you to choose the right eBooks for your Library

Add Routledge titles to your library's digital collection today. Taylor and Francis ebooks contains over 50,000 titles in the Humanities, Social Sciences, Behavioural Sciences, Built Environment and Law.

Choose from a range of subject packages or create your own!

Benefits for you

» Free MARC records
» COUNTER-compliant usage statistics
» Flexible purchase and pricing options
» All titles DRM-free.

 REQUEST YOUR FREE INSTITUTIONAL TRIAL TODAY

Free Trials Available
We offer free trials to qualifying academic, corporate and government customers.

Benefits for your user

» Off-site, anytime access via Athens or referring URL
» Print or copy pages or chapters
» Full content search
» Bookmark, highlight and annotate text
» Access to thousands of pages of quality research at the click of a button.

eCollections – Choose from over 30 subject eCollections, including:

Archaeology	Language Learning
Architecture	Law
Asian Studies	Literature
Business & Management	Media & Communication
Classical Studies	Middle East Studies
Construction	Music
Creative & Media Arts	Philosophy
Criminology & Criminal Justice	Planning
Economics	Politics
Education	Psychology & Mental Health
Energy	Religion
Engineering	Security
English Language & Linguistics	Social Work
Environment & Sustainability	Sociology
Geography	Sport
Health Studies	Theatre & Performance
History	Tourism, Hospitality & Events

For more information, pricing enquiries or to order a free trial, please contact your local sales team:
www.tandfebooks.com/page/sales

 Routledge
Taylor & Francis Group
The home of Routledge books

www.tandfebooks.com